FIGHTING THE
U - BOATS

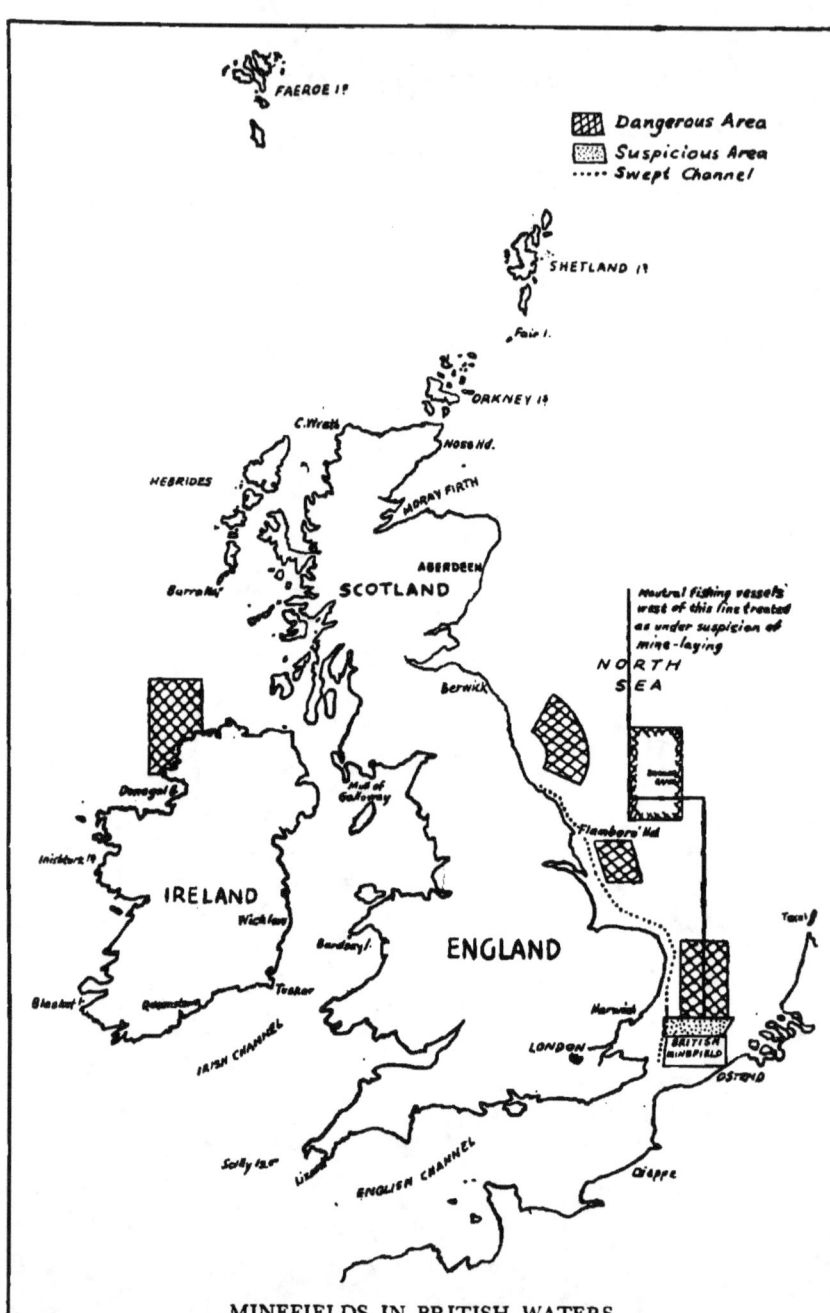

MINEFIELDS IN BRITISH WATERS

This shows the larger areas at the end of 1914. The hatched areas indicate the Southwold, Humber, Dogger Bank, Tyne, and Tory minefield respectively. The area of British mines across the Dover Straits, and the suspicious region above, are also indicated.

FIGHTING THE
U-BOATS

By

E. KEBLE CHATTERTON

The Naval & Military Press Ltd

Illustrated

Published by

The Naval & Military Press Ltd
Unit 5 Riverside, Brambleside
Bellbrook Industrial Estate
Uckfield, East Sussex
TN22 1QQ England

Tel: +44 (0)1825 749494

www.naval-military-press.com
www.nmarchive.com

In reprinting in facsimile from the original, any imperfections are inevitably reproduced and the quality may fall short of modern type and cartographic standards.

PREFACE

THE following chapters contain one of the most exciting dramas in the history of human endeavour, but they are full of maritime lessons for those who care to trace results back to their motives.

It has been my object to record in detail the fate of every enemy submarine sunk during the period 1914 to the close of 1916; to show how German and Austrian U-boats individually were fought, and how the enemy's effort to conquer our marine might was waged through little ships. The period 1917 and 1918 will be issued as a separate volume entitled, *Beating the U-boats*; in these two volumes we have before us the full and detailed history of that war against submarines which finished in the greatest surrender to us, the victors.

When the German War began again after a new generation had grown up, we needed not merely new weapons but a careful understanding of the past enshrined in those eventful years. It has required nearly a quarter of a century to produce the following chapters, of which the information has been derived from every possible angle: British and German sources, first-hand information given by many of the characters who actually took part, personal knowledge of the ships and men; correspondence with naval officers who played prominent roles in the anti-submarine campaign, or with some whose mercantile vessels led to their Masters becoming prisoners of war.

It is hoped that, apart from the pleasure of general reading, and of seeing the results of certain inventions, this study may become of permanent value to the historian.

E. KEBLE CHATTERTON.

CONTENTS

		PAGE
	PREFACE	7

CHAPTER		
1.	PRELUDE TO THE GREAT STRUGGLE	11
2.	THE FIRST ACTIVITIES OF U-BOATS	17
3.	THE SUBMARINES LEARN THEIR STRENGTH	23
4.	THE LATEST DISASTERS	31
5.	GERMANY RAIDS GORLESTON	37
6.	THE DOGGER BANK	45
7.	TRAWLERS AND U-BOATS	54
8.	RUTHLESS ATTACK	62
9.	CHANGE OF POLICY	71
10.	THE "LUSITANIA" SEQUEL	80
11.	NORTH SEA STRATEGY	87
12.	THE MINELAYERS	96
13.	TRAPPING THE SUBMARINES	104
14.	WHAT A SUBMARINE CAN DO	113
15.	WHAT THE RAM DOES	118
16.	TRAPPING THE U-BOAT	127
17.	THE ENEMY DELUDED	134
18.	DECOYS AND DESTINY	142
19.	THE COMING CHANGE	150
20.	IN THE MIDDLE SEA	160
21.	AMERICA INTERVENES	169
22.	GERMAN DEVICE	175
23.	TO THE BOTTOM	187
24.	THE STORY OF SCHWIEGER	196
25.	DODGING DEATH	202
	INDEX	208

LIST OF ILLUSTRATIONS

	FACING PAGE
ONE OF THE PATROL DRIFTERS	36
ARMED DRIFTER	100
ONE OF THE SLOOP CLASS	100
THE FIGHT WITH U-27	148
HOW GUNS WERE HIDDEN	172

In the Text

MINEFIELDS IN BRITISH WATERS	*Frontispiece*
	PAGE
PATROL AREAS	48
GUARDING THE TROOPS' TRANSPORT ROUTE	83
THE FORK-SHAPED LINE	88
SUBMARINE DESTINY	92
N.E. COAST SINKINGS	138
MAN OF ACTION	147
"BARALONG" SINKS U-41	155
DOVER STRAITS	159
THE NEW ZONES	168
U-BOAT TRAP	178
THE U-BOAT WHO FAILED	184
GUARDING DOVER STRAITS	194
FRUSTRATED EFFORT	203
SINKING OF UB-19	204

Chapter I

PRELUDE TO THE GREAT STRUGGLE

IF it be true that personal characteristics do not greatly change in the course of one human being's progress through life towards death, so likewise a nation does not materially alter its tendencies from one generation to another. A modification of regime cannot basically transform these marks which are the outstanding features of national prejudice, national hatreds, national ambitions, however secretly they may for a while be hidden. Whether the man in Berlin is a subject of the Kaiser or of the Führer will be of less consequence than whether he is a German : as to essentials, and particularly with regard to disposition, the Nazi is fundamentally much the same as our enemy of 1914. The jungle creature is unable to change his spots physically, or to adopt internally a complete set of new ideals, merely because there has been a change of the forest's ownership.

To be precise, the German is always a German, with the inevitable implications. That is why the war of 1914-1918 has so much in common with those hostilities which followed when a new generation had grown up. Teutonic brutality, callousness, ruthless vigour, mechanical efficiency, remarkable organization, were just as notable during the first period of warfare as the second —except that the greater encouragement of paganism, and a decline of moral values, intensified the desire to conquer at all costs.

Industrialists in Britain during the last two decades noted with regret that in matters of commerce the German trader was even less inclined to respect the sanctity of agreements : obligations seemed to possess but the slightest restraining influence. Again the aim was to be top dog regardless of every principle, moral or social.

Consequently we find that, with all his trickery, the German of Hitler has been repeating with only greater emphasis those dispositions manifested to the world under Emperor William. He torpedoes at every opportunity every hospital ship, he destroys men, women and children as heartlessly as in the previous contest ; and the same juggling with facts and figures in his propaganda is common to both wars. In brief, we are fighting the same enemy, and merely the intensity of explosives really separates the old from the new. So then, as we trace the struggle clearly focused by U-boat warfare of August, 1914, and onwards, we are watching also that warfare which began to menace us in September, 1939, with a fresh ardour.

It was on July 15, 1914, that the German High Sea Fleet started for Norway, and five days later the Kaiser through his Foreign Office secretly informed directors of the Hamburg-Amerika Line as well as of the North German Lloyd Line that the Austrian ultimatum was expected on July 23; so that "in view of incalculable and perhaps sudden consequences" these two leading corporations might accordingly "make their dispositions, and issue orders to their steamers abroad." That they took the royal hint, made arrangements as well for security in neutral American harbours, as for commerce raiding on the Atlantic and for supplying raiders with fuel or food, is a matter of plain history.

But events began rapidly to develop. On July 25 the Kaiser had ordered the High Sea Fleet to remain concentrated in Norwegian waters, Admiral von Ingenohl on arrival at Sognefjord in the Fleet flagship was summoned aboard the royal yacht *Hohenzollern* after information had been received that the Austrian ultimatum had been sent to Servia. Therefore—about 6 p.m.—the Admiral was ordered to proceed that day with his whole fleet towards the German Baltic, in order to deal Russia the first blow should war break out; for Austria would certainly mobilize, and Russia in her turn would mobilize against Austria.

That is why the High Sea Fleet left Norwegian waters for Kiel.

Meanwhile on the next day, July 26, Captain Erich von Müller (German Naval Attaché in London) telegraphed that the British Admiralty had cancelled leave, and that the British First Fleet was at Portland, but on the 29th he cabled further that this fleet had left for an unknown destination. It is to be noted that the Kaiser in his *Hohenzollern* hurried from Norway to Kiel, and ships of the High Sea Fleet were by July 30 detached to guarantee Kiel Bay's protection, whilst the line Wangeroog–Heligoland–Eider began to be patrolled by destroyers throughout the night and by cruisers during daytime.

So far Germany counted on British neutrality. On the last day of July Germany's Fleet Flagship, certain other battleships plus her 1st Submarine Flotilla, passed through the Kiel Canal to the North Sea end, whilst some battleships steamed round the Danish coast. The possibility of Great Britain "suddenly abandoning her attitude of aloofness" began to cause the Germans anxiety: in fact at 5 p.m. on that July 31 von Ingenohl was informed by wireless he might expect war against France, Russia, and ourselves.

By 6 a.m. on August 1 the vessels which had come from Kiel were at the naval base of Wilhelmshaven and the submarines were already patrolling off Heligoland, whilst three light cruisers were keeping a look-out some 50 miles from Heligoland; but the battle-cruisers were kept at anchor outside the bar in the River Jade's Schellig Roads, or off Wilhelmshaven itself, ready to rush forth and support the cruisers if the latter should wireless for help; whilst the battleships could also slip from Wilhelmshaven should further aid be required.

Germany was nervous. On August 2 Russia opened hostilities, but at 7.30 p.m. (German time) of August 4 our enemies entered into a state of war with Britain. The Teutons greatly feared that a sudden attack might be made by British submarines and minelayers, wherefore measures were instituted for laying German minefields off the Ems, Jade, Weser, Elbe, as well as the Lister Tief, whilst a barrage of blockships stood by at Cuxhaven also for defending the Elbe.

In short, then, Germany at the commencement of war had through her Commander-in-Chief of the High Sea Fleet made the following distributions: the 1st and 3rd Battle Squadrons based on the Jade, the 2nd based on the Elbe inside the Cuxhaven boom; a flotilla of destroyers on the Ems; whilst the Heligoland Bight besides being defended by destroyers was also looked after by minesweeping divisions and aircraft.

But that was not all.

Let it be stressed that neither Germany nor Great Britain yet appreciated the immense potentialities of the submarines. Certainly the former looked upon this sort of craft as somewhat coy, of vague reliability, and possessing a certain value as observers, but little beyond these attributes. The Submarine Flotilla which came through the Kiel Canal on July 31 was in charge of Commander H. Bauer and included U 5, 7, 8, 9, 14, 16, 17 and 18. It may be mentioned that each of these eight was destined during that war to take part in many a thrilling incident, and that Bauer himself later was to become Commodore of the High Sea Fleet submarines, thus commanding not a mere flotilla, but whole divisions. To his foresight and his organizing ability the progress of Germany's U-boats owes much: the force became in time no longer a doubtful possibility, but one of immense strength, as months went by. But at the moment Admiral von Ingenohl contented himself with ordering four of them to be in immediate readiness for undertaking long-distance cruising up the North Sea.

Thus the German Navy, with their units of battle-cruisers, battleships, light cruisers, and destroyers duly assigned to stations, arranged immediately also for the operations of two other categories: (1) armed merchantmen, but working along the trade routes disguised; (2) armed merchantmen also disguised, but intended principally as minelayers. Now since both (1) and (2) have been discussed with great detail already in my volume, *The*

Sea Raiders,[1] it will suffice if we call attention to the working of the German mind as expressed by the naval officer commanding the *Konigin Luise*, first of the Teutonic minelayers to create damage. At a later date our enemies were to learn that it was easier, and far less risky, to lay these explosives by submarines.

It is an historical fact that use of mines had never been favoured by the British Navy, and that outbreak of hostilities in August, 1914, found us consequently quite unprepared for an extensive policy based on this weapon. We possessed at that date only a few thousand naval mines, and seven second-class cruisers for laying them. These were slow of speed, could carry only a hundred mines each, so that eventually they had to be paid off and replaced by half a dozen converted merchantmen.

Actually the Russo-Japanese War of 1903-4 was the first occasion which demonstrated the use of mines for strategic and tactical purpose, as distinct from the original purely coast-defence employment, so the British Navy took a new interest and ordered a stock of mines for deep-sea purposes: yet both Germany and Russia were far ahead of us regarding the development and knowledge of mining possibilities. We were to learn in the Dardanelles campaign, to our severe cost, that Turkey possessed a stock of efficient German mines which could sink alike British and French capital ships.

But there was always the international aspect of this mining to be considered, though we know full well how little respect Germany pays to such considerations. By the Hague Convention of 1907 it was forbidden to lay anchored contact mines which do not become harmless as soon as they have broken loose from their moorings: every possible precaution must be taken that, after anchoring automatic contact mines, the security of peaceful shipping is assured. Germany signed and ratified this convention, but did not agree that it was forbidden to lay these off an enemy's coast and ports solely to intercept shipping.

Now the *Konigin Luise* (2163 gross tons) was a 16-knot vessel owned by the Hamburg–Amerika Line, employed in peace-time for running excursions to seaside resorts. On the afternoon of August 1 she was lying at Cuxhaven, and there began fitting out for the German Navy. It took twelve hours before her cargo of explosives was completed. After anchoring off Wilhelmshaven on August 3, she steamed out next day and brought up a little nearer England in the River Ems. At the fateful hour of 7.30 p.m. of August 4 she received the following order by wireless:

"Proceed at utmost speed in the direction of the Thames. Lay your mines as near as possible to the English coast. Do not lay mines off neutral coasts or further north than 53° N."

These were the instructions to Commander Biermann, her

[1] London, 1931. Hurst & Blackett.

Captain, and he intended to foul what is known as the King's Channel,[1] but got a little out of his navigational reckoning with the result that he did not deposit the mines where he estimated. Indeed, the Germans for years persisted in confusing the alleged with the real position.

The *Konigin Luise* was armed with rifles, pistols, and two 3·7-cm. machine-guns. She passed abreast of Borkum at 10 p.m. of August 4, then made for the Terschelling Lightvessel, and after the Haaks Lightvessel steamed down the Dutch coast, being about the latitude of the Maas at 8 a.m. (German time) next day. She then altered course for the East Anglian shore and began laying the mines at 10.40 a.m., sending out a wireless report homeward at 1.15 p.m. that she had accomplished her duty "in square 125 Alpha", though more accurately in Lat. 52.10 N., Long. 2.20 E.

This two-funnelled craft, however, was to have a speedy end. She was turning gradually to the southeast, and was less near the shore than intended, when suddenly a British force interrupted. It was a trawler which had informed H.M.S. *Amphion*. The fishermen had seen a suspicious ship off Aldeburgh "throwing things overboard". When, therefore, *Amphion* and the 3rd Destroyer Flotilla some 30 miles east of Orfordness arrived on the scene, she sank in about 52.10 N., 2.25 E., the German at 12.20 p.m. (German time), taking prisoners Commander Biermann, all executive officers, but four officers and seventy-three men were killed.

Survivors related that though *Konigin Luise* had laid a line of mines eastward, many of these "eggs" still remained aboard; but in truth she deposited them about 12 miles north of the position where Biermann believed himself to be. Thus he did not block the King's Channel, and the minefield was located in an ESE. course slightly zigzagged from Aldeburgh Napes. Not more than twenty-six mines were dropped and sweeping subsequently proved that very few remained, though unfortunately the *Amphion* herself was to founder on one of them.

However, the German plan had failed to entrap the long line of mercantile traffic which throughout the war passed north and south yet carefully avoided the Aldeburgh area. But an interesting example of German trickery was manifested in *Konigin Luise*. Why had this ship been chosen?

The answer is that in general appearance, and as to her funnels, she might easily seem at night, or not too near by daylight, to be one of those Great Eastern Railway steamers running for years from the Hook of Holland to Parkeston (Harwich). She, therefore, before setting out had previously repainted herself to resemble such a ship, and also from the Maas followed the course which one of these vessels would pursue.

[1] The King's Channel is one of the main approaches of the Thames Estuary leading out of the North Sea.

And a curious confirmation was fated to add life to this story.

Many readers will remember the name of Captain Edward Sycamore, a well-known skipper of racing yachts whose home was in Essex. Five days after the above incident he reached Parkeston as passenger in a Danish steamer. That season Sycamore had been skipper racing the yacht *Isabella Alexandra* for a German owner, and just before declaration of war, when the crisis seemed inevitable, *Isabella Alexandra* was given a tow into the Elbe by a German destroyer. Sycamore kept his eyes open, and did not fail to notice that the *Konigin Luise*, with a couple of other steamers were his neighbours in harbour surrounded by fishing craft. He watched the fishermen dabbing the white hull and yellow funnels of the excursion steamer a dead black during July 31 and August 1. so that he was struck by the similarity to a G.E.R. steamer.

And there can be no doubt that our enemies intentionally made use of this for fooling mariners. The Maas Lightvessel became a favourite locality for U-boats to be lurking at night, but sometimes the sharp forefoot of a Harwich steamer combined with a master mariner's daring spirit sufficiently availed to make the U-boat wish she had chosen some other spot for ambush.

CHAPTER 2

THE FIRST ACTIVITIES OF U-BOATS

THE initial German naval policy in August, 1914, may be summed up quite succinctly. Whilst her converted merchantmen were to do their worst along the trade routes, the High Sea Fleet was to remain at present on the defensive, any offensive operations to be carried out by destroyers and submarines.

Implanted in our enemy's mind was an expectation that the British Fleet would at once commence a *close* blockade of Heligoland Bight, and against this line of encirclement the surface and underwater torpedo craft would essay their attacks; but it surprised the German Navy that August 5 revealed something quite different. If the British main strength was not commencing its stranglehold in the Bight, then (it was argued) a *distant* blockade must have begun at some position farther up the North Sea.

Something must be done to make absolutely sure, and ten U-boats, therefore, were to inaugurate an enterprise northward. The selected boats were those eight mentioned in the previous chapter under Commander Bauer, plus U-13 and U-15. It was assumed that there must be a British blockade line permanently patrolled across the North Sea, which should be carefully reported on, and any units that presented a fair target were to be assailed.

These ten left Heligoland and at 4.40 a.m. on August 6 in their first sweep, their objective being an imaginary line drawn from the Shetlands across to Bergen. With high hopes did low-lying craft start off at dawn, yet it was an ambitious adventure full of uncertainty. We know from Captain Gayer, himself a celebrated German submarine specialist, that at outbreak of war his section of service owned for any military employment only U-5 with consecutive numbers up to U-25, but that U-5 to U-18 were driven by petrol engines which were not particularly efficient. We are aware also from another source[1] that U-5 was not long in developing engine-trouble, so she had to turn back home and thus there were nine.

The flotilla were still pressing northwards and never a British ship did they see until August 9, when at 5.45 a.m. (German time) U-18 (Lieut.-Commander von Hennig, senior officer) sighted one of our cruisers. Ninety minutes later U-9 (Lieut.-Commander

[1] *Der Krieg Zur Zee.*

Weddigen) sighted also a British destroyer, the exact position being Lat. 57.45 N., Long. 3.40 E., but at 3.40 a.m. H.M.S. *Birmingham* both sighted and rammed U-15, sending her to destruction, and thus bringing about the first of those U-boat losses which ultimately reached such large numbers.

It was no casual incident, for on August 8 reports of sighting submarines had each been made by the battleships H.M.S. *Monarch*, *Orion*, *Ajax*, *Dreadnought*, and *Iron Duke*. Indeed, because of this sudden U-boat menace, Admiral Jellicoe that day had ordered all his heavy ships to the northwest of the Orkneys, but *Birmingham* as one of the light cruiser squadron screening the battle-fleet (being then in Lat. 58·35, Long. 1.56 E.), made such a quick, complete job that Lieut.-Commander Pohle (although he fired a torpedo at a battleship) sank to the bottom with his men forthwith. Nor was that all.

Some time that day U-13 (Lieut.-Commander Graf von Schwinitz) disappeared also. Exactly how fate overtook her is, and always will be, a mystery. Whether she struck a mine, or whether another steel forefoot decided the issue, she disappeared leaving behind no clues. The net result of this expedition of U-boats was that they discovered no permanent patrol line and came back to Heligoland on August 11 little wiser than before. One of the flotilla had broken down, two had paid the death penalty, but the five days of cruising—longer than any period attempted during peace-time—had established among German officers a unique confidence in their boats. This should be emphasized, for from that adventurous experience much was to follow later and even already a second cruise by other U-boats was started on August 8, though to the southwestwards.

For it was decided that U-19, 21, 22, and 24 should sweep up to the line joining Maas Lightvessel with the Outer Gabbard Lightvessel. These were Diesel-engined craft, but such an exploratory cruise did no better than allow U-22 to contact a British destroyer patrol near the Maas Lightvessel. The aim was largely that of attacking the British Expeditionary Force which was to land in France, yet the submarines for this purpose failed for two reasons: (1) the German boats were back at Heligoland by August 11, and (2) the B.E.F. did not cross till several days later by a more western route. And in this connection we may well notice how badly informed was the German secret service. For in his diary of August 7 Admiral von Pohl (who at this date was Chief of the Naval Staff) whilst in Berlin wrote the following words:

"Conference with Admiral Behncke regarding attacks on the transports of the British Expeditionary Force, which, according to positive information, has begun its crossing to French and Belgian ports."

And on the 8th is this entry:

"8 a.m. the Fleet is notified by me that the ships of the 2nd and 3rd [British] Fleets, which are covering the British transports towards the North, offer a good target for the light forces. 11 a.m. Audience of His Majesty at the Palace, at which this procedure is approved. His Majesty lays special stress upon the employment of submarines. . . . His Majesty has ordered the light forces to be used offensively. . . . 4 p.m. Report from Admiral von Ingenohl on submarine operations."

How lacking in knowledge was the German Secret Service in those early days is shown by the alleged claim to "positive information". For actually—apart from various advance parties—the main British Expeditionary Force did not even *begin* to cross until August 12.

Still, the Germans were far from content. Admittedly when hostilities had broken out, only U-5 to U-25 were available for war service, and two enterprises did not seem to justify the Kaiser's hopes, but by August 15 three U-boats left Heligoland to make a further effort. They consisted partly of U-20 and U-21, and swept towards an imaginary line extending across the North Sea from Peterhead to Egersund, which the Germans considered to be the British blockade line. The enemy first advanced to about Stavanger, then U-21 went to the vicinity of Peterhead, up north to the Orkneys, back again south to the Moray Firth and Fifeness, thence by August 21 to Heligoland again. U-20 had examined the south-west of Norway before returning home, and the third boat, U-22, cruised to the Dogger Bank, from there to the neighbourhood of Flamborough Head, down the Yorkshire coast till abreast of the Humber entrance, and so once more to Heligoland.

Quite obviously these were trips made with the desire for obtaining precise information—not merely as to the Grand Fleet movements, but to bring back news of what might be the movements of commercial shipping in the North Sea and especially of our fishing trawlers. Why? Because the enemy were about to lay three important minefields a few days later, and greatly wished to know what sort of detection might lurk afloat. They were more than a little suspicious of our trawlers still engaged in fishing off the Dogger.

The culmination occurred during August, 21 and 22, when the German light cruisers *Rostock* and *Strassburg*, together with a flotilla of torpedoboats, swept towards the Dogger Bank and thus sank eight of our working trawlers, taking the crews as prisoners. It is to be noted that this expedition was supported by the *Hamburg* as well as the three submarines U-5, U-16 and U-17.

Having, then, "cleaned up" the area, it was possible for the two vessels *Albatross* and *Stuttgart*, with an escort of destroyers, to leave Heligoland at eight o'clock on the evening of August 24, and after midnight of August 25–26 *Albatross* began laying her mines some miles off the Tyne mouth, half a dozen Grimsby trawlers being sunk by the destroyers to prevent information reaching us; but almost simultaneously the *Nautilus* laid a minefield seaward of the Humber between 11 p.m. of August 25 and 1.50 a.m. of the 26th. Seven more fishing trawlers were sunk for the reason mentioned.

Thus the preliminary reconnaissance of U-boats had brought valuable data on which the German Navy acted promptly, for these two minefields—though luckily soon discovered—were destined to be dangerous nuisances of uncertain extent.

Yes: but how was it that Germany's surface ships, her High Sea Fleet, did not this month concentrate on interfering with the B.E.F. whilst being transported across the sea? One would have thought that it would have been more than worthwhile attempting the task.

Certainly the problem had been considered, yet the reason for this apparent neglect of an obvious chance is as follows. Nothing could be more illustrative of Teutonic military arrogance. For at the beginning of hostilities, the Operations Section of the German Admiralty asked the German Military authorities whether they laid stress on interrupting the British troop transports. The Military Chief of the General Staff answered that the Navy must not allow its own operations to be interfered with on that account, but it would be advantageous to the German Armies in the West if the latter were allowed to settle with 160,000 English soldiers at the same time as French and Belgians were defeated. In fact, our enemy considered the numerical size of the B.E.F. so small as not worthy of attack whilst afloat.

The British Admiralty, however, in consequence of the *Konigin Luise* minefield off Southwold and the foundering thereon of our destroyer *Amphion* the day after, began from August 7 the organizing of a naval base at Lowestoft under Captain Ellison, commanding officer of H.M.S. *Halcyon* hitherto engaged in fishery protection duties. The primary intention was to establish a permanent flotilla of eighty minesweeping trawlers who were to keep swept a channel from the Outer Dowsing down to the South Goodwins, and presently this long stretch was buoyed and constantly patrolled by drifters. It was thus that we inaugurated a reasonably protected fairway along which traffic could proceed between the eastern end of the English Channel and right up to the Humber.

A secondary development was to arm trawlers for the special service of hunting submarines off the East Coast because, whilst the potentialities of the U-boat were still not fully realized, yet there was a certain uneasiness as to what might happen to our men-of-war. The sighting of foreign submarines by Grand Fleet units in the first week of hostilities was accentuated when on August 16

H.M.S. *New Zealand* saw a U-boat in Lat. 55.5 N., Long. 5 E., and two days later another ship chased U-27 when 15 miles east of the Spurn.

Many technical details had still to be assimilated in the employment of trawlers. It was soon decided that they were not to be painted grey, like other naval ships, but would the better resemble genuine vessels still fishing if they preserved their usual appearance, even with fishing numbers on the hull still retained. Yes : but since they carried neither ice nor fish, did they not betray their true character by being well out of the water forward ? Certainly they would have done, yet this was largely counter-balanced by placing the gun on the fo'c'sle.

The fog of war had completely settled down over the North Sea within the first fortnight, and each side was trying to discern the other's intentions, yet many incidents continued unrevealed till long after hostilities. For instance, it is now ascertainable that on August 17 the light cruisers *Strassburg* and *Stralsund* made a reconnoitring sweep towards East Anglia, but did not get nearer our coast than 39 miles east of Great Yarmouth. It is also interesting to know that they were accompanied by the submarines U-19 and U-24 which at later dates were to have notable careers. Did not the former, before the war concluded, sink such naval ships as the *Dundee* and *Calgarian*, whilst Schneider in U-24 became notorious by torpedoing in different months H.M.S. *Formidable* and the White Star liner *Arabic* during the year 1915 ? This expedition of the two cruisers was just to ascertain what sort of British naval strength might be expected north of the line Lowestoft-Ymuiden, so that the Germans having arrived back home by August 19, it was possible for *Strassburg* to refuel and start off on the Dogger Bank enterprise with *Rostock* two days later, as already noted.

Thus the method of our opponents was rather that of cautiously feeling their way and laying ambushes, consisting of minefields, outside certain ports or in such areas as were likely to entrap not merely battleships but trawlers, destroyers, and such like. They laid in the Humber minefield a couple of hundred black "eggs" at a depth of 2 metres (7 feet) below low water ordinary springs, and at the same depth about that number off the Tyne. By no means an extravagant cargo, since the *Albatross* with her 2200 tons and 21 knots was capable of carrying 400 mines, and the slightly smaller *Nautilus* (1970 tons and 20 knots) could also carry 400 mines. Incidentally, it will be remembered that *Albatross* was destined, eleven months later, to end her cruising ingloriously. Whilst serving in the Baltic, she was driven ashore by the Russians on Gothland, the date being July 2, 1915, but subsequently salved and interned by the Swedes.

Now it was extremely wise to allow trawlers—not taken up for naval service—to continue their normal North Sea work. Why ?

Apart from supplying the country with food, they were doing valuable work unintentionally. Firstly, their external markings did not distinguish them from the anti-submarine trawlers, but secondly, there is no better way of discovering a mined area than to let vessels steam about with their trawls down. Sooner or later a mine will either explode, or foul the trawling gear. (This happened over and over again during these four war years.) Or it may be that a herring drifter finds her nets suddenly so heavy that something far weightier than fish must be the reason.

The first intimation of the Tyne minefield was when the fishing vessel "SN184" at 7.15 p.m. of August 26, some 30 miles from that river's mouth, fouled her nets and lost them. A few hours later her report was sent to the Admiralty. So also at 10 p.m. of the 26th, when the *City of Belfast* was shooting her nets at a spot 15 miles north of the Outer Dowsing Lightship, two mines exploded, whereupon the skipper cut away his nets, reported the occurrence to a patrol vessel, and thus the Humber area was made suspect.

This, however, did not prevent disasters happening, for presently in the same year, *Speedy*, *Linsdell*, and *Revigo* all sank on the Humber minefield, and the *Alberta* as well as *Orcades* in April, 1916 : for it is one thing to know that a minefield exists, though quite another matter to be aware of its limits north, south, east, and west. Such exact dimensions must be found only by the long and laborious process after minesweepers have made a thorough, if dangerous, investigation.

These points, then, are stressed at the outset because we shall note that later on Germany, whilst giving up the practice of laying such ambushes by means of surface ships such as the *Albatross* and *Nautilus*, did carry on the same idea, but by the operation of minelaying submarines. This will be detailed in due course.

CHAPTER 3

THE SUBMARINES LEARN THEIR STRENGTH

BY the beginning of September no fewer than two hundred and fifty hired trawlers and drifters had been diverted from their fishing avocation, and were instructed that it was quite legitimate not to hoist the White Ensign until such time as they opened fire against the enemy. That trawlers drew about 13½ feet, and drifters about 9 feet, of course exposed them to dangers of blundering on to mined areas.

From September 2 an important step was taken in more thoroughly organizing what came to be known as the Auxiliary Patrol, consisting of armed yachts, trawlers, drifters, and motor craft round our coasts. Gradually this grew and increased till a few days before the war ended it numbered 3714 vessel—yachts, patrol gunboats, whalers, trawlers, drifters, paddlers, and motor launches in the Narrow Seas, the Mediterranean, and elsewhere.

It was the surreptitious minelayers which originally demanded a more complete watch and guard by our small craft, but now the U-boats accentuated this need. Let it be mentioned that certain senior naval officers of the old school still despised the submarine as a new thing grossly overrated, but September brought a fresh surprise and unpleasant shock towards reality.

On an earlier page we mentioned U-21, and henceforth the reader is invited to make a special note both of this submarine and of her enterprising captain, Lieut.-Commander Otto Hersing, one of the greatest pioneers in submarine history ; and because of his daring adventurous spirit that section of the German Navy developed a confidence which became the greatest menace that ever threatened our shipping. In personal appearance Hersing looked more Italian than Teutonic, with dark eyes, a big nose and large mouth. Somewhat sullen in expression, tall and slender, this undaunted pioneer was the kind of fellow who is not nervous of doing something original.

Just before that war he had the deck of U-21 strengthened by extra plating, so that she could carry a gun. At the end of August, having done so well on his previous cruise in Norwegian and Scottish waters, he now once more came up the North Sea, quietly stole along the Firth of Forth under cover of darkness with the intention of destroying the massive Forth Bridge. Germany for some time had conceived the intention of demolishing this important means of connection with northernmost Britain, and indeed one of her principal spies was known to have examined the nature of its foundations.

About 10.30 p.m. on September 2, two of our batteries—one at Carlingnose and the other a machine-gun nest just below—fired on what they took to be a submarine's periscope proceeding under the bridge. It is significant that these two batteries opened fire independently, for both were convinced of its reality. At this time there happened to be very few vessels in harbour above the bridge, but the battle-cruiser *Invincible* was senior ship, and acting on the report, sent picket-boats to hunt the alleged submarine. It should be remembered there were no nets at this time across the Forth, no defences on Inchcolm, so the U-boat had only to give Inchkeith Island a wide berth and be suspicious of Carlingnose.

After investigating the scare, it was considered to have been a baseless rumour and that the batteries must have mistaken a floating piece of wood for the periscope, yet it was strange that both batteries should have made the same error at the same time. Actually their promptness prevented Hersing from committing any hostile act; he came out of the Forth, and on September 5 was in the neighbourhood of St. Abb's Head when he espied in the distance, at 3.45 p.m., H.M.S. *Pathfinder*, a flotilla leader commanded by Captain Martin Leake who was in charge of the Forth Destroyer Patrol. Hersing made a long shot with his torpedo—over 1600 yards, in fact the biggest range so far attempted, the German submarines having generally been accustomed to not much over 500 yards—and *Pathfinder* was so accurately struck that she went down in four minutes with nearly all hands.

This was the first loss of the British Navy by submarine onslaught, and it had a most depressing effect on the nation, whilst simultaneously at last convincing the most reluctant that U-boats were something to be considered most seriously. History, however, plays strange tricks in the careers of human beings. Captain Leake was among the few saved, though wounded; he recovered and was later appointed commanding officer of H.M.S. *Achilles*, a light cruiser. In that capacity he, together with the Armed Boarding Steamer *Dundee*, sank the German raider *Rena* (alias *Greif*) that was trying to run the North Sea blockade[1] one March day of biting wind and snow squalls. Subsequently he was promoted to Commodore, and served at Queenstown. Now this very courteous and charming officer, who had experienced most of the risks of seafaring, and after an exciting war left the Navy as an Admiral to enjoy a well-deserved retirement in the country, did in fact perish in peace-time along a rural road because of a mere bicycle accident. He belonged to a

---

[1] The full account of this action will be found in Chapter XVII of my book on *The Sea-Raiders*.

family conspicuous for its brave men, and I recollect his telling me that one of his kinsmen had been awarded the V.C. during the South African war, and another V.C. in the war against Germany.

When Hersing returned to Germany it was to receive very hearty congratulations on this initial victory against the British Navy, and henceforth he became marked out for great things. He had set out in company with U-20, but the honours fell to Otto Hersing.

But what were our own submarines doing all this time? Were they not paying visits to the Heligoland Bight and achieving daring exploits, collecting valuable information of shipping movements and using their torpedoes also? Soon after daybreak, on September 13, Lieut.-Commander Max Horton at 600 yards range sunk the German cruiser *Hela* of 2000 tons from H.M. Submarine E-9, and already Lieut.-Commander Godfrey Herbert on August 21 had at 600 yards just missed torpedoing from D-5 the four-funnelled German cruiser *Rostock* when outward bound with *Strassburg* to sweep the Dogger Bank of trawlers. It was not Herbert's fault that both torpedoes ran below the *Rostock*. Why? Because the war-heads of our torpedoes were found to be 40 lbs. heavier than the practice-heads with which exercises had been conducted.

As to such activities in the Heligoland area, it is enough again to quote Admiral von Pohl referring to the German Naval Commander-in-Chief:

"A letter from Admiral von Ingenohl, dated 13th September, in which he complains that British submarines control the German Bight. The attack on the *Hela* took place in a strong westerly wind and seaway."

It will be recollected that the Germans had reason for feeling miserable. On August 28 had been fought the Battle of the Bight which was not a German victory, and the Kaiser's policy of holding the High Sea Fleet in defensive reserve was much criticized by their own officers who admitted the loss of 649 men killed or drowned, 361 captured, and 140 wounded. On that occasion no German submarines had been allowed to operate. That explains why U-20 and U-21 so shortly afterwards had been sent to the Firth of Forth, why also on September 3 the four boats U-19, 22, 24, and 28 were despatched to the Ems so as to be in a position quickly to advance northwards and make a flank protection to the Heligoland Bight at the westward.

On the other hand we, foreseeing that certain well-known lightships might be likely to assist minelayers or submarines in fixing the latter's position, now took steps either to remove these navigational aids, or shift them to another spot, or obliterate their lights. During September the following were altered by the 7th: Smith's Knoll as well as Inner Dowsing and Outer Dowsing removed; Sandettie extinguished; and all East-coast lights extinguished between Orford Ness and Wick. During October the Ruytingen was removed, both the Galloper and Longsand put out, but the Outer Gabbard and Shipwash each continued to burn their lights during this year, though the North Hinder in October was shifted.

And now we come to the most startling events that hitherto had happened in sea warfare either to us or the Germans, yet how strangely do we observe one thing leading to another in the manner least expected!

Just now we saw how anxious was the Chief of the German Admiralty Staff to interrupt by U-boat attack the British trooping activity towards Ostend; but owing to bad weather no submarine could be despatched immediately. It was, however, decided to select U-9 (Lieut.-Commander Otto Weddigen), and at 5.15 a.m. (German time) of September 20, she left Heligoland to take up a position between Ostend and the West Hinder lightship, thus being well placed for attacking any British transports likely to approach the Belgian coast from England.

Now it is one of the curious links in the chain of events how an equinoctial gale kicked up such a vicious sea, that U-9 made very slow progress southwards when bound for her allotted beat. She was quite a small craft, displacing on the surface 500 tons, with a speed of 14 knots in smooth water. However, the sea was anything but smooth, the submarine became well-nigh unmanageable, yet the presence of surface vessels caused Weddigen to keep diving; so it was not until early on the 22nd that he reached that neighbourhood of the Maas lightship which throughout the war was an important landmark for shipping bound to or from Rotterdam, but likewise for such patrols as German submarines and British destroyers. It was especially valuable for these vessels to verify their position.

At 6 a.m. (German time) Weddigen through his periscope espied three surface ships conspicuous in the murky morn and recognized them to be British cruisers two miles apart. He determined on attack against *Aboukir*, the centremost; her companions, *Cressy* and *Hogue*, steaming in line abreast northwards doing 10 knots. At 7.30 a.m.—this Central European time being one hour ahead of Greenwich—Weddigen reckoned *Aboukir* to be right ahead, distant about 500 yards. He fired his No. 2 tube, saw *Aboukir* roll heavily, then capsize, so next he made for the *Hogue*, the easternmost vessel which had come to the help of *Aboukir* and was standing by rendering all assistance, with boats out. She was practically stopped.

According to Weddigen's own diary of the event, he fired Nos. 1 and 2 torpedo-tubes at 7.55 a.m., the *Hogue* being right ahead, the range about 350 yards. He saw the ship roll, and within ten minutes she disappeared. But that was not all. Preparations were made for attacking the *Cressy*, which was the westernmost ship, also stopped and engaged in saving lives. It was now 8.20 a.m., the range about 1000 yards, and at five seconds interval Nos. 3 and 4 tubes were fired though only one explosion—and that a very violent one—was heard. Possibly the missile had entered the magazine!

But through the periscope could be seen a huge smoke cloud, and after four minutes she was observed no longer to be on an even keel, then a final torpedo was despatched to make sure. Shortly after 9 a.m. she was seen lying right over on her side, turned turtle, and sank. Our North Sea tragedy had been completed.

Weddigen had surpassed anything that he, or the Germans, or the British, had ever expected. He had failed to obey his original orders because he never reached the destination and had used up all his torpedoes. At 8.50 a.m. he was on his way back towards Germany and observed that at least five vessels were rushing succour to this ghastly scene. Dutch steamers and Lowestoft fishermen succeeded in rescuing over 800 officers and men, but more than 1100 were drowned. With pain we remember the loss of so many young midshipmen barely accustomed to seafaring, of many more men grown old in the service who had come back from retirement.

It was a hard lesson that we learnt: not only that a big ship must not go to the assistance of another mined or torpedoed, but also that the submarine instead of being held in derision by older and senior officers was to be regarded as a very great potentiality of danger. Reports of seen U-boats were coming in from all kinds of ships too frequently for entire disbelief, and many deep-water sailors began to look at the problem afresh.

What then was the submarine which in one hour could wipe out three big cruisers? We could say that when on the surface such a craft drew roughly 14 feet, and that with periscope awash (that is, say, about 2 feet of this tube showing) the draught to this periscope was some 24 feet. But she could quickly hide herself below the surface, and this invisibility was quite another matter. Apart from the definite sinking of U-15 by H.M.S. *Birmingham* on August 9, and of H.M.S. *Pathfinder* on September 5, by U-21, it was certain that H.M.S. *New Zealand* on August 16 sighted (in Lat. 55.5 N., Long. 5 E.) a submarine with her deck almost awash, but also on August 28 H.M.S. *Lowestoft*, *Fearless*, and *Lion* all made similar claims; that the monitor H.M.S. *Severn*, whilst coming across from Ostend to Dover, had a torpedo fired at her; that a torpedoboat off May Island in September was the target for two torpedoes, but on September 27 (within a week of Weddigen's effort) our light cruiser *Attentive* was most certainly assaulted by submarine in Dover Straits. This was the work of Lieut.-Commander von Hennig in U-18 (one of the flotilla who had left Heligoland for the north on August 6). I remember entering Dover Harbour on September 29 and hearing the Admiral giving certain instructions, for it was the first time that a German submarine had penetrated these straits.

What was to be the fate of this daring U-18 we shall see presently.

It is, however, to be borne in mind that neither the Germans nor ourselves were free from muddled reasoning at this time. For instance, the following written remark by Admiral von Pohl on September 17 should be read in conjunction with the desire that sent Weddigen towards the Belgian coast:

"The War Minister, who is now the representative of the Chief of the General Staff, has asked me", says Admiral von Pohl, "whether it would not be possible for our submarines to interrupt the passage of British transports to Ostend: I showed him on the charts how impossible it was for submarines to operate off Ostend on account of the sand banks, but I have drawn the attention of the Commander-in-Chief, High Sea Fleet, to this suggestion of the Army leaders and have requested him to give it his attention."

In plain language it needed a sailor and his charts to convince distinguished military personages they were talking about a subject they did not comprehend. Weddigen did not get to the Ostend vicinity, and the British Navy operating in that district never believed that U-boats off the shallow Belgian coast would risk themselves so near to shore.

Did the German Navy make no mistakes, then? Of course they did. When they laid the Tyne minefield on August 26, alleging that its northern end began just south of Blyth and its southern end a little north of Sunderland, the whole line being thought to be from 2 to 6 miles off the land; the position was hopelessly wrong, although the Germans believed the veracity of their statement till long after the war. Actually the German minelayer that night laid his cargo *over* 30 *miles from the land*, having got badly out of his reckoning.

But we know that the Germans are bad losers, that unfavourable news seriously affects their outlook, that the Battle of the Bight on August 28 had depressed the spirits of the High Sea Fleet. Contrariwise, when U-20 and U-21 were sent to the Firth of Forth at the beginning of September, and on September 5 Hersing accomplished the first submarine success in history by sinking H.M.S. *Pathfinder*, the German naval spirits went up; and the Weddigen incident assured the Teutonic mind that here was a really great, but hitherto unsuspected, weapon of offence.

For once it was thoroughly established that the modern cruiser and battleship were not safe to roam the sea, except when screened by destroyers. The *Pathfinder* was lost because she was patrolling in a regular area and without any screen. The three *Cressys* certainly possessed a destroyer force, but the equinoctial weather intervened on September 17 and necessitated their seeking shelter in port. Not for five days was it possible for an anti-submarine screen to be sent from Harwich, but by then it was too late. In those days it took quite a time to convince naval officers that both the *Pathfinder* and *Cressys* were not the victims of mines, but this was quite natural when the North Sea minefields off the Tyne and Spurn accounted for so many disasters.

Life at sea had indeed become difficult since these snares had been laid to entrap fishermen, who by their trawls often became the first to announce the fouling of an area. But sometimes it would turn out not quite as expected. Take the case of the fishing trawler *Kilmarnock* which came out of the Humber on September 19 (1914), and from the Spurn steamed ESE. at 8 knots. About 2 p.m. the Skipper was at the wheel steering, and all the crew on deck (excepting the engineers and trimmers) getting the net ready, when suddenly they sighted a mine.

Thereupon the Skipper in the wheelhouse rang down to stop engines, and the log was hauled showing they had run 31 miles from the Spurn. Another mine was also sighted 40 yards away, so a dan buoy, with an old deck-brush lashed to the end of the staff, was dropped to mark the spot : it was time now to search out the minesweepers and put them wise. They were not too far away.

Course having been altered to the southward, *Kilmarnock* went cautiously at half-speed, and the news she carried would be valuable for ascertaining limits of the dangerous area. Six or seven more mines now appeared, so *Kilmarnock* carefully steered to go between them, when the terrible thing happened. Suddenly she struck a mine about amidships, where she drew most water, and everything seemed to occur. The Mate, named John Frederick Outhouse, was right forward at the time with three other hands, when off vanished the trawler's stern whilst the fore foot was lifted two feet from the sea. Down went the Mate blown bodily off the ship, and sucked into the depths, but happily he came up again, grabbed a piece of board and held on to it till 3.40 p.m.

Lucky for him that his strength did not give in, for the minesweeping trawler *Kaphreda* came this way, sighted him, and saved the man who was able to send warning of these dangers. Of course, trawlers drawing so much as $13\frac{1}{2}$ feet of water were not the most suitable sort of ship for sweeping : paddlers, normally employed as excursion steamers with about 6 feet to $7\frac{1}{2}$ feet draught, were found much more useful for sweeping quickly the areas of mines. And it was also an advantage that powerful engines gave them high speed.

Consequently the Admiralty chartered on September 27 at

Bristol such paddlers as *Brighton Queen* and *Devonia*, whilst *Westward Ho!*, *Glen Avon*, *Cambridge*, and *Lady Ismay* from that port soon followed. It was amusing enough to see such ex-pleasure craft now painted Navy grey and doing strange antics within Grimsby locks, but soon they performed most excellent and perilous work, and their speed of 19 knots was some 8 or 9 knots superior to that of the trawlers.

Chapter 4

THE LATEST DISASTERS

THE Germans settled down to relying on the mine and submarine as the principal naval weapons, yet for the present it did not seem fitting to combine the two : but the successes in September of Hersing and Weddigen urged a new belief that at last the Germans possessed a weapon which would eventually bring those hateful English to their knees.

German submarine activity during October, 1914, increased considerably, and H.M. ships either were attacked by, or merely sighted, enemy submarines at least thirteen times. The earliest this month was when H.M. Submarine B-3 on October 2 was quite close to Dover's eastern entrance. At 12.35 p.m., when 2 miles SE. of the Goodwins, an enemy submarine spotted and fired a torpedo which luckily passed some yards astern of the British craft.

It was, of course, a further proof that U-boats were going to become tiresome in the Straits, if not further westward. Thanks to Admiral Jellicoe's zeal in this matter, it was decided to lay a big minefield at the approach to the Dover Straits. Having regard to the statements in the previous chapter about a submarine's depth, it is interesting to remark that these British mines were laid 20 feet below low water (ordinary springs). Theoretically, then, this ambush disposed of any submarine proceeding submerged. We have to state, however, that not for a long time were our mines either satisfactory in themselves, or furnished with reliable mooring arrangements. Therefore (if the reader will pardon anticipation) one may remark that this eastern minefield gradually got adrift, and its round objects of explosion mostly drifted up the North Sea before wind and current until beaching themselves on Holland and even Sweden, as I can personally testify.

The first line of these mines was laid on the night of October 2–3 by H.M.S. *Apollo*, *Andromache*, *Iphigenia*, and *Intrepid*, who were steaming at 10 knots at the time in bright moonlight. This initial night they dropped 264 mines at intervals of 120 feet, but by the night of October 21 the total number of mines deposited was 2464 in seven lines.

There could be no doubt that in the meantime Germany through her submarines was keeping a vigilant lookout on the Dover Straits, for in the neighbourhood mentioned a submarine was seen on October 6 by the destroyer *Mohawk* near the South Goodwin lightship and attacked by a German torpedo. The climax came a few days later and in another part of the sea, but by immense luck it is Weddigen who again comes into prominence.

He had set out again in U-9 after the sensational sinking of the three *Cressys*, and at this time those old-fashioned but bad sea-keeping *Edgar* class of cruisers were employed[1] in the north as the 10th Cruiser Squadron. It was 10 a.m. of October 15, and the position Lat. 57.47 N., Long. 0.12 W., the sea being calm; the periscope framing three of these *Edgars*, the colourful bunting hoisted for exchange of signals, and the indiscreet lowering of a boat. Weddigen took the proferred chance as the hove-to *Hawke* waited to collect her mails from *Endymion* and then had barely restarted when the explosion burst. She heeled over as Weddigen remembered the *Cressys*, and she went down with about 500 men to the depths. That same day H.M.S. *Theseus* (also of the 10th Cruiser Squadron) was attacked in Lat. 57.50 N., Long. 0.33 E., and narrowly escaped. Next day that famous destroyer *Swift* was engaged rescuing *Hawke's* survivors, when the *Swift* was attacked by U-boat no fewer than three times.

But Weddigen was really on his way north to attempt the eastern entrance to Scapa Flow, and had achieved (as in the *Cressys* incident) something else. When therefore on the 16th he found himself off the eastern entrance (in Lat. 58.43 N., Long. 2.5 E.) he sighted H.M.S. *Alarm* and fired a torpedo which fortunately missed. Almost immediately he saw H.M.S. *Nymphe*, also missed, and the Switha Battery reported him about 4 p.m. Weddigen did not get through into Scapa, but he was able to return home with one certain victory and some near-victories.

Now at this time there was also operating in the North Sea Lieut.-Commander Feldkirchner aboard U-17. She was one of those boats which on August 6 had made a trip up the North Sea, and now she had gone across this area so that on October 20 she was 14 miles WSW. of Skudesnaes. She here sighted the British S.S. *Glitra*—quite a small ship of 866 tons—captured, and scuttled her. This was the first of all the merchant vessels which for the next four years Germany was to sink. It thus marks a notable occasion in warfare attack on vessels other than men-of-war.

There was likewise about now another important event: it was the first loss during hostilities of a British submarine, E-3. Like certain others she came over from Harwich to the Heligoland Bight, and most excellent work they all performed in bringing home valuable information: on one occasion she had even brought back the pilot of a German seaplane caught on the surface. Some time, however, in the earlier half of October, E-3 was caught and sunk in

---

[1] Full details of their experiences will be found in my book *The Big Blockade*.

the Bight, for on the 18th of that month her loss was claimed by Lieut.-Commander Wegener in U-27 off Borkum, the torpedo literally blowing our boat in two.

But Wegener was destined to have a hectic career as we shall follow in due course. He carried on towards the Dover Straits, which now were becoming popular with these adventurers, and a few days later also came U-19. As usual this latter hugged the Dutch coast, and on the night of October 24 was in Lat. 52.51 N., Long. 4.12 E., but so was the British destroyer *Badger*. The German was actually bound for Zeebrugge (which had now fallen into enemy hands) and tried in the darkness of a black night to settle the *Badger* by means of a torpedo. The latter, however, avoided the missile and using her forefoot rammed the U-boat.

Steel against steel? Of course something had to give in such a contest. But which was the victor?

The answer is that, despite the awful clash and crunching, both escaped destruction, but each received serious damage. The *Badger's* bows were crumpled, but she got safely into the Medway. U-19 had to turn back for Germany and there undergo repairs, so she was relieved in the meanwhile by U-24. The nocturnal excitement had simply proved again, as instanced through all the ages, that ramming is usually as damaging to the rammer as to the rammed. Even galleys of the ancients are fair examples of this.

Shortly after the above incident Germany sent to Zeebrugge U-5, U-11, and U-12. Of U-11 it is enough to state that she perished on a mine off Zeebrugge in December with all hands, and that U-12 was rammed and sunk by H.M.S. *Ariel* on March 19, 1915. I recollect seeing that destroyer returning to Leith immediately after the incident, but of course *Ariel's* hull had been severely damaged by the impact and already was badly down by the bows.

Well, then, since U-24 had now to operate in the Dover Straits neighbourhood, she appeared off Cape Grisnez on October 26. The 4590-ton French steamer *Amiral Ganteaume* was carrying to France from the Low Countries hundreds of Belgian refugees. It was a dastardly attack, yet only forty of the panic-stricken passengers lost their lives, and the torpedoed vessel was towed into Boulogne, about two thousand refugees being rescued by the S.S. *Queen*.

Our immediate interest with U-12 is that she soon motored out of Zeebrugge into Dover Straits, where she found H.M.S. *Niger* off Deal Pier on November 11, but here was a gunboat of ancient vintage and lying at anchor: so there could be little merit in sinking such a vessel. On the other hand, we had not yet got into our minds—firmly and clearly—the submarine danger, the lurking peril that might come when least expected. We had allowed H.M.S. *Hermes*, a seaplane carrier, to be torpedoed and sunk on October 31 some 8 miles WNW. of Calais whilst crossing over from Dunkirk intending to make for Dover. That the attacker was none other than U-27, shows that her repairs from the *Badger* wounding were but slight, and that Wegener was a glutton for destruction ; but also we saw that something more drastic would have to be done in protection of our shipping.

And now two major events occurred which affected the general naval outlook rather than the particular. Firstly, there was the Scapa Flow difficulty. At last in mid-October there were so many discussions about the Grand Fleet, and the daring of the U-boats, that something shaped itself in the Commander-in-Chief's mind. Perhaps in the present condition the sanctity of Scapa was in danger of being violated by a U-boat ? The Grand Fleet must therefore be moved to the western side of the British Isles, until Scapa had been made reliable. Thus it came about that Lough Swilly in the North of Ireland was decided upon, and we can picture these ships approaching that coast.

Suddenly H.M.S. *Audacious* at 8.50 a.m. of October 26 struck a mine, the exact position being 18 miles NE. of Tory Island. With great difficulty, and not without the display of immense resource and gallantry, she was towed towards the shore when she finally blew up and sank at 9 p.m. The previous day at 2.15 p.m. the British S.S. *Manchester Commerce* had also struck one of these mines and foundered, but this important news did not reach those concerned until 1.8 p.m. of October 27.

To cut this episode short, the Fleet was compelled to remain inside Lough Swilly whilst minesweeping trawlers were telegraphed for from Milford and Larne, so that before that month ended these trawlers were sweeping a safe exit for the Grand Fleet from Lough Swilly westward. No mines were found there, and at last the Grand Fleet emerged safely. But the whole of this suspense and anxious period of days had arisen through the desire to come westward entirely because of the submarines. In other words, at last the U-boat had been recognized as a dangerous foe.

The Tory Island minefield was located in the Atlantic swell by the trawlers not till five days before Christmas, and after monotonous sweeping, interrupted by bad weather, most of these dangers were swept up by the following April or, at least, had drifted chiefly northward. The Tory Island area was presumed to be clear in June, 1915, though even in 1916 one mine was destroyed in its original neighbourhood.

Who laid these mines ? At the time there was not a little which was mysterious, and even after the event there existed a great difference between where the Germans *thought* they laid them and where they actually were placed. It is agreed that the minelayer was the North German Lloyd liner *Berlin,* 17,324 tons, which previously used to run to New York capable of carrying 3630 passengers but was taken over by the German Navy and repainted. Her particular object had been to foul the North Channel off Ireland

and entrap a convoy of thirty-three steamships bringing from Canada thousands of troops. These were saved, because at the last the convoy was directed into Plymouth.

Altogether 200 mines were laid from Tory Island, but the incident was so shrouded in mystery that official announcement of the *Audacious* loss was not made till three days after Armistice—November 14, 1918—and the Germans were kept in ignorance that in November, 1914, the Fleet which their submarines wanted was somewhere else but precariously situated. Nowadays when we are apt sometimes to feel that fate deals against us with a heavy hand, it is well to remember how grievous was the burden of our dismay which had to be borne. In many a ship and ward-room this *Audacious* affair was of course common knowledge which could not be discussed, and the incident was so well guarded by the Press that no mention was made of the matter, save in an American journal which also published a photograph of the stricken battleship heavily listing, with decks awash, boats rowing about, and destroyers standing by as a screen. The White Star S.S. *Olympic* waited for a while, but nothing could prevent her American passengers from viewing and photographing the scene.

Admiral Jellicoe, who in his memoirs has left a record of this tragic sinking that has been read by thousands of our contemporaries, at first thought a submarine had done the deed : in fact, the battleship *Monarch* quite erroneously reported sighting a U-boat : an announcement which shows how valueless were some allegations in those days. It may definitely be affirmed that no such craft was nearer than the Dover Straits.

All available destroyers, trawlers, and tugs, were sent out as well as the collier *Thornhill*, suited for towing, together with the Fleet Messenger *Cambria* in which Vice-Admiral Sir Lewis Bayly (presently to be mentioned in another connection) proceeded to the spot and with great skill directed the impossible salvage operations. The wind was from the WSW., force 4 to 5, with a long swell, when she struck the mine. At the time the *Centurion* (flag) was leading, then followed the *Ajax*, next the *Audacious*, and finally the *King George V*. The *Audacious* had turned a little inside the *Ajax* ; otherwise we can understand how narrowly was a heavier disaster caused, weakening our battle strength till the High Sea Fleet superiority would have imperilled our nation.

At first the dull noise aft had been thought on board to be one of the after guns fired by accident, but it was next noticed that the ship did not right herself as she should have done after the helm had been eased, so she was hauled out of line to starboard head to wind and sea. The port engine had to be stopped for the port wing engine-room was flooded. In this condition she limped at 9 knots towards Lough Swilly, with six feet of water rising in the dark, lamp-lit, compartment and the whole place covered with oil. Then about

11 a.m. the great ship ceased to steam, she laboured heavily in the Atlantic swell, gear was beginning to get adrift—two boats washed overboard and the main derrick taking charge dangerously until lashed—and the sequel could be forecast painfully.

Finally about noon the cruiser *Liverpool*, several destroyers, and *Olympic* sent boats to remove all engine-room ratings, daymen, and most of the Marines. About 250 seamen now alone remained. It was about 2 p.m. that the *Olympic* got her in tow, the line being taken to the latter by H.M.S. *Fury*, a destroyer. But alas! everything went wrong, the *Audacious* declined to be steered, became utterly unmanageable, and actually parted the tow rope.

First, then, *Liverpool* tried but the tow fouled one of her propellers, and had to be cut. Then *Thornhill* tried, but when the strain came, the line again parted. So at 5 p.m. when it was getting dark and the quarter-deck well under water volunteers were called for, and out of them were chosen 8 officers with 56 ratings. The others were removed from the ship, but presently the hull rolled so deeply that even the sixty-four had to be taken off.

The last of these crises occurred about 9 p.m. when the *Audacious* blew up with a terrible explosion, the hull turned bottom uppermost and she sank stern first. Every one of the 852 officers and men were saved, though when the flames had burst out they reached a height of 400 feet and the explosion could be heard 15 miles away in Lough Swilly.

So that was the end to a fine modern unit of our Battle Fleet, yet whilst more U-boat rumours were being spread and even more patrol vessels and minesweepers taken up all round the coast, a second sensation was destined to occur. Until now we had either in commission, or fitting out, some thirty-seven yachts; whilst we numbered of armed trawlers, either patrolling or getting ready, 130; besides 246 minesweeping trawlers, 42 drifters and a few paddle minesweepers, also serving. Till the end of October only half a dozen trawlers and drifters of these auxiliary warships had been lost through mines since the war began.

Nevertheless, whilst the great ships of the Grand Fleet were resting silently within Lough Swilly, and sweepers were exploring waters close to the coast, the S.Y. *Lorna*—at some future date fated to sink UB-74 west of Portland—with her six trawlers patrolled off Lough Swilly entrance.

But on the East coast of England came a startling visitation.

ONE OF THE PATROL DRIFTERS
Many were armed as here shown

Chapter 5

GERMANY RAIDS GORLESTON

WE now see the Germans with their surface ships purposely coming across the North Sea under cover of night, laying mines off the English east coast, and advertising that fact by bombarding land property, then scurrying off seaward and returning home.

In this undertaking we perceive more than one objective : it was intended to create the local demand of pegging down one well-gunned ship to the spot for that illogical purpose of "coast defence", but apart from the display of Teutonic frightfulness the desire was to entice warships on to the mines left behind. Let us view November 3 from our own vessels.

The biggest of the latter was H.M.S. *Halcyon*, 1070 tons, a familiar sight among visitors to East Anglia. Nothing wonderful as a fighter with her pair of 4·7-inch guns, for though classed as gunboat and usually secured well up harbour at one of the Lowestoft quays, she emerged in peace-time now and again to look after the North Sea fisheries, but at 6.15 a.m. of November she was coming out of Gorleston—the next harbour further north—and her mission was to search for mines.

Nearly an hour passed, she had navigated north of Corton Sands, had worked up to 11 knots when at 7.8 a.m. she sighted to the northeast a four-funnelled cruiser, then four battle-cruisers, and three more cruisers. A German raiding squadron, which under protection of the night had come across from Germany. They altered course at the Cross Sand Lightship from SSW. to SE., but who were they ? *Halcyon* was not quite certain, so flashed a challenge but an immediate reply from a shower of 11-inch shells left no further doubt. By 7.20 the *Halcyon's* steering compass was shot away and, for a while, her helm jammed.

By altering course frequently, the enemy's salvoes were avoided further and at 7.40 *Halcyon* was no longer the target. To the southwest of *Halcyon*, about two miles from the Corton Lightvessel were two destroyers patrolling : *Lively* and *Leopard*, of 400 and 385 tons respectively, but old-fashioned, the biggest gun being only a 12-pounder. These three lightly armed vessels were obviously no match for the German squadron.

Now on sighting the enemy, both destroyers made towards the

Germans at 24 knots. It was a typical North Sea morning, with November mist, and the raiders were belching much smoke from their funnels which made it difficult for them to be discerned as one ship from another, the visibility aboard *Lively* being reckoned as 6 miles. The latter took station about one cable on *Halcyon's* port quarter, in order to make a smoke screen for the latter since the 11-inch and 6-inch shells were firing at the fisheries vessel from 7.15 till 7.25 at a range of about 6500 yards, but it had begun at 10,000, decreased to 8,000, and diminished still further. At 7.32 the Germans ceased fire entirely and accelerated their speed on a southeast course, but the two destroyers leaving *Halcyon* to find her way back to harbour, went in chase of the retreating enemy. The intention was at least to maintain touch, but soon the Germans were lost to sight in the mist.

It is remarkable that *Halcyon* received so little damage, and the destroyers were not hit at all. The Germans laid 140 mines, and fired about 200 shells. Next day when the minesweepers got to work one of them, the *Mary*, blew up; though so late as November 9, 1916, whilst clearance of this area was still going on the paddle minesweeper *Fair Maid* thus foundered. But that does not complete the story.

In actual money value the enemy lost heavily by this Gorleston raid. One of the German vessels subsequently supporting was the *Yorck*, armoured cruiser, and on reaching her own waters she was groping through the mist when she hit one of the German mines off the Jade. The explosion caused her to capsize and founder with the loss of half her crew. And this was confirmed in a curious manner.

For on June 26, 1918, the submarine UC-11 ended her days on a mine in the Harwich area, but her young captain, Lieut. Kurt Utke, was saved and taken prisoner. At the time of the Gorleston affair he was serving as a midshipman, but was below and saw nothing of the bombardment.

But Utke says that when entering the mouth of the Jade on November 4 she struck two mines of the barrage, the weather being very thick and the sea smooth. The first explosion happened roughly abreast of the bridge, and *Yorck* was immediately turned, but during this manœuvre she detonated a second mine further aft. She then heeled over to port and sank in five minutes after capsizing. She was never salved.

Yes: this Gorleston episode was responsible for yet another sequel, and it is strange that things should so work out. Let it be mentioned that during this first autumn Gorleston, besides harbouring many drifters and some trawlers, was also the temporary base for certain of our D-class and E-class submarines bound for the Baltic or elsewhere. I laid my ship exactly opposite to these boats on October 4, and presently there arrived D-3 and D-5, this latter being commanded by Lieut.-Commander Godfrey Herbert, one of the ablest naval officers who incidentally on August 21 had fired two torpedoes at the German cruiser *Rostock* in Heligoland Bight when the latter was bound up the North Sea. Herbert missed, but the fault was not his and we have already explained on an earlier page that the warheads of our torpedoes were 40 pounds heavier than the practice heads we had been accustomed to use.[1]

Now it so happened that on November 2, the Senior Naval Officer at Yarmouth gave Herbert permission to leave D-5 and go up to Norwich for the night, provided he could return at an hour's notice if wanted. Hiring a car, therefore, he went but soon after 7 a.m. the next morning was rung up on the 'phone by Lieut. Donald Brodie his next in command. The announcement was that the German raiders were off the coast, so with great speed Lieut.-Commander Herbert dashed through the county, joined his craft without delay, and took her out to sea, making in the same direction where the Germans had been last seen.

Perhaps it might be possible to torpedo at least one enemy vessel?

Meanwhile, at 9.50 a.m., having as he told me "finished a belated breakfast", he came up to the conning tower and sent Brodie down to get ready the torpedoes. Twenty minutes later came disaster full and complete. The submarine blew up with a terrible explosion, for D-5, out of all that North Sea space, struck a mine under her stern and in less than a minute changed from a submarine to a submerged piece of wreckage. One extraordinary feature is that five people were saved, that Herbert was one of them but Brodie was not. It was the watchful Skipper of a herring drifter who from a distance of 4 miles sighted the explosion, rushed to the rescue, gave the survivors hot coffee, wrapped them up in blankets, and landed them in Gorleston. Yes, it had been an odd sort of day, and mines had been laid by the Germans plentifully.

But the oddest fact of all is that D-5 foundered on a British mine, for this was one of those which we saw being laid at the entrance to the Dover Straits and had such indifferent holding gear. Thanks to the autumn gales, this among other mines had broken adrift and was now making a passage up the North Sea; but that was sheer bad luck when it hit the submarine though history showed in this war how very rarely a vessel hit a mine end-on, for the hull's suction and the indraught of her propellers drew the object aft.

Taking it by and large the German raid brought about totally unexpected sequels, though to entrap Commodore Tyrwhitt's Harwich Force which would be expected to arrive on the spot was one of the main intentions. We know from German sources that the enemy relished this Yarmouth exploit "as a means of maintaining the spirit of the *personnel*". Originally it had been intended

[1] See page 84 of my volume, *Amazing Adventure*, 1935.

to take place any time after October 29, but the bad weather interrupted until they set out on November 2 at 4.30 p.m. under Admiral Hipper.

It is claimed in the German official, post-war, account that the mines were laid by the *Stralsund*, the purpose being to block the Haisborough Gat. Admiral Hipper had some difficulty in making out his exact position, but as he neared the coast and saw first the *Halcyon*, and next those two destroyers, he feared for a torpedo attack. There was a misunderstanding among his own ships as to the signals he now made, the North and South Star Batteries were engaged, but what he especially expected was a submarine onslaught so he kept moving at high and varying speeds.

There can be no denying that the usually efficient Germans failed still further, for this squadron had consisted of *Strassburg*, *Graudenz*, followed by the *Seydlitz*, *Moltke*, *Blucher*, *Von der Tann*, and the smaller *Kolberg* with *Stralsund* as minelayer. Now, on the way home engine trouble developed both in the *Von der Tann* and *Kolberg*, then as the squadron was approaching Terschelling where they were being awaited by U-boats, the latter were so convinced the squadron consisted of British units that only just in time did they avoid a fatal mistake. Then, too, having reached Schellig Roads, occurred the loss of the armoured cruiser *Yorck* belonging to the supporting main fleet.

At the back of the British war mind was very much present the thought that this Gorleston raid was but the precedent of some attempted invasion, nor did this conviction lose its belief during the whole winter. The necessity for taking up more trawlers for sweeping mined channels, for maintaining vigilant patrols round our coasts against invaders and submarines, was thus so urgent that these fishing vessels accustomed to keep the seas in all weathers were being enrolled everywhere.

On an earlier page we mentioned the sending of three German submarines to Zeebrugge after Belgium fell into the enemy's hands, but we have already explained that U-11 was destined to go down on a mine off that breakwater and it is also believed that U-5 disappeared this December for the same reason. For the present we have been content to record the blow by U-12 against H.M.S. *Niger*, ere that submarine was compelled to pay the penalty. And now another pioneer, U-18, was to have her career brought to a sudden stop.

It was in the early hours of November 22 that the Grand Fleet, being back once more within Scapa Flow, came out for making an incursion down the North Sea. It happened that on the next day Lieut.-Commander von Hennig in U-18 made his ill-timed effort. So far he had won fame by (1) attacking H.M.S. *Attentive* in Dover Straits, (2) being the first German submarine to penetrate that area, and (3) being thought to have been the craft which just failed to torpedo B-3 off the Goodwins on October 2. Therefore his daring might lead him with success against the Grand Fleet.

After passing into Pentland Firth, he followed a steamer into Scapa Flow approaches, noticed the boom defence in the Hoxa entrance, and that the Grand Fleet was "not at home", so out he came again. Now began his trouble, for the trawler *Tokio* off Hoxa Head caught sight of the periscope and then she was rammed by the minesweeping trawler *Dorothy Gray* (Skipper A. Youngson, R.N.R.). A very fine bit of work, for anybody who has tried knows how difficult it is to manœuvre a straight-keeled, single-propeller, slow-moving trawler straight for a partially submerged and moving obstacle. But fishermen are clear-eyed and quick to act.

As a result of this impact, U-18 was rammed shortly after midday, her damaged hydroplane made her nose-dive, she hit the sea-bed, then broke surface and was properly in a dilemma ; for H.M.S. *Garry* (a destroyer) appeared and also rammed, so that finally she hit the bottom again, broke down and was driven on to the rocks. Her rudder was bent, her batteries caught fire when *Garry* first saw her. After the Germans had let off star signals for assistance and hoisted the white flag, she gave up the contest off Muckle Skerry. The valves were opened, and she sank ; all the twenty-eight officers and men (except one) being taken off by *Garry* and another destroyer.

This destruction of the enemy was chiefly credited to the *Dorothy Gray*, and it was the cause of the First Lord (Mr. Winston Churchill) telegraphing from the Admiralty : "Hearty congratulations to trawler" followed by the award of £500 to Skipper Youngson and crew, with £100 to the *Tokio*. The U-boat's crew had left Heligoland only eight days previously, and now found themselves in a prisoners-of-war camp. There von Hennig bided his time till the years ended and he returned to the German Navy, so that when the Second War started in 1939 he was already an Admiral.

On this same November 23 Hersing in U-21, having come down the English Channel so far as the neighbourhood of Havre, sank the S.S. *Malachite* bound from Liverpool with a cargo for the Army in France. She was only of 718 tons, and the interesting feature is that the deed was done not by torpedo but gunfire. So also three days later when Hersing waylaid the S.S. *Primo* off Cape d'Antifer, he achieved another sinking by gunnery. This was a technique which was eventually a speciality of some U-boat captains, and saved the more costly torpedo whilst enabling the submarine to extend her period of activity. The best instance was that "ace of aces", Commander Lothar von Arnauld de la Perière, who was the greatest U-boat specialist Germany possessed and was credited with sinking 400,000 tons chiefly by gunfire and keeping his distance. He was killed in France in 1941, having reached the rank of Admiral.

By the end of November the submarine situation was beginning to take form and indicate that it could be grappled with. Guns were being mounted more and more in trawlers, and there was no doubt that the *Dorothy Gray* incident had given every man a fresh encouragement. For instance, two days afterwards, though it was clear that an attack on Scapa Flow had by no means been shelved, trawlers were chasing submarines in the neighbourhood of Lat. 58.42 N., Long. 2.39 W. Even Admiral Jellicoe was praising the trawler patrols. Such units as the *Brutus* and *Hamlet* would chase a submarine till finally—relying on superior speed whilst above surface—she got away and dived from sight.

It was learnt, too, that the minelayer *Berlin* had from the Tory Island field entered Trondhjem Fjord by November 16 where she was now interned and disarmed. Trawlers kept assembling at Buncrana for minesweeping Tory Island minefield, but there were many days when sweeps could not be used in the heavy weather which prevailed, and some vessels were sent for that purpose to Lough Swilly.

But now in December another, and more important, minelaying surface raid was to be attempted. The enterprise had been fixed for the end of November, though eventually it had to be postponed about a fortnight. Before such occasions the Germans usually despatched one of their submarines to make a report on the neighbourhood, and for this purpose selected Lieut.-Commander Wegener who (we have seen) already had in U-27 sunk our submarine E-3 and H.M.S. *Hermes*.

Before valuable capital ships, drawing much water, could be risked off the Yorkshire coast it was essential that U-27 should ascertain whether the British had there laid any mines and to what extent they were patrolling. Wegener brought encouraging news, so that at dusk of December 15 the German *main* fleet left Germany at 15 knots proceeding across the North Sea. Admiral von Ingenohl, Commander-in-Chief of the High Sea Fleet, had a grave suspicion of the North Sea trawlers working between Heligoland and the Dogger Bank. Although practically all of these fishermen were of Dutch nationality, he still believed they were in some ways serving the enemy's purpose and that numerous mines were by them laid. It is rather curious to remember exactly the same suspicion was frequently expressed by Admiral Jellicoe and others. For instance, when the Tyne minefield had been mysteriously laid, the First Lord of the Admiralty openly, but erroneously, accused Dutch fishing craft of depositing these mines; and whenever Admiral Jellicoe took the Grand Fleet down the North Sea, he would send destroyers from his screen to examine suspected fishermen seen at their job. So, also, we know that when the Germans were sending minelaying vessels for the Tyne and Humber areas they were careful first to clear the Dogger Bank of fishing trawlers that had come from Boston and Grimsby.

We have learned from no less an authority than Admiral Scheer that the results of German minefields—off Southwold, Tyne, Humber, Tory Island, and Gorleston—were unknown to the enemy. The Germans had been working as if blinded later. When, therefore on December 15, the big cruisers under Vice-Admiral Hipper sailed with orders to bombard (1) Scarborough and (2) Hartlepool, farther north, they were to lay also mines because of the traffic between East Coast ports. A further reason could be pleaded that in hoping to attract also the Grand Fleet in this neighbourhood, they plotted for another purpose.

"The big cruisers," says Admiral Scheer,[1] "then divided into two groups . . . the northern section, the *Seydlitz*, *Moltke*, and *Blücher*, making for Hartlepool. An officer of one of the U-boats, who had reconnoitred the area beforehand, rendered good service in locating the place." As to the southern group consisting of *Von der Tann* and the *Derfflinger*, these "made for Scarborough, which was easily distinguishable", and "the light cruiser *Kolberg* laid her mines at the appointed place without much difficulty, although the ship heeled over to 12 degrees."

Now "the appointed place" was off the Yorkshire coast between Flamborough Head and Scarborough, the line of mines being roughly in an L-shape, the intended German base of the L being approximately parallel with the coast. And the *Kolberg* laid one hundred of these mines in a zigzag plan across the supposed track of shipping—roughly NE.—the first mine being laid close to the shore 3 miles NW. of Filey.

The *Kolberg* was one of Germany's most successful light cruisers, an excellent seaboat and very reliable steamer, drawing 17¾ feet, with her turbines giving her 25 knots. This 4350 tons vessel on December 16 did her job so efficiently that a series of mercantile minings began when the Norwegian S.S. *Vaaren* sank that morning and the British S.S. *Princess Olga* disappeared 5 miles ENE. of Scarborough, the collier *Elterwater*, and so on. At 8.25 a.m. (German Time) the *Kolberg* reported that she had laid the mines "in spite of the unfavourable sea". The S.S. *City* reported that the sea off Scarborough was "strewn with mines" and she had on board several of *Elterwater's* dead.

The traffic between Flamborough and the Tyne was halted on the 17th until the 19th, when a Grimsby trawler unit began sweeping close to the shore. Three old gunboats (*Skipjack*, *Jason*, and *Gossamer*) were on passage from Sheerness to Scapa, and were ordered *en route* to stop the regular traffic and sweep northwards from Flamborough. So at 8.30 a.m. they swept up two mines, which they found 6½ miles southeastward from Scarborough signal station. It was thus that they sighted the Grimsby unit, and *Skipjack* closed the trawlers. Then the excitement began.

[1] *Germany's High Sea Fleet*, chapter VI. London, 1920.   [2] Wegener.

Almost immediately the trawlers got amongst thickly laid traps—within five minutes at least eighteen terrible mines were accounted for, and such an experience as few ships have ever been called upon to endure. On either side violent detonations were shaking each vessel from stem to stern, and in the general mêlée of trawlers were parted sweeps mingled with drifting mines. It was the worst picture of suspense and death, two trawlers having just struck mines and one other sank slowly, her mast nearly submerged whilst moving through the sea like the periscope of a submarine. The other was down by the head, badly on fire.

This flotilla was in the midst of a thickly dangerous region and low water was not far off, so they were ordered to anchor. As if to make the experience more horrible, some of the mines drifted close to the anchored ships, and now the weather became hazy. But eventually luck followed pluck, the actual clearance of the minefield was done entirely by trawlers, and the old gunboats explored the route to Hartlepool, finding no mines, and then carried on to Scapa. Two more trawlers were mined during these operations, which were not completed until April 23, 1915.

There were not many of *Kolberg's* mines unaccounted for : of the 100 there were 53 swept up this month alone, but by the date given the number had risen to 69, and I remember being at Grimsby at the time when they brought in a German carbonit mine which was of great interest. It was finally reckoned that this Scarborough minefield caused the loss of 7 British mercantile steamers, 7 neutrals plus 2 trawlers, 4 minesweepers, and the damaged armed yacht *Valiant*. I saw her, too, and after watching her on the Humber noticed her a few days later safe off Portsmouth on her way to Liverpool. But the most impressive sight of all was when one of the trawlers was brought into the Humber with a hole at her side big enough to admit a motor car.

Yet how futile were such incidents as the bombardments of Gorleston, of Scarborough and Hartlepool (when the battle-cruiser *Seydlitz* was hit three times), and later on of Lowestoft ! Even the Kaiser in September, 1916, had realized the utter uselessness of such activity which got the Germans nowhere.

"Surprise bombardments of the enemy coast and other spectacular exploits of that kind which seem to provide an argument for the value of very high speed," minuted a high official of the German Admiralty at the time, "are, when all is said and done, for us only episodes : limited successes which are valuable for morale, whereas the general action is an event of historical importance that may have a decisive effect."

And this reference to the episodic character of surprise bombardments so struck the Kaiser that he marked the reference with pencil twice in the margin.

Chapter 6

THE DOGGER BANK

NEW YEAR'S DAY, 1915, opened with one of the most remarkable deeds of the submarine campaign. It is a strange story, and one with which I was able to be acquainted at first hand.

The principal actor in this great drama was Vice-Admiral Sir Lewis Bayly, who at the beginning of hostilities commanded the 1st Battle Squadron, with his flag in the *Marlborough*. A great tactician—the use of a smoke screen was among his original ideas—he was a keen student of naval history, a firm disciplinarian whose aim was efficiency at all costs. Essentially a "big ship" man of the genuine blue-water school, it was with a slight contempt for the submarine that he began the war. But also he entertained certain opinions concerning the capture of Borkum, and this became one of his fixed ideas. Even months earlier, when the nation was still at peace and his flag hoisted aboard the *Lion* where Sir David Beatty presently succeeded, I remember him in conversation again and again stressing this Borkum proposition. "It may cost me ten thousand Marines, but we still must capture such an essential post," was one of his remarks.

I called his attention also to the great possibilities of Zeebrugge, suggesting that this harbour which had been just opened was going to play an important role in the coming war. "Surely the Germans will find it very useful as an advance base for destroyers?"

"Never heard of the place," replied the Admiral gruffly. "Zeebrugge? Where is it?"

And having recently visited Zeebrugge, spent the nocturnal hours there taking soundings, I came to certain conclusions: but he and his bowler hat would also visit the port this summer, and learn things for himself. Unfortunately, the Great War intervened, and the Admiral took his squadron up to Scapa.

During that autumn Zeebrugge came into his mind prominently, and increased his consideration as the first five months went by. It even rivalled Borkum for interest, since the Germans having occupied the coast and possessed themselves of Zeebrugge and Ostend, the use of their destroyers and submarines would follow naturally. We know how deeply impressed was the great tactician, and whilst at Scapa he used every opportunity for discussing with Admiral Jellicoe the blocking of Zeebrugge harbour by sinking ships across the channel. "Sir Lewis Bayly considered the scheme feasible, and wrote to me on the subject. I then suggested to the Admiralty that such an operation should be carried out. It was not considered practicable by the Admiralty at the time."[1]

So Admiral Jellicoe recorded: but still this planning haunted him, so finally the Admiralty about Christmas allotted him a totally different job. From the 1st Battle Squadron in the Grand Fleet he was given what appeared on paper a bigger and even more responsible office—Commander-in-Chief of the Channel Fleet with his flag in the *Lord Nelson*. But you may guess how Admiral Bayly interpreted the change.

"The Admiralty have what they call promoted me", he wrote to me from on board the *Marlborough*. "But I am heartbroken, and Jellicoe is furious."

However, sick at heart, he took over in the Medway, and the first resolution was to exercise in gunnery and tactics what was known then as the 5th Battle Squadron (eight battleships and two light cruisers), but he must find out whether it were safe to expose such ships in the English Channel, and secondly demand a destroyer screen. The request was easily complied with: he left Sheerness on December 30, 10 a.m., at 15 knots. During December it is noteworthy that U-boats lately had been exceptionally quiet: in fact throughout December no British men-of-war, or mercantile ships, or fishing craft, had been sunk. That seemed encouraging, but for greater prudence (Admiral Bayly informed me) the squadron was to be screened by six destroyers (sent from Harwich) through the Dover Straits so far as Dungeness, when these were to turn back whilst the battleships carried on.

So the latter proceeded west of the Wight on the last day of the old year, and very heavy weather was working up with a hard southerly wind. At 2.20 a.m. on January 1, 1915, the squadron was 15 miles from Start Point when H.M.S. *Formidable* was suddenly torpedoed in Lat. 50.11 N., Long. 3.6 W. abreast foremost funnel. Quickly she sank, when 547 out of 780 officers and men were lost, including the Captain and his little dog.

It was a sad blow and cast a gloom everywhere, but it threatened to ruin Admiral Bayly's career as a sea officer. Quite rightly the squadron scattered (in accordance with the instructions issued after the incident of *Cressys*) and Admiral Bayly brought his battleship into Portland, but from Lord Fisher (First Sea Lord) went the curt order that Admiral Bayly was to haul down his flag and come ashore.

End to a brilliant career! The closing scene to much striving! Never was a great man so deeply touched by disappointment. Convinced of his rightness in decision, he demanded a court martial and was refused. So we find the sailor compelled to serve ashore

[1] *The Grand Fleet, 1914–16*, page 154.

whilst the Great War on sea waged furiously and the U-boat was threatening its worst.

It was Lieut.-Commander Schneider in U-24 who fired the torpedo, the officer whom we remember as having previously attacked the *Amiral Ganteaume*. In December he made his base at Zeebrugge, but what stands out is the fact that a submarine had come right down the English Channel far beyond Dover Straits to the Devonshire coast. He had been trying all this afternoon for an attack.

We must expect any development now. The U-boat had proved itself capable of working much farther away from her base—be it the Heligoland Bight or Zeebrugge. No longer was it a purely defensive weapon fashioned against invaders: it would depend on two ·factors for its success—fuel endurance and the personal venturesomeness of her commanding officer. Also the mind could envisage the torpedo or gun being brought countless miles against merchantman or U-boat, and underwater hostilities might be extended even to the Mediterranean. If, then, over the private ambition of the U-boat captains we superimpose the driving force and encouragement of their superior officers in Germany issuing commands that gave them new cruising limitations, we shall presently find the submarine not content with the English Channel, or the Irish Channel, or the North Sea—or any part of the tide-swept Narrow Seas.

Meanwhile round the British Isles the coast for greater efficiency had been divided into twenty-one areas of the Auxiliary Patrol, the finest of our steam yachts were now patrolling against submarines, whilst drifters no longer needed for herrings were selected for using wire netting which was supported by glass floats, but a hydroplane buoy was also attached to indicate any submarine which might foul these meshes. In two areas especially were such drifters and their towed wire nets employed: the Dover Straits, and that other restricted area between Southern Scotland and Northern Ireland known as the North Channel. Of course, we must realize that whether drifters lay to nets from the bows, or towed from the stern, this was an unprecise method for catching the submarine, though in the darkness their propellers might become entangled. On the whole, then, we must admit that this method would finally mean failure out of all proportion to the huge number of crews and craft employed. Much simpler, more scientific, and far more effective, was the employment of depth charges. But our solution of a big problem had not thus far reached that stage, and the process of "trial and error" must for many a month be experienced.

And there was occasionally some human element, which many a naval officer at first failed to appreciate. Whereas the crew of a trawler might be obtained from perhaps nine different towns, the men who formed a drifter's personnel almost exclusively came from

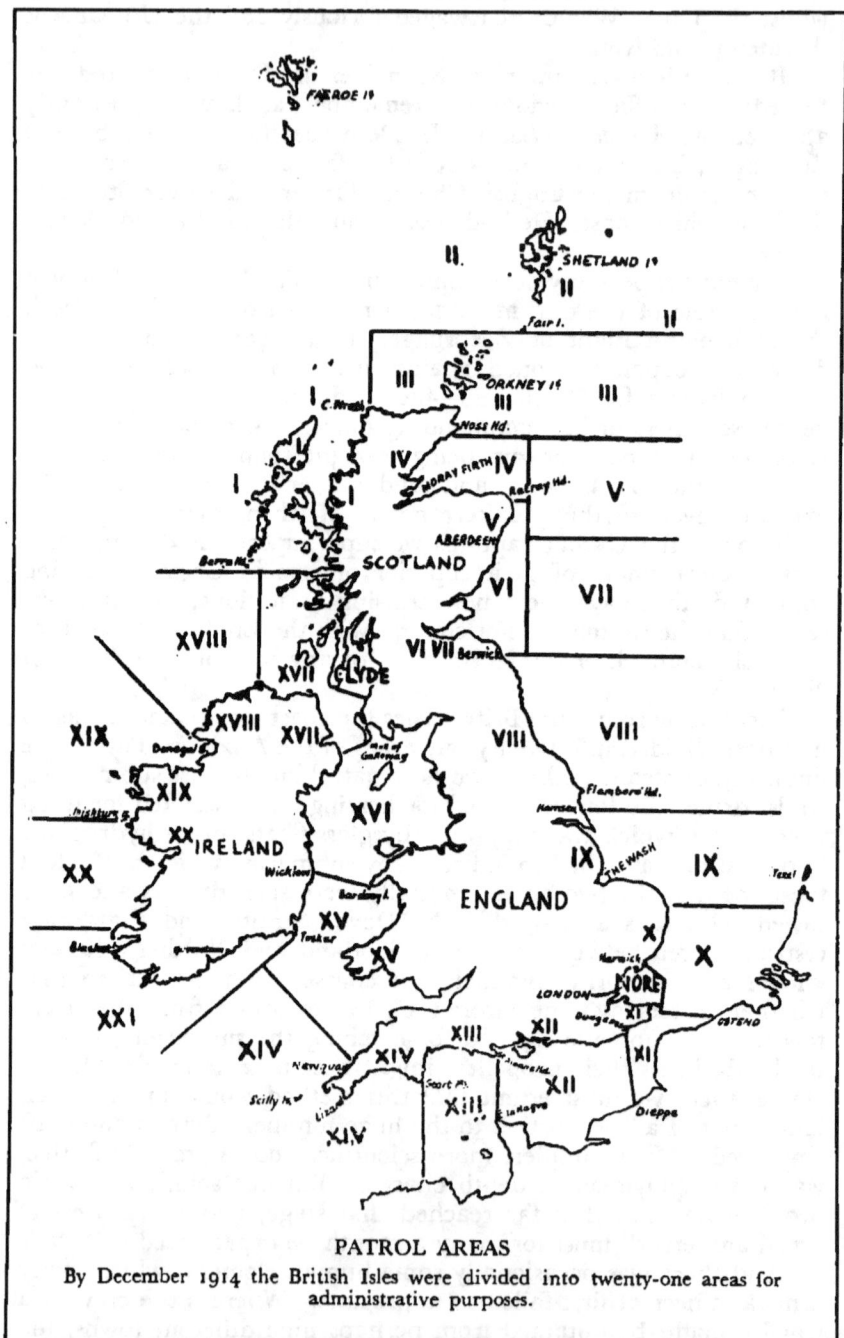

PATROL AREAS
By December 1914 the British Isles were divided into twenty-one areas for administrative purposes.

some North Sea port, shared the ownership of this drifter, and worked together. Among the party of nine men they would not rarely consist of brothers, brothers-in-law, cousins, and so on. Nearly always they came from the same town, and especially so when the port of register was some corner of the Moray Firth, but they had to be treated with respect for their customs and traditions as a whole. Certainly the Skipper was Skipper and they all understood that much, but running a drifter was the nearest thing to working things on a communal basis.

On the 1st of January, 1915, there were twenty German submarines operating in the North Sea, and seven in the Baltic. Some time during this month Germany was certainly unlucky with several of her boats. U-7, which had been employed since the beginning of war, was torpedoed and sunk off Holland by U-22, with one survivor. A fatal mistake of thinking she was a British submarine had been made after two challenges. About the same time U-32 was injured but got home, and U-31 failed to return. We all of us hate unexplained mysteries, and no one can state positively what happened, but with so many minefields off the British and German coasts, the frequent prevalence of a January fog, the well-known "wandering" tendency of a submarine's compass which so often jeopardized a boat near the shore ; it is almost certain that U-31 blew up with all hands in a minefield.

The Germans, in the absence of positive facts, have, however, invented a wonderful story which surpasses sober history, descending even into the realm of thriller creation. The German author, Captain A. Gayer, suggests that U-31 was found in January "by the English, drifting in a closed condition, completely dry inside, and the crew dead". Gas poisoning is also suggested. But wonderful as this discovery reads, the one missing link is that not one British subject has been produced to support this yarn.

Perhaps this unknown finder, in an unspecified region, on opening the steel coffin, tumbled dead in the sea after encountering the fumes from chlorine gas and German corpses !

In various ways the requisitioning of vessels from civil occupation created all sorts of amusing situations. There was one well-known majestic yacht which was not taken up by the Admiralty without exerting some stern pressure. The Duchess refused to let the vessel go unless she herself went with it "to share the perils of the crew". Of course this could not be entertained, and the vessel was taken over to be commissioned in the normal manner. Another well-known titled owner was so lacking in patriotic spirit that he tried dodging the ship's arrival from abroad, but a smart look out and the issue of a warrant for arrest soon settled that difficulty. It was a difficult matter always to supply doctors, for there were forty-four yachts in the Auxiliary Patrol by the first week of January and other such vessels were coming along, but some "half-stripe" doctors were obtained from among hospital dressers just as in some cases they were required for destroyers.

And it meant not a little brave endurance that a zealous, but very sea-sick, expert should have to do his best with injured men awaiting surgical operations after German shells had done their worst. There was, too, such a shortage of guns at this time that only two per yacht were allowed, and I remember one very fine vessel being thus compelled to surrender four of her 6-pounders. She had the satisfaction some months later of knowing that these weapons, after being mounted on other craft, rendered magnificent aid against the Germans.

Dover was in process of becoming a big base for net drifters. Complaints were made that these fishing craft would arrive in a manner somewhat novel to the Royal Navy. Improperly ballasted, with defects in hull and machinery; inadequately supplied with lights, spare lamps, bedding, good warps and a spare anchor; the Skipper would even be found wearing a "little 'ard 'at" and old clothes, whilst the crew would look even worse clad. As to sea discipline, they had their own which differed very considerably from that known in the Royal Navy. But the service would look after this, rough North Sea fishermen began to respect old traditions; and the Navy soon respected the courage, the heroism, the marvellous pertinacity of these hardy fellows. In the meantime the Admiralty had done well in getting these south from the East Coast to work in the Dover tideway, where even by mid-January it was clear that the British minefield had not succeeded in preventing U-boats from finding their way at least as far as the Start. So a drifter would be fitted with 500 yards of "Indicator" nets, the establishment grew considerably from week to week, and the flotillas increased; but Poole and Milford were to become important for their drifter bases, whilst other centres were established at such places as Cromarty, Peterhead, Firth of Forth, Yarmouth, Harwich, Portsmouth, Portland, Falmouth, and Devonport.

So rapidly did this organization grow by January 21 that it numbered 161, of which there were 54 drifters working out of Poole, but that was only a beginning. By the afternoon of January 23 activities were being prepared in Germany which were not devoid of meaning. U-19 (which was once rammed by *Badger* on January 21) sank off the Dutch coast the British S.S. *Durward*, 22 miles NW. of the Maas Lightship. It had become a favourite locality for this submarine to hang about, and the intention now was to prevent the steamer bringing her cargo into Rotterdam. U-19 came back into the Ems two days later as did U-33; and U-32 (to be mentioned again presently) was 15 miles north of Borkum whilst Hersing, in U-21, left behind the busy naval dockyard of Wilhelmshaven on the 21st, bound for a cruise quite as important as when he sank *Pathfinder*, but with more historic sequels.

We will return to the matter again.

It is to be remembered that January 24 is memorable for that famous Battle of the Dogger Bank when the first encounter between super-Dreadnoughts took place in the war. On the previous evening at 6 p.m., Admiral Beatty with his flag in the *Lion* left Rosyth, the first contact with the enemy was made by *Aurora* and light cruisers from 7.20 a.m. By 8.34 a.m. the British battle-cruisers were doing about 29 knots, and ten minutes later the German battle-cruisers were opening fire on their enemy, which consisted of *Lion* (Flag), *Princess Royal, Tiger, New Zealand, Indomitable* battle-cruisers, with the light cruisers *Southampton, Nottingham, Birmingham* and *Lowestoft*, whilst Commodore Tyrwhitt and the light cruisers *Arethusa, Aurora,* and *Undaunted*, together with the destroyer flotillas, were ahead.

The wind was NW., light, with extreme visibility, and the long chase which had been commenced was varied by the German battle-cruiser *Blücher*, fourth ship in the enemy's line, receiving the first hit from *Lion* at 9.9, but about 9.22 the *Lion* also received a hit. The enemy with *Moltke, Derfflinger, Seydlitz,* and *Blücher* concentrated his fire on the head of the line (*Lion*) with perfectly sound tactics, in the hope of throwing this line into confusion as the Japanese succeeded at the Battle of Tsushima.

It was at 10.18 that the *Lion* was so mauled that she seemed almost to stop, but the *Blücher* had been so battered as to get on fire. To her fate Admiral Hipper decided she must be left. She was in the rear, the most exposed position, and she was the weakest of the four ships. But by 10.35 the *Lion* received more damage, then one of the turrets was in a state of conflagration.

The *Blücher* hauled out of line with a heavy list, the *Lion* was still further injured than previously, and finally she was brought into the Forth much wounded, but still afloat, though *Blücher* had sunk in the North Sea whilst the other three of Hipper's vessels scurried back home. The German submarines paid no part in this battle, but they were on duty off the Ems and Borkum in case the home-comers were pursued by British units.

Admiral Scheer has left on record that the object of this expedition had been the reconnoitring near the Dogger Bank for any of our light forces to be destroyed forthwith. And he also mentions that a valuable lesson was that day acquired when *Seydlitz* burst into flames. They learned something which we did not learn till the Battle of Jutland. As Scheer expressed it,[1] the lesson obtained was "for the future in dealing with reserve ammunition, and it was applied in subsequent actions".

He was, of course, thinking of the fire which spread to the munition chamber of each turret.

Now because of undoubted penetration of the English Channel

---

[1] *Germany's High Sea Fleet*, page 76.

by submarines passing through the Dover Straits—especially at night—the Navy was developing a genuine uneasiness at last: there prevailed even a strong suspicion that U-boats passed through the Downs at night. But it was U-21 which again had become prominent, and Hersing was nothing if not original.

He came out of Wilhelmshaven on January 21, found his way through the Dover Straits and now was right down the English Channel into the Irish Sea. At 8.15 p.m. he was sighted[1] about 3 miles NW. of Bardsey Island on January 28 by the armed drifter "R.R.S." (Sub-Lieut. A. E. Williams, R.N.R.), whilst on the 29th U-21, before 2 p.m., bombarded Barrow, but the Walney Island battery returned the fire. The submarine had been firing at 6800 yards' range, and the battery replied with eleven rounds. The German was visible for quite a considerable time, the crew on deck, and apparently taking keen observation. Evidently the U-boat was aiming at our airship sheds, but all her shots fell short.

She made off again to the southward and sank three steamers next day—the *Ben Cruachan*, 15 miles NW. of Morecambe Light; the *Linda Blanche*, 18 miles NW. from Liverpool Bar Lightship; and the *Kilcoan* also, in almost the same place as the last, was destroyed. U-21 had, in fact, done so well in destroying shipping, and proceeded so far, that all standards for submarines were broken. Hersing came safely down past the Welsh and Irish coasts, had no difficulty in retracing his way up Channel and through Dover Straits, but on arrival back in Wilhelmshaven was received with iron crosses for such a meritorious service. Henceforth not the North Sea, nor the English Channel, could contain the ambition of a keen officer. The Narrow Seas were indeed to be a U-boat's sphere, and she could navigate in all parts of England.

So, barely had Hersing proved this to be so, and his return convinced senior officers, that Admiral von Pohl (Chief of the German Admiralty Staff) declared by a notice in the official *Reichsanzeiger* on February 4 that the waters around Great Britain and Ireland were herewith in the War Zone; and that from February 18 every merchant ship met with in that zone would be destroyed.

At this date there were several submarine captains from whom Germany hoped to expect many things, given this freedom of action. One such was U-20 (Lieut.-Commander Droescher), who on the 30th of January torpedoed three steamers—*Ikaria*, *Tokomaru*, and *Oriole*—in the eastern portion of the Dover Straits, and on February 1 fired a torpedo in the evening (5 p.m.) against the hospital ship *Asturias* when 15 miles NNE. of Havre. At the beginning of February, 1915, the Germans had twenty-three submarines

---

[1] It is also true that the armed yacht *Vanduara* whilst on passage from the Clyde to Portsmouth was attacked by U-21 some 33 miles NW½N of Fishguard at 8.30 a.m., but also fired at the submarine.

in the North Sea to inaugurate their blockade, and there were in hand (though not ready for service) forty-two large and one hundred and twenty-seven small submarines being built. Ten big minelaying submarines at the beginning of the year were also laid down.

Gayer points out that owing to the retreat from the Marne of the German Army, a decision had to be sought at sea. How? Either by a purely submarine war—as was now to be attempted—or by the High Sea Fleet in conjunction with the submarines. Nevertheless the Germans never seem to have gone "full out" on February 18; their date was ill-chosen because for some time to come they did not possess a sufficient number of U-boats. Twenty-three was a ridiculous number for inaugurating what was, in all but name, a blockade.

Submarines are very delicate, very tricky, creatures requiring a thorough overhaul after four weeks of constant heavy war service: and they put a heavy strain on the nerves of their personnel. It took a U-boat one week on passage from Germany to the western British Isles (Ireland), and they spent a fortnight thereabouts in heavy Atlantic weather, which left only another week for going home when the refitting and dry-docking would begin. Thus out of twenty-three there were at any given moment only five or six submarines available against the entire British Isles.

The Admiralty on our side were, however, alive to the danger which Dover Straits presented as a gateway not merely for submarines going down Channel. In spite of certain objections, a barrage was laid in February, from Dunkirk to the North Foreland, entirely to thwart the passage by surface ships: not against submarines travelling under water. The laying of this obstruction was begun on February 4 by H.M.S. *Intrepid*, *Thetis*, *Andromache*, *Latona*, and about four thousand mines were put in strategical position this month, but the job was not concluded until the following October when nearly six thousand mines had been laid. This barrage was left down and unswept until the spring of 1918, and there is reason to suppose that by this time all our mines in the barrage had ceased to exist.

CHAPTER 7

TRAWLERS AND U-BOATS

THE first submarine to copy U-21's example was U-30 (who, however, passed round the north of Scotland) and began her share in the campaign by sinking the British S.S. *Cambank* (3112 tons) on February 20, 10 miles east of Point Lynas in the Liverpool region. So that with U-30 already on the way, and U-8 as the only boat ready to sail on February 18, the Blockade had begun weakly.

Scheer says that a blockade as such was not declared, because Germany had not enough submarines to make it effective. The instructions issued now to U-boat commanders are as follows, but we should emphasize the fact that Germany certainly did not, as time went on, respect the limitations indicated, as for instance the regulations Nos. 3 and 4:

    1. To prosecute the U-boat campaign against commerce with all possible vigour.

    2. Hostile merchant ships to be destroyed.

    3. Neutral ships to be spared.

    4. Hospital ships to be spared; also those of the Belgian Relief Commission.

    5. If mistakes are made, the commander will not be responsible, provided he had used great care.

Some idea of the kind of life being lived by these submarine commanders, thus assured of their freedom to cruise as they wished, may be gathered from U-16 which early in February was off Heligoland waiting for orders. On February 9, ten hours after reaching the Maas Lightship, she came to the surface, stopped, but released, a 6000-ton steamer. Next day appeared the British S.S. *Laertes*, who hoisted the Dutch flag and hurried away. Ignoring U-16's signal to stop, and after being chased by the latter, *Laertes* escaped by dusk, leaving the German indignant at the "misuse of the Dutch flag". Captain Propert, the master of *Laertes*, was afterwards decorated and given a commission as Lieutenant R.N.R.

"Misuse"? How curious an assertion! For the use of false colours, and the employment of disguises by merchant vessels attempting to escape, was a custom well established in the history of naval war; and the Masters were indeed encouraged so to act.

U-16 proceeded to Calais, where the weather was so thick that she remained under water for hours, but on coming to the surface turned the crew out of a small British boat and torpedoed her quickly, for French destroyers were coming up. Still remaining off the French coast, though farther down Channel, she stopped and torpedoed the 3289 tons S.S. *Dulwich* on February 15 without warning 6 miles north of Cape d'Antifer, whilst the steamer was bound for Havre—the British crew having taken to the boats—and next day halted the S.S. *Ville de Lille* off Cherbourg, towing the boats nearer to Barfleur and blowing the ship up by bombs. Then, on February 18, the day when the Blockade began, she torpedoed off Dieppe the French S.S. *Dinorah*, carrying horses and guns. Finally, the submarine returned to Heligoland and well pleased with herself, for she believed that her action would thus have the effect of sending up freights, insurance, and seamen's wages.

In view of this new activity by U-boats, the Admiralty decided to close the Straits of Dover by means of nets worked by drifters; and, when that had been done, to deal with the North Channel (between Scotland and Ireland) in a similar manner, but generally all available 12-pounders and 6-pounders were to be mounted in yachts, trawlers, and drifters. On paper, of course, this looked very well, and it seemed nice to imagine submarines getting their propellers foul of the nets, whether the latter be moored permanently by means of buoys or kept on the move when towed by 9-knot drifters.

Matters get out of focus where the expert is not so much the man-in-the-office as the man afloat. Any practical seafarer ought from the first to have convinced the theorist firstly that a 5-knot tide is bound to make the net-line not as rigid as a red mark on a sheet of paper, and secondly that there must be gaps through which a submarine by night and a little enterprise could wangle her way. That was the fundamental error in both these areas for a considerable time, and therefore in neither region were U-boats completely excluded though there were brief periods when a German captain bound down the English Channel preferred to go right round the North of Scotland than be caught in Dover nets.

It may be at once asserted that during the First War with Germany in 1914-1918 as well as in the Second War, this North Channel was always much favoured by the U-boats. As the reader will see from the accompanying plan, the tide varies from 5 to $3\frac{1}{4}$ knots. The intention for a period was so to work drifters that the area MNOP was entirely theirs, but that much activity should be displayed by small craft in the areas AMNB and PDCO. In other words, advance patrol lines at either end of the netted area would be so impossible for submarine navigation, that a U-boat must either navigate southwards of Rathlin Island or, having dived to 90 feet below the netted area, would arrive in the Lough Larne

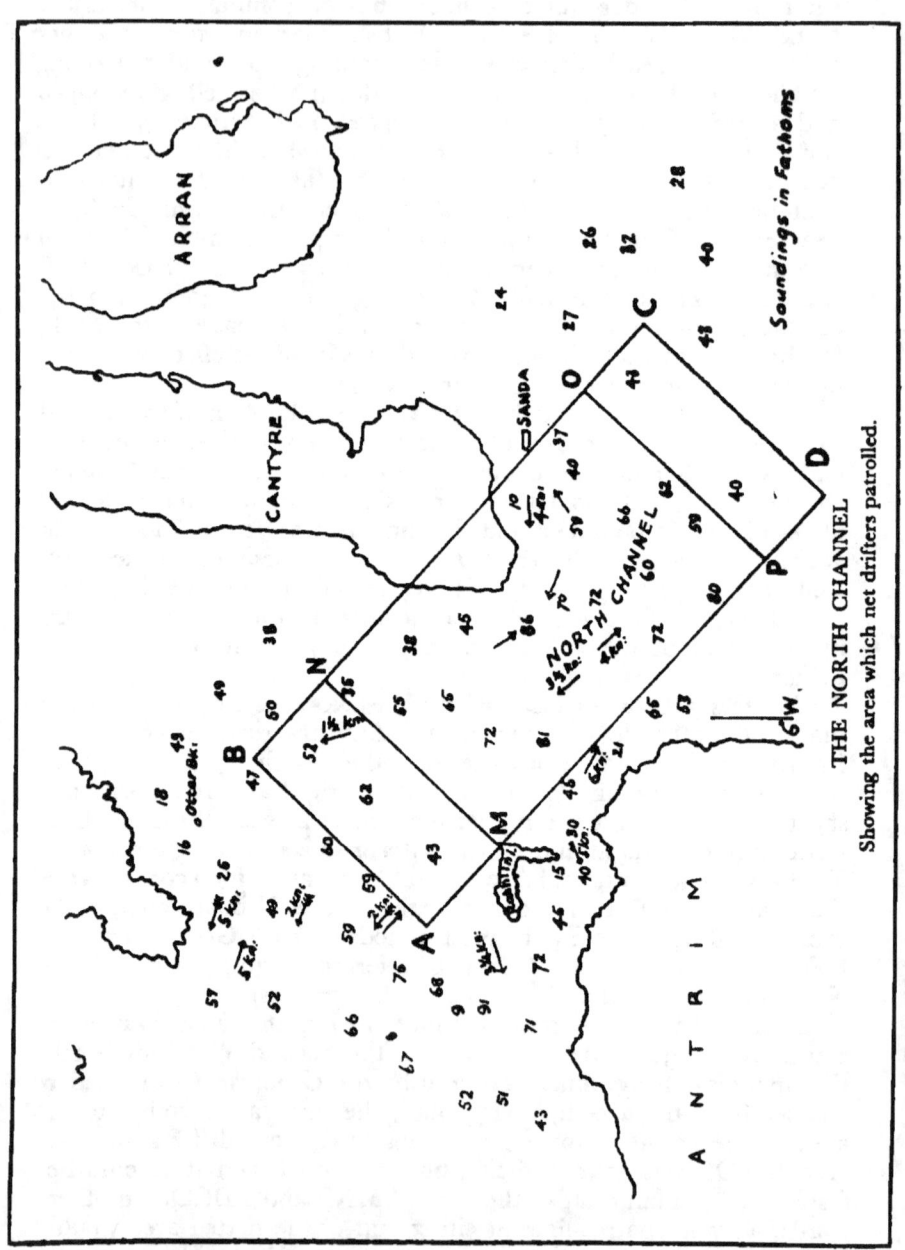

THE NORTH CHANNEL
Showing the area which net drifters patrolled.

vicinity at the end of her submersion powers and, therefore, at the mercy of the patrols on the surface. And it was pleaded that though a drifter might have perhaps 800 yards of net out astern, this would from a distance of 600 yards be invisible to any submarine.

But in spite of the meticulous care expended, the risks drifters ran in hugging the shores at night with these awkward nets, and the manner in which tides or gales of wind would turn their 800-yards' tow into a hopeless tangle, the theory eventually after proper trial was not a practical success. Other drifters operated across the Irish Sea, involving a large employment of ships and men, but their cumulative effect was slight and not to be compared with the later depth charge.

We know from the German submarine authority Captain Gayer,[1] that already before February 18 the U-boats in negotiating Dover Straits, used to lie on the seabed north of the Ruytingen Bank, and wait till the tide turned west (if bound down Channel). Otherwise they would pass *by night on the surface* after the tide had eased a little. The British mines (emphasizes Gayer) hardly inconvenienced them, as these obstructions were mostly on the surface, and could be avoided. The Germans say they were surprised at the delay before the British took steps to block the Dover Straits passage.

During February armed drifters were patrolling the northern part of the Downs, watching an area of nets kept drifting when the weather permitted. Buoys, all lighted, had been laid across Dover Straits, numbered from 1 to 8, but this was really the beginning of an alteration, for when moored nets should become available they were to be moored 10,000 yards in a 93 degrees direction and thence from Ruytingen No. 7 buoy for 4500 yards.

Yet it showed how immediately unsatisfactory was this kind of defence, because the first thing which happened was the loss of ninety nets in a three days' gale, whilst sixty-eight nets were lost in a couple of nights' fine weather. Nothing, in fact, seemed certain and definite, except that submarines could sink ships—yes, but even the former might just succeed or just fail. Let me give an instance.

We mentioned just now U-30, who passed round the north of Scotland. Well, on February 23 the steam trawler, *Alex Hastie* of North Shields, was about 3 p.m. some 105 miles ENE. of the Longstone Lighthouse, the gear had just been put down and the crew busied themselves with the trawl because of being a genuine fishing vessel. All available hands on deck were working at the catch of fish just previously emptied on board, when suddenly one man called attention.

"Why! What's this 'ere?" he wondered.

"Periscope! That's what it is."

[1] *The German Submarines*, volume II.

"And it's moving, too."

Eyes were concentrated on the thin object, and it could be seen that the submarine was attempting to pass close astern of the trawler, but in so doing fouled the trawl's wires which twanged and creaked with the strain. In fact it was such that presently the submarine came to the surface on her beam ends; for neither periscope nor conning tower seemed to be visible. After twenty minutes the submarine sank, leaving behind a large quantity of oil on the water's surface. A report was made and sent in to the Admiralty, and whilst the incident was slightly uncertain, the Authority decided that £100 should be awarded between owners and crew.

But the sequel is that this U-30 did get back home quite safely. Her periscopes had indeed fouled the trawler's wires (about $2\frac{1}{2}$-inch), these periscopes being strained and causing the glands (through which the periscopes pass into the hull) to leak. Thus water got into the hull too, and prevented her from attaining her upright position until some time later she came to the surface. There was no sinking.

It was not until February 25 that U-20 and U-27 both left the Ems to do their share in the Submarine Blockade. The former went down Channel, the Bristol Channel and Irish Sea, for a little later this year she became notorious in sinking the *Lusitania*; whilst U-27 went via Scotland, the North Channel, and Isle of Man to the Irish Sea, and eventually sank one of our armed merchant cruisers, *Bayano*,[1] on March 11.

It is notable that when the Submarine Campaign against merchant shipping began, losses due to mines became less numerous and did not become prolific until September, although now and again some North Sea mines from the Scarborough and Moray Firth areas did their damage: for instance, even on February 24, the British S.S. *Deptford* foundered 3 miles E. by N. of Scarborough.

But the Germans in future displayed their ability in their new-found strength, the submarine, and at once began building new hulls that winter, which in the summer of 1915 would be ready for service. In the meanwhile this month U-boats were reported everywhere—off the Lizard, the Start, the Owers, Cape de la Hague, Portland Bill, the Channel Isles, Anvil Point, Rame Head, Ilfracombe, Dungeness, Teignmouth, St. Alban's Head, St. Catherine's, Ushant, the Scillies, and so on. Some of these apparitions were false alarms, yet all the same there were plenty of well-substantiated sightings.

Of these genuine affairs we may draw attention once more to U-8, which had left Zeebrugge for the English Channel, passed the Dutch coast, and having laid a course to work the tides through Dover Straits, got held up by the nets off the Varne, burst her way through and reached the neighbourhood of Beachy Head, where

---

[1] See my *The Big Blockade*.

she promptly torpedoed four British steamers—*Oakby, Branksome, Chine, Rio Parana*, and *Western Coast*—during February 23 and 24. She even tried to sink the hospital ship *St. Andrew*, but luckily did not succeed.

Stoch, the Commander, then took his boat back to Flanders, filled up with stores, and early on the morning of March 4 set out from Ostend for another trip. It was to be no pleasure cruise for either Stoch, his three officers, or his twenty-four men.

We can picture his boat as displacing 620 tons when below surface, in which condition she had a speed of 8 knots (for one hour), but above surface—displacing merely 500 tons—she could do her 13 or 14 knots.

For armament she relied on two torpedo-tubes in the bows and another couple aft.

The trouble began when she got past Dover that same afternoon in the strong tide and found herself some 6 miles to the southward near the NE. buoy of the Varne shoal, which lies midway in the English Channel, steering down the fairway with hull invisible, but periscope showing.

This for a German U-boat always meant a most anxious bit of navigation, keeping on the alert for eager patrols and dodging commercial traffic.

Stoch, through his lens, observed, not without anxiety, several British destroyers and drifters, but hoped to avoid their attentions : if that could be achieved during the next mile or two all might turn out happily. For with the widening of the English Channel his course would be far less restricted.

Yet fortune seemed to be on his side definitely : the weather was inclined to be foggy with the first promise of Spring, and this protective cloak came as a great gift when most wanted.

But Stoch, one of the most experienced submarine commanders in the German Navy and among the few who had served seven years as a specialist, now made a terrible mistake.

He allowed his craft to get foul of nets laid by fishermen crews which the Navy had enrolled.

• This became manifest to H.M. Drifter *Ma Freen*, on duty near the Varne soon after 12.30 p.m. As she looked towards the line of pellets which marked the nets, suddenly something seemed abnormal : although the tide now happened to be running in a westerly direction, these pellets were travelling easterly against a 4-knot velocity.

Pretty sure evidence that some mechanical power was at work !

The drifter's skipper did exactly the right thing, made certain this had not been caused by any shoal obstruction, took soundings and found 19 fathoms. Then he reported the affair to H.M.S. *Cossack*, who got busy, and that destroyer wirelessed the news to Captain C. D. Johnson, R.N., in charge of the destroyers at Dover.

This officer, about 1.30, rushed out of harbour in the destroyer *Maori*, and followed H.M.S. *Viking*, who, like a terrier chasing a rat, was going full speed against the enemy.

Now this last-mentioned destroyer, commanded by an officer to-day famous everywhere, had sighted at 1.10, distant a mile off, the undoubted shape of a submarine rising to the surface during one brief clearing of the fog.

Commander (now Admiral) Edward Evans, with his characteristic instancy and determined energy that had been so marked in the Antarctic, sped the *Viking* towards its objective, got right abreast, tried to ram but missed, opened fire, then the submarine dived, and even now the chase continued.

For half an hour the enemy was thought to be indicating her presence, since a series of swirling pools moving northwest could certainly be discerned. Presently these turned westerly, and *Viking* followed for quarter of an hour; then they altered to ESE. until, at 3.50, Commander Evans fired his explosive sweep.

The swirl carried on 150 yards farther, then ceased completely when 4½ miles from the NE. Varne Buoy.

Now when *Maori* arrived on the scene Captain Johnson ordered four other destroyers to search on various bearings from *Viking's* position. At 3.22 a periscope was distinctly observed 1 mile north of the buoy, and twenty-three minutes later a similar sight appeared more southerly. Destroyers were now churning the English Channel at high speed radiating like sparks to the northwestwards of the Varne Lightship and covering a wide area between them.

A glorious thrilling episode for officers and men with zest and human hearts fast beating, whilst down below the ears of twenty-nine Germans could listen with trepidation to the lashing of propellers getting nearer and desperately nearer every moment.

Sea drama in its most tense modern expression!

These additional destroyers comprised *Ghurka*, *Syren*, *Mohawk*, *Ure*, but the *Maori* at 4.40 received the great joy of espying the elusive periscope, though not for long.

Twenty minutes afterwards *Ghurka* fired her sweep, waited but thirty seconds, and then there rose up at an angle of 45 degrees the unmistakable stern of a submarine, till gradually it came to an even keel with conning tower in full view.

The enemy had, as a result of perfect combination by her pursuers, been chased out of the water and now lay an ideal target.

Guns barked furiously, men in the *Maori* and *Ghurka* began deluging the conning tower with shells. Victory was theirs.

As usual, the Germans showed little stomach to fight a losing game, and several of them emerged on deck holding up their hands in impotent surrender.

"Cease fire!"

All destroyers approached and encircled, one by one Stoch, his three officers, all of his twenty-five men who were rescued and taken prisoners, though U-8 herself sank to the bottom.

While the success directly was attributed to Lieut.-Commander R. W. Richardson, R.N., in charge of *Ghurka*, yet the skipper of *Ma Freen* and all the others had played their contributive part.

Even chance had its share, for it so happened that this day had been selected for removing the Varne Lightship, and a Trinity House steamer was busily so engaged between 3 p.m. and 5 p.m.

Were the Germans thoroughly shaken up? The depth hereabouts varies from about 70 to 90 feet. Stoch had taken U-8 down to about 60 feet when the sweep exploded over them.

It fell "as if a lump of iron had fallen on deck."

Water poured in through the thick glass bullseyes of the conning tower, some of the mechanical connections were shattered by the impact, short circuiting followed, and the electric juice failed to revolve the propellers.

Two compartments were soon flooded, and immediately the submarine rose to surface Stoch was hurled by compression through the conning tower.

Although Engineer Officer Pelz blew the main ballast tank after explosion had perforated the hull, the boat was doomed at once, and a second detonation confirmed this quickly.

But you can draw your own conclusions as to the ubiquity of what to-day are commonly known as "Fifth Column" men. Even before the last war Germany placed her men in places convenient for obtaining first-hand information.

It was learned that among this crew was one who lived formerly just outside Portsmouth, in Southsea, where he pursued employment unsuspected as "boots" at a certain establishment.

But the coincidence remains to be told. U-8 was not alone, and on leaving Ostend had voyaged in company of another submarine. That, indeed, was the one over which *Viking* fired her sweep, yet who she may have been we have no idea.

That she managed later on to get home again after such a narrow escape doubtless helped to bring about that intense respect for Dover's patrols, which presently became so marked.

From the questions asked by U-8's prisoners concerning certain other specified submarines, it was quite obvious that, though their losses had occurred months previously, these men still remained in ignorance.

Chapter 8

RUTHLESS ATTACK

THE war of the U-boats was now being waged by them with something more than a mere hope, but the fishermen had learnt that success over the Germans produced a very real effect. Did not the Admiralty distribute £500 between the trawlers and drifters for their share in destroying this U-8?

We learned from the latter's prisoners how for a considerable period our patrols had harried her, and this fact gave our drifter men great encouragement. For within the first few days of March eighty drifters had been collected at Larne for the North Channel area, and it looked as if this region might be efficiently netted—until it was ascertained that these boats did depend definitely on the weather. Since gales blustered in from the Atlantic generally too bad for reliable patrolling, the North Channel parallelogram looked doubtful defensively.

But next we return to Scotland, where U-12 had proceeded under Lieut.-Commander Kratsch from that advanced post of Zeebrugge. We remember her as having sunk the *Niger*, but now she had begun working between Peterhead and St. Abb's Head. For expert advice as to the coast and its shipping, Kratsch brought an officer of the German Mercantile Marine named Völckner, but somehow that did not convey immunity. Indeed, the so-called "War Pilot" occasionally had no more knowledge of the locality than a mariner in some cargo steamer learns in one voyage from Germany and back: at other times it was one who was very familiar with local ships and men.

Now during four days U-12 was hunted by armed patrol trawlers and a steam yacht off Eastern Scotland. The submarine had on March 10 got down to the Firth of Forth neighbourhood and finally was sighted near Fifeness by the destroyer *Ariel*. The latter did not waste the golden opportunity, rammed her heartily, disabled her with gunfire before the German craft finally sunk, and ten survivors were rescued including Völckner. Presently that afternoon *Ariel* much damaged at the forefoot came limping, but triumphant, into Leith harbour, her stern, of course, high out of the water. It was one of the most welcome arrivals that I had ever witnessed. Völckner, six months later, was clever enough to escape from captivity, and reached the east coast of England, where he managed to obtain a sailing-boat and, sailor-like, started off to cross the North Sea. Escapes from camps of U-boat prisoners were not exceptional, and by means of an ambiguous message in a letter well ahead of time a rendezvous would be given for a submarine to pick a man up. Actually U-16, then under charge of Lieut.-Commander Aillebrand, fell in with him and so brought the pilot back to Heligoland.

The sinking of U-12 was an instance of the detailed preparations sometimes necessary before the hunt could result in a genuine kill. The chase had been spread over a distance of 120 miles : only the great perseverance and skill of officers and men in yachts and trawlers and destroyers afloat, but also in Naval Centres and War Signal Stations ashore, plus the promptitude in passing on information and in anticipating the submarine's probable movements, combined to bring about the perfect result.

Conversely like a thief in the night a submarine could swoop to her deed and hurry away before being caught. On the very next day (March 11) H.M.S. *Bayano* on her way to coal at Liverpool, was torpedoed whilst steaming at only $8\frac{1}{2}$ knots about 5.15 a.m., the exact position then being 10 miles NW. by W. from Corsewall Point. She was steaming without lights, the low speed being due to the necessity of arriving at the netted area of the North Channel[1] after light. U-27 (who had previously sunk H.M.S. *Hermes*) was the culprit, but in due course we shall see the fate which was coming to her captain.

So also we must call attention to H.M.S. *Antwerp* (alias *Vienna*), which was the first "mystery ship" consistently to be employed by the Navy against submarines. She was really one of the Great Eastern Railway steamers on the Harwich to Hook of Holland route. Commanded now by Lieut.-Commander Godfrey Herbert, R.N.,[2] this "decoy ship" was lying on March 12 at Falmouth when she came out bound for Pembroke, having learnt that three steamers had been sunk in the Land's End region. It was therefore worth the *Antwerp's* while to try her luck : for she looked innocent enough, and her two 12-pounders were invisible. At 3 p.m., when about 12 miles north of the Bishop Rock Lighthouse, he saw U-29 steering for a steamer on the horizon, then the *Antwerp* closed a sailing ship and found she had on board the officers and crew of the Ellerman S.S. *Andalusian* (2349 tons) which that day had been captured and scuttled some 25 miles from the Bishop Rock.

Now Captain Malley of the *Andalusian* was on board the sailing-ship and he stated that U-29 had taken them for a while aboard the submarine, so from 4.10 p.m. the *Antwerp* gave chase. But *Antwerp* coming up within 4 miles of the still floating *Andalusian*—though the latter was about to sink—was bereft of her prey, for the submarine next dived and was not seen again.

[1] See Chapter 7.   [2] See Chapter 5.

And the stranger was actually Weddigen, the man who sank the three *Cressys* but had since been given a newer boat. Otto von Weddigen was not devoid of seamanlike brotherhood, made profuse apologies for having to sink merchant ships, said that he didn't like doing it but orders must be obeyed and even rose to the courtesy of handing round cigars. Had this popular Germanic idol then received a hint of that which was to follow after a week? Was the famous submarine hero given a word of some impending fate?

For what happened may be stated succinctly.

U-29 at once moved out of the area and made for the North Sea. Six days had intervened, so it was now March 18, and the Grand Fleet happened to be out and Weddigen essayed to increase his reputation when he fired a torpedo at H.M.S. *Neptune*, but he missed, and the battleship carried on. Then came the Fourth Battle-Squadron, in which was H.M.S. *Dreadnought*, and the great drama happened in Lat. 58.20 N., Long. 0.57 E. One of this vessel's officers told me it was whilst the Wardroom were at lunch that Lieut.-Commander B. H. Piercy on the bridge sighted a periscope. Perhaps Weddigen was confused by the *Dreadnought's* course, for it is hardly likely this German lost his head. In trying to get out of the way and dive he was too slow, and the Englishman was one jump ahead—even though the handling of a great battleship takes time and accuracy.

Straight for Weddigen's craft sped the bows and the thousands of steel tons; a heavy horrible crunch ensued as U-29 was rammed amidships, cleaving the smaller craft in two, and those who came running up from lunch had just time to see one half of U-29 glide past the ship's side and sink.

It all happened as quickly as that. The loss of three *Cressys* had been avenged, and there was no German to narrate how this had happened.

Now on March 15 the gradually accumulating submarine units at Zeebrugge and Ostend were formed into the Flanders U-boat Flotilla: working independently of the submarine based on Heligoland or Wilhelmshaven, these were to build up a reputation of their own independently. And it was a hint of things to come when to the southwest of Cape Clear (in Lat. 51.10 N., Long. 9.52 W.) a submarine was actually sighted off that part of Ireland and engaged at 7 a.m. by H.M.S. *Partridge*. Then the U-boat menace and Submarine Blockade threatened to beat the radius which Hersing had extended to Walney? Some day were our Western Approaches to become the main operational area for the enemy?

Within two months the name of *Lusitania* would always be associated with tragedy.

But U-34 and U-35 at the beginning of March left Heligoland to pass through Dover Straits, which for some time were always an uncertain obstacle to the enemy: they were thankful to have

cleared the white cliffs of Albion, but always a little surprised despite
themselves. And there was, too, U-37 (Lieut.-Commander Wilcke)
which left Heligoland to go through the Dover Straits but never
returned. How and why we shall see presently. Of U-34 it may be
borne in mind that her commanding officer (Lieut.-Commander
Rücker), after sinking vessels in the Western Approaches, later took
his craft for a spell to the Mediterranean where he found success for
a while before coming home and receiving promotion to U-103;
in which, however, he was signally defeated by the White Star
S.S. *Olympic* during May, 1918, and became a British prisoner for
the rest of the war.

U-35 (Lieut.-Commander Kophamel), after operating in the
English Channel, likewise was sent to the Mediterranean, and of her
also we shall speak in due place: but our immediate concern is
with Freiherr von Forstner who had charge of U-28 and by his callous
brutality earned notoriety. Let us glance at this unchivalrous
pirate and note that whilst yet in the North Sea this March he sank
the S.S. *Leeuwarden* off the Dutch coast, next day captured a big
neutral steamer carrying foodstuff for the United Kingdom, and
sent her with a prize crew into Zeebrugge.

Wending his wicked way down the English Channel, he sank the
Dutch S.S. *Medea* off Eastbourne and by March 27 set to work
heartlessly against British shipping off the Cornish coast, well
knowing that between Lundy Island and the Scillies plenty of
steamers could be found on their lawful occasions.

Thus on that day he had no difficulty in sinking the 3837-ton
South Point, and the 2114-ton *Aguila*. But presently, being some
38 miles west of Trevose Head, he spotted another unarmed English
trader. She was the *Vosges*, 1295 tons, coming up from Bordeaux
for Liverpool with general cargo and seven passengers of whom one
chanced to be a woman.

U-28, being of 870 tons, with a speed of 16 knots on the surface,
carrying fuel enough for over 5000 miles, was one of Germany's
biggest and most powerful submarines. Moreover, besides her
eight torpedoes, she mounted on deck a couple of 22-pounder
guns. Altogether a formidable foe.

But if the *Vosges* possessed not so much as a rifle, she had a stalwart
North Country crew that would defy Baron von Forstner and fight
to the very last. Her Master, Captain John R. Green, was as full
of grit as resource. Seaman and tactician. Surrender his ship to a
German? Allow her to be captured? Not likely.

It had just gone 10.15 a.m. when the submarine showed its
whale-like form, and Captain Green took one look at the low-
lying creature, then at the rough sea. What to do? Bring the enemy
well astern, keep him there, go full out with engines, and the *Vosges*
might yet escape. Why? Because whilst offering the smallest
target, and by steering to windward, the steamer would cause the

U-boat to be washed down by every wave and annoy the German gunners.

Therein lies the one advantage which a surface vessel always owns over a submersible. Repeatedly it has been proved, and successfully, during this second war.

Of course, Forstner had several knots' superiority of speed, though the *Vosges*' engineers were coaxing machinery to do wonders.

"Give her all you can," the Captain exhorted.

Firemen off watch hurried down below to help, all the male passengers assisted too. The steam pressure sent the gauge mounting steadily. But already U-28 had begun sending her shells across. The first failed to hit, the second made a hole in the stern. Forstner was annoyed. He tried to get on the steamer's beam and settle her with his torpedoes, but Green each time altered course to keep the submarine dead aft. Maddening to the haughty German that a little bit of a steamer should be so defiant!

Try again? The Freiherr never ceased, but always the Liverpool Skipper counter-manœuvred.

Yet the poor *Vosges* was having a hot time. Again and again during this hour and a half the 22-pounder projectiles fell smashing against the ship. One pierced the starboard side and made a two-foot hole; another opened the starboard quarter; bridgehouse was smashed to splinters, funnel resembled a cook's colander, leaks were starting along the waterline. Second Mate on the bridge had been wounded in the arm, Chief Officer and the Captain suffering hand injuries.

Still these British seafarers carried on, and still they dodged away from the faster opponent.

"Stick to it, lads!"

Harry Davies, the Chief Engineer of *Vosges*, was standing by the stokehold door, he had barely uttered this exhortation to firemen and volunteers, when another shell shot through the hull, struck him in the chest and robbed him of life immediately. Things were looking pretty bad, water pouring in too plentifully, and one of the firemen wounded in his wrist—awkward place for him wielding a shovel. The mess-room boy received a bit of shell in his leg, and even the lady passenger was hit in the foot.

What next? How much longer? Pumps could not contend with the inpouring sea. The *Vosges* was doomed. Captain and crew had done their uttermost. And now it was 11.45 a.m.

Then, of a sudden, something wonderful occurred.

"Why! Look! She's had enough! Old Fritz is shoving off!"

Angry and disappointed, the Baron was giving up the chase to seek another victim. The Liverpool steamer had defeated him.

So the *Vosges*' crew set to work afresh, and Captain Green headed for Milford Haven. Lots of beaches, inside where she could be temporarily put ashore ! Patch up the holes, and then home to the Mersey !

Hope, however, perished when leaks turned into a deluge. The ship was sinking definitely and quickly. It was time to leave her. Heavy rain, boisterous sea, blustery wind. Passengers and crew took their places in the ship's boats, nerve-tried, but without excitement. Over to the northwest of Trevose Head patrolled the armed yacht *Wintonia*, and luckily she saw the boats before they could become separated. So rescue speedily followed, though the gallant little *Vosges* disappeared bows first at 2 p.m.

"If only we'd had a gun," Captain Green bewailed, "we should've sunk the submarine." But even 3-pounders were scarce in those days. For his splendid and heroic struggle, the Admiralty awarded him a commission in the Royal Naval Reserve, the King presented him with the D.S.O., gold watches were sent to each officer, and each member of the crew received £3 each.

Nor does the story end there.

Forstner, after quitting *Vosges*, submerged and was seeking a fresh prey when the unarmed steam trawler *Eileen Emma*, out of Milford Haven, sighted the periscope of U-28.

If the fisherman had no gun, at any rate his steel bows might do something.

"Full speed ahead", he rang on the telegraph and essayed to drive his ship at the stranger. It was now 12.30 p.m. At one time it looked as if Forstner were done for, and only with considerable difficulty did the latter avoid an ugly collision. A duel for positions ensued, and an interesting occasion, for *Eileen Emma* could do little more than 9 knots, but U-28 when submerged had a speed of less than 10 knots. Rather than be baulked by a trawler, the Baron therefore blew tanks, increased buoyancy, and speeded off to look for a more worth-while prey.

He found what he wanted one day later, but by then his temper had reached bursting point. After chasing the S.S. *Dunedin* (4796 tons), which—by superiority of speed—got clean away, he hoisted the British ensign and made for a passenger liner steaming down the St. George's Channel, outward bound from the Mersey for Sierra Leone. Her name turned out to be *Falaba*, 4806 tons.

After lowering false colours and showing the German flag, he stopped the liner and ordered the Master to abandon ship, the hour being just before noon. Within six minutes, even whilst boats were being swung out for human beings to be saved, U-28 with incredible brutality loosed off a torpedo at 100 yards range, and down went *Falaba* at 12.10 drowning 104 persons including the Master. Not content with this dastardly crime, German sailors laughed and jeered at men and women struggling for existence in the choppy sea or dropping like flies one by one as the steamer sank to her doom.

This was the first time in history that a submarine had destroyed a passenger ship, but the news created such a wave of indignation as to sweep through the whole civilized world. Records of the last war show that this jeering and laughter occurred on other occasions as victims hovered between life and death.

U-28 seemed to be having all the luck, but the time for vengeance had to come some day. She was not working alone: for U-34 and U-37 were co-operating with her off our Western Approaches. Sometimes she talked to them by wireless: sometimes, when within visible distance by flags. The Cornish area had become too dangerous, so by the end of the month, they both cleared across to the French coast where armed trawlers patrolled.

On March 30 the leader of this new patrol, *Sainte Jehanne* by name, was steaming in the direction of Fécamp when U-37 showed up on the surface. Circumstances were exactly right, the trawler perfectly situated. She went straight for her objective, and down dived the submarine involuntarily. That quickly ended one submarine's career.

It looked as if U-28 would still evade destiny, for the trawlers were after her. She got away but her gyroscopic compass broke down. How would she get back to Zeebrugge without foundering on a hidden sandbank?

She bleated on her wireless for help, out flew an aeroplane, which then from the sky piloted the submarine home.

It was April 5, 1915, only a few days after Forstner had left the Cornish coast, and the steam tug *Homer*, owned in South Shields, had been sent round to Queenstown to fetch the French barque *General de Sonis*, which had recently arrived across the ocean loaded with grain. As sailing ships go, the latter with her 2190 tons was quite a big vessel, having been built in 1901 when canvas had not yet been banished afloat. But this kind of ship with lofty masts, wide-spreading yards, and a maze of rigging meant an awkward, risky, thing to tow through the submarine zone—up the English Channel and so past the east coast to Sunderland.

All went well for the first three days, till the afternoon of the 8th when tug and dumb sailor were 25 miles SW. by S. of the Owers Lightship. They were still outside the Isle of Wight at 3.30 p.m. when Captain Gibson, Master of the *Homer*, noticed a U-boat on the surface approaching from the port side, but now a mere 400 yards away. Not too pleasant a picture! For two vessels could scarcely be in a more defenceless condition than tug and towed.

He looked again. Seven Germans were on deck, and the signal "Abandon Ship" was flying. Gibson ignored the demand, and thought out an idea. But the Hun commander waxed furious and shouted loudly, pointing to the flags. Still the tugmaster pretended not to hear.

Thereupon the submarine crossed the cavalcade's bows, came up the starboard side, motored on a parallel course and commenced firing a machine-gun; again bellowing sharp orders for the Englishmen to get into their boat.

Captain Gibson held his peace, sent a man aft to be ready for slipping tow-rope, instructed the helmsman what to do, waited a few more seconds till only a hundred yards separated the stranger ... then:

"Leggo, aft!"

"Aye, aye, sir."

Away went the snake-like hawser into the sea, and *Homer* became a free agent.

She was a brand new steamer, built that year, engines in perfect condition and able to do 12 knots. Being 95 feet long and of 157 tons, this steel tug signified weighty force, and now steered direct for the German. Hundred yards! A thrilling situation.

"Steady as she goes, there. ... Steady!"

The German never suspected such impudent daring, suddenly turned from offence to the defensive, saw the foaming bows make determinedly towards him; then, barely in time, the U-boat put helm hard-a-port and saved an impact. Only a matter of three feet prevented *Homer* from ripping a deep gash in the submarine's stern.

Goodness! A near thing, that time!

The German's Maxim gun rattled out a shower of bullets spitefully, whilst Gibson reversed helm and was going to have another try; but the enemy preferred keeping his distance and increasing his fire. In this dilemma, it were useless for the tug to go back and pick up the tow: that would mean the loss of both vessels. Better hasten ahead and find some naval patrol.

So the *Homer* steered towards the eastern end of the Wight, and a race for life was now on. Steam versus motors. Fierce going. A contest worth watching. Lucky the tug, with clean bottom and first-class machinery, made a grand performance. The Hun, likewise, went "full out", but gradually, decidedly, Gibson drew ahead.

"Look out!"

A torpedo shot forth, and well aimed, but though it passed close to the tug's starboard quarter that was another miss. During the length of one exciting hour the contest persisted until *Homer* had increased her lead by a good half-mile. There was a hard westerly wind lashing up considerable sea, but at last the U-boat gave up the chase and departed, butting into the waves resolved to demolish the French barque. Captain Gibson counted his damage and found seven bullet holes, and before rounding the Wight glanced astern. The last he observed before the cliffs intervened was a cloud of smoke enveloping *General de Sonis* between fore and main masts.

That German had done his worst.

Off Bembridge Captain Gibson spoke a destroyer, reported the incident at once, but the enemy by this time had cleared off. Then a most extraordinary occurrence followed. The French crew mastered the fire, they began setting sail, took advantage of the fair wind, scudded up Channel to Dungeness, where a Dover tug brought her into port.

So really the bullying U-boat had a poor day. But the Admiralty were so pleased with *Homer's* plucky achievement that they presented Captain Gibson with a gold watch and a letter of appreciation on vellum, whilst each of his crew received a gratuity.

CHAPTER 9

CHANGE OF POLICY

DURING the winter Germany had been constructing at the shipyards of Kiel, Hamburg, and Bremen ever since the previous autumn a smaller species of submarines. The intention was that these two smaller species should be able to operate from Zeebrugge and cut across the North Sea to East and Southeast England—such areas, in fact, as the neighbourhood of Lowestoft, Yarmouth, and Harwich; the French coast near the Dover Straits, off Boulogne, and so forth. Their radius of action was limited, their displacement limited, so they could never attain very considerable success, but the desire was to produce what was possible by the Spring.

Two kinds of boats were thus evolved: the UB type, which displaced 127 tons on the surface and 142 tons when submerged below water. Their speed was a steady 5 knots for 1650 miles on the surface, they were somewhat slower submerged, were fitted with a couple of bow torpedo-tubes, one machine-gun; their complement consisting of one officer and thirteen men. The second type was the UC class displacing 168 tons on the surface and 183 tons submerged, fitted with six chutes for carrying a dozen mines, one machine-gun; but their endurance was only 850 miles at 5 knots on the surface with occasional spurts of 8 knots, and their personnel numbered the same as the UB's.

Now the first of these minelayers to be commissioned was UC-11, which appeared in April but she did not join up with the Flanders Flotilla till early in June. You can imagine that she could be sent with her cargo of mines across the sea with regularity, lay them under cover of night in some harbour approach, then hurry back to Zeebrugge—only submerged when near the land but generally enjoying the freedom of the sea on passage. UC-11 was sent on a successful mining enterprise to the South Goodwins Lightship, but East Anglia as far north as Yarmouth was very much her area.

The submarine must always be a problem to the defenders, because of her elusiveness, but it was hoped that the further mining of Dover Straits, the care in keeping this area netted, would make that defile too difficult. Unfortunately we know that the submarine captains endowed with a certain venturesomeness and love of the risky, were not finding the Straits too difficult this April. Lieut.-

Commander Gansser in U-33, Lieut.-Commander Spiegel Freiherr von Peckelsheim in U-32, and Lieut.-Commander Schneider in U-24 (who had previously sunk *Formidable*)—all three very able at their job—successfully negotiated the Straits this month.

From Gayer we know that Gansser found the danger from mines had considerably increased between the Ruytingen and the Falls, but that these obstacles were mostly on the surface. Nevertheless, U-32 whilst traversing the area (submerged) at the beginning of April became foul of a net, was compelled to go to the bottom and wait for dark when she came to the surface and investigated. The net was found tangled up ahead of the conning tower, and festooned on either side. In consequence of this alarming experience, U-32 did not return by this route but came home northabout past Scotland. U-24, however, did pass Dover about the same time as U-32, with better luck by night and on the surface.

But because of this incident to U-32, a new order was issued to the submarines : the Northern route was to be used exclusively, though the UB's and UC's from Zeebrugge were exempt : their slight displacement would render any wriggling through peril a slight risk. Indeed, the first shot fired by these little craft of the Flanders Flotilla was on April 10 near the North Hinder Lightship, when UB-4 torpedoed and sank the British S.S. *Harpalyce*. By the end of this—their initial—month these boats from Zeebrugge had sunk 9713 tons of shipping, but such mass-produced and hastily fabricated machines had various constructional troubles.

Britain also was taking greater precautions against submarines. The negotiations ended on April 9, 1915, when a contract was signed for the first fifty Motor Launches to be built by mass production in America, and this order was on July 9 further increased, to 550.

As ML's they were in future known ; the contract insisting that they were to be 80 feet long and to be delivered by November 15, 1916. Built in New Jersey, U.S.A., in Quebec and Montreal, Canada ; they were given each two engines of 220 h.p. respectively, manufactured in the United States. The pattern boat was made at Bayonne, New Jersey, where all the fabrication was done, the Canadian plants being used only for assembling. These craft were transported to England four-a-time on the deck of some steamer— to Portsmouth, to Italy, even to Egypt, and the West Indies— and the whole contract of 550 were built in 488 days.

These ML's were not beautiful and were much criticized, yet until 1918 they performed good work round the coasts despite disadvantages. Perhaps the most remarkable feature was that they lasted so long, for many survived both in British and foreign waters as conversions into yachts until this second war of 1939 began.

Now when in the first autumn of war Admiral Tirpitz had ordered seventeen of the UB class and fifteen of the UC class,

Germany was able by the following April to export some of these small craft to the Mediterranean (in sections) by train and relaunch them into the Adriatic. Thus arrived UB 1, 3, 7, 8, 14, 15 together with the four minelayers, UC 12, 13, 14, 15, at the headquarters of Pola. From them were selected UB-3, UB-7, and UB-8 sent under their own power from the Adriatic to the Aegean and so to Constantinople; and of these UB-3 was last heard wirelessing her report when 80 miles from Smyrna. It is practically certain that on April 9 she was blown up when entering that area, having fouled the Turkish minefield in the Gulf. But the other two—UB-7 and 8—safely navigated from the Adriatic to the Aegean, and via the Bosphorus into the Black Sea; UB-8 not arriving at Constantinople till June 4 and was handed over to the Bulgarians.

Being only 98 feet long, drawing just under 10 feet, their speed through the Dardanelles current did not allow much of a safety margin, but at least being friendly craft they could be allowed by the forts to navigate on the surface against the current. It was, however, wisely realized that such frail little boats must never be employed outside the Sea of Marmara against our Fleet. UB-7 survived only till the autumn of this 1915, when she hit a Black Sea mine, but during that summer, UC-13, 14, and 15, came round to Constantinople bringing arms and ammunition from the Adriatic.

It is clear from Gayer[1] that at any rate UB-14 was this summer using Orak Bay, near Budrun, Gulf of Kos, Aegean; and that UC-14 also utilized that place. Why? Well, it was situated on the flank of the Dardanelles traffic route (so busily employed by our warships and transports), yet it happened to be hidden away in this lonely spot. On the other hand, it was an ideal corner for several reasons: the German crew could be given opportunity for exercising their limbs after being cooped up in these small vessels, there was plenty of cattle to be got from the nearby farms, general provisions were also obtainable, and it would be a good place for effecting repairs.

In fact we have here a clear instance of the Germans utilising to the full their thorough knowledge of local geography.

So, then, the spring of 1915 saw the Germans striving to make the smaller UB's and UC's of special help against southeast England and in southeast Europe, but it must be remembered that these very weak and light displacement boats were of decided limitations. Far more capable were the U-boats, as, for instance, U-6 (Lieut.-Commander Lepsius) which captured our fishing steam-trawler *Glencarse* in the North Sea and took her across to Lister Deep with which she entered on April 20. Yet five months later Lepsius was to pay the penalty for this daring when the British submarine E-16 settled her account off Stavanger.[2]

The Dover area still caused anxiety, yet we could never be

[1] See volume II.   [2] See below, under September 15, 1915.

exactly sure of the way submarines were getting through, so on April 13 Rear-Admiral R. H. S. Bacon, C.V.O., D.S.O., was given charge of this extremely important region with its patrols, its mines, and even its extensions to the Belgian coast. But that the nation had still, after nine months' hostilities, to complete preparations for her defence is well instanced this April by arming defensively valuable liners against U-boats. For instance, the Orient Line *Osterley* was able to mount in her stern a 4·7-inch gun, and so she proceeded to the Mediterranean : but at Gibraltar this weapon was hoisted out, and two Reserve ratings with it, to be put aboard the same Company's S.S. *Orsova* bound homewards across the Bay of Biscay. Economy was necessitated by the fewness of guns.

Even now the U-boat by its uncertainties still was regarded as something of a mystery, and instances of this surprising behaviour are numerous enough. In mid-April submarines were certainly busy at the western end of the Channel when the S.S. *Wayfarer* was torpedoed 60 miles WNW. of the Scillies, though they managed to get her towed into port. So also the next day a U-boat had the temerity to circle round the Belgian trawler, No. 0131, when in Lat. 50.30 N., Long. 7.45 W. It was night time—10.30 p.m.— but after having a good look, the submarine decided not to waste a £1000 torpedo on her, so sheered off. The North Sea always was more or less the haunt of U-boats, especially off the northeast coast, and when on April 13 H.M. Submarine C-39 was one mile east of the Tees Fairway a few minutes before seven o'clock that morning, she distinctly saw the conning tower of a U-boat which dived a minute later. When at 4 a.m. of April 14 two trawlers caught sight of U-16 on the surface off Hartlepool, perhaps she was already making her plans for taking Völckner back to Heligoland.[1]

But the changes and chances of this U-boat business were never better illustrated than by the months of April and May when North Europe saw not one of these submarines sunk. Falmouth became an important base this April with armed steam yachts, trawlers, and drifters because of the increasing submarine activities at that part of the English Channel. On the other hand the Germans had recently laid by surface ships a minefield which ran in a 117° direction from Lat. 53.55 N., Long .1.33 E. It became known as the Outer Silver Pit Minefield because of its geographical position round that spot, the first discovery being made when the Dutch S.S. *Olanda*, bound from Seaham to Rotterdam, foundered on a mine some 30 miles east of the Outer Dowsing. This was on April 18, but the loss of the fishing trawler two months later really caused the ambushed area's discovery.

Other disasters that summer followed, and the probable reason was to foul the track of shipping bound from England to Rotterdam,

[1] See Chapter 8.

Amsterdam, Christiania. According to the Germans, these mines were set for 4½ metres, but an officer engaged in the sweeping tells me they were set for 6 metres. Interference with our trade was in itself a powerful enough reason for its existence, but the Swarte Bank minefield evidently was laid about the same time.

But now we come to an entirely new development, the voyage of a U-boat whose enterprise and daring gave a new twist to events.

I am not concerned with writing a history of the naval operations at the Dardanelles: that I have already attempted in my volume *Dardanelles Dilemma*,[1] but the Mediterranean does concern us intimately because of this new connection with the U-boats. As time developed, the story of the U-boat was to grow bigger and more notable but at first it was quite a small affair.

Already Germany by the spring of 1915 had become apprehensive of what might happen to the cause of her and Turkey, if the British in their Dardanelles campaign should succeed. And though the Turks could not be supplied with a submarine, yet we have seen that Germany was willing to send here via Austria some of the smaller types. So seriously was the matter still further regarded that finally the German Admiralty determined to try a most original experiment. Could one of their ordinary U-boats voyage from home to the Adriatic, there refuel and refit, afterwards proceeding round the corner into the Dardanelles and up to Constantinople?

It might be possible to reach an Austrian port, provided arrangements were previously made for replenishment with fuel, but the first question to settle was whom they should send on such an uncertain project.

Obviously there was one whose qualities had marked him out both as a daring man and a first-class seafarer. And we who have considered in the preceding pages the stealth of one who crept up to the Forth Bridge, who a few days later sank the *Pathfinder*, but at a later stage was also able to blaze the trail up the Irish Sea creating a precedent among steamers which were sunk near Liverpool, but returned home a great hero; was the very person to attempt this Mediterranean madness. Yes: Lieut.-Commander Otto Hersing should have the job, and he should make his effort in U-21.

His boat was given a thorough overhaul, and though older than those smaller and slower creatures of the UB and UC classes, she was far more seaworthy. Measuring 210 feet long, with a surface draught of 12 feet, displacing 840 tons submerged and 650 on the surface, she carried eight torpedoes and after that still could use a couple of guns. Her speed gave her 15 knots over the surface, and 9 knots when submerged. U-21, far from being the latest thing built, was first commissioned in 1913.

Granted that Hersing and his boat were thoroughly efficient in all senses, it still remained to be proved that the long outward

[1] Published in 1935.

voyage to the Mediterranean were possible. As Germany possessed no bases, and since the Dover Straits were considered too dangerous for a craft of her size (so that she must cross the North Sea, give the coast of Scotland a wide berth, plunge down the Atlantic away from Ireland, make her progress down the Bay of Biscay past Portugal and Spain through the Gibraltar Straits), her first base could be no nearer than one of Austria's ports in the Adriatic.

And that would mean a lengthy voyage of roughly 4000 miles.

Consider the strain on cooped-up personnel! Consider the endurance of bad weather from north to south! Otto Hersing, tall, slender, dark-eyed, sullen, and hawk-like would require all his capability to win through; but all the luck if he were to survive this seafaring and settle down once more to the life of a country gentleman at Rastede, growing potatoes and ignoring the damp environment which encourages rheumatism.

He left Wilhelmshaven on April 25, the very day when our troops landed on the beach of Gallipoli. He got safely past patrols and through the Fair Island passage, but always at the back of his mind was that fear of running short in his oil fuel. Still, he had managed to start his journey with 56 tons of oil fuel and arrangements had been made by the Admiralstat in Berlin through the German Embassy in Madrid that this amount should be supplemented *en route*. How was it to be done? As if this were a realistic detective novel, a small steamer was to come out from the Spanish cliffs with oil fuel, lubricating oil, drinking water, and provisions.

The name of this vessel was the *Marsala*, 1753 tons, owned in Hamburg. I have had inquiries made along that coast concerning this adventure. Let it be said that Spain and this littoral were favourable for illegal undertakings, that strict neutrality was not enforced, that with a little enterprise and some secrecy a rendezvous was quite within the range of possibility. German trickery and German bribes could brush aside many difficulties, though apparently not even Teutonic meticulousness nor the man at the Embassy could prevent the avoidable.

Hersing made a successful voyage, met the *Marsala* off the coast, and together they retired within Corcubion Bay which is just one of those many indentations along this rock-bound shore between Cape Finisterre and Vigo. Of his 56 tons Hersing had used up 31 in the Wilhelmshaven–Corcubion progress, and now under cover of a warm May night he took aboard 12 more tons of oil fuel replenishing also with 2 tons of lubricants. The steamer let go the ropes, the low-lying U-21 stole out past the high cliffs, the long voyage was resumed. The submarine knew that 25 plus 12 tons of fuel ought to see her well up the Adriatic.

But the great mistake now was revealed. It was the wrong sort of engine oil, which the *Marsala* had brought! The flash-point was not suitable for Diesel motors! And any mingling of the old with the new convinced the mechanics that this spelt failure to the best laid scheme of Spaniards and German tricksters.

Only 25 tons of the original Wilhelmshaven fuel available! Should Hersing still try to reach Cattaro? Or give up this undertaking because some idiot had bungled the most essential factor?

It is to Otto Hersing's credit that, despite this discouragement, he determined to take the gamble and carry on. Germany counted on his reaching the Mediterranean. Turkey was expecting him to do great things in the Dardanelles, and on a bigger scale than had been attempted by the little UB's and UC's. But if he were to get from Corcubion calling at Cattaro, he must husband every drop of this precious fuel, avoid diving, do most of the mileage on the surface and at economical speed. Therefore his hope lay in avoiding all patrols and any traffic which might report his presence.

But the German may expend the most careful means on behalf of efficiency, only to do the most senseless thing presently. Just as the fuel had been foolishly provided, so Hersing seems to have erred badly. When 36 miles NW. by N. of the bleak Burling Islands, right in the track of shipping, U-21 was sighted on the surface with no colours flying. It was the British S.S. *Teiresias,* who wondered at this wave-breaking conning-tower, and did not hesitate to report the stranger's southbound progress. Suspicion had thus been bred.

Still, U-21 continued, the Mediterranean was entered, the Gibraltar Straits passed, but Hersing had not been able to voyage entirely with secrecy: it was even believed that she might rendezvous some fuel-carrying vessel near Alboran Island, for which reason therefore the Gibraltar Patrol was given the task of specially watching this area. In command of this patrol was Lieut.-Commander W. Ward Hunt, R.N., who was afloat in Torpedoboat No. 92, and he tells me that on May 6 about 3 p.m. he sighted U-21 some 40 miles west of the island.

There was a fresh easterly wind blowing, so as Hersing butted into the waves his craft threw showers of spray from the bows and made her still more conspicuous. She was 7 miles distant, No. 92 went full speed, but when 3 miles off the submarine dived. At 200 yards the German showed her periscope, again dived and could be seen plainly in the water below the torpedoboat's keel: in fact, the latter even damaged the periscope, and marks of the same were found on No. 92's bottom when the time came for docking.

U-21 did not like being compelled to waste oil by diving, and in her wrath fired a torpedo—which missed: but it may be again mentioned that these were the days before the advent of depth charges, or the torpedoboat could have settled Hersing's fate readily. All the same, the incident had proved that the German submarine was now in the Mediterranean and might a few days later be expected up the Dardanelles. Probably not earlier than the night of May 11–12.

Actually it was to be later, because he intended to call first up the Adriatic. In the meanwhile he sighted a second British torpedo-boat, a French steamer off Cartagena, and a French destroyer, till finally passing north of Malta he entered Cattaro on May 13. He had made a record voyage of eighteen days, but with the narrowest margin. Barely half a ton of oil remained in his fuel tanks: he had fared luckily, and we may mention one interesting fact. Hersing created precedent by negotiating the Gibraltar defile "in the grey light of dawn", and I have found that German as well as British officers confirm this to be the general practice of U-boats in the future down here. The bearings of Spartel and Trafalgar lighthouses, and the steady 4-knot current, were more friendly than the Dover Straits to any German who knew that beneath him was deep water and no mines could be laid in Spanish territory.

Hersing refitted his craft and rested his crew in Cattaro's secluded bay, then went up to Pola where the boat could have her periscope repaired and her thirty-five men enjoy the delights of civilization. Not for long, since U-21 set off again on May 20 and then passed up the Aegean: she had been sent from Germany to counteract the British campaign in the Dardanelles. Hersing sighted, but failed to attack, our ally the five-funnelled Russian cruiser *Askold*, and was actually seen on the morning of May 22.

Three days later about noon she torpedoed the battleship *Triumph* and sank her, although the latter was lying with nets out off Gaba Tepe. The ship in her final agony had turned turtle, and over fifty officers with men were drowned. Rear-Admiral Stuart Nicholson transferred his flag to the *Majestic*. Next day was May 26, then came the dawn of May 27 and at 6.40 a.m. U-21 from a distance of 350 yards fired a torpedo in clear calm weather, striking abreast the mainmast so that the 15,000-ton *Majestic* likewise capsized and among the survivors was Admiral Stuart Nicholson, but no officers were lost and only forty-two men.

Hersing had thus quickly after his arrival sunk two British battleships in three days: his name was more famous than the man who wiped out three *Cressys*: but Admiral de Robeck now sent his biggest ships into the security of Imbros and Lemnos, and Hersing did not sight another target till the evening of May 30 about 6 miles east of Strati Island off the Asia Minor Coast. He was surprised to see H.M.S. *Tiger*. Just after 8 p.m. he torpedoed her, she had to be abandoned, but—strange to observe—her 13·5-inch "guns" would not sink. Why? Because this was not the real, but the "dummy" *Tiger*, actually the S.S. *Merion* cleverly disguised. Only four men lost their lives.

Somehow Hersing's luck had changed and targets seemed all too few. After going into Smyrna Gulf for the day—a custom already outlined—and then failing to torpedo the homeward-bound Cunard trooper *Carmania*, he finally went up the Straits, negotiated the

Chanak Narrows into the Sea of Marmara, and on June 5 reached Constantinople where he was received with great enthusiasm as the man who saved the Dardanelles—"Der befreier der Dardanellan"—and was given the German decoration corresponding to our Victoria Cross.

Such, then, was the introduction of submarine warfare to the Mediterranean. Hersing and the smaller boats which had arrived by train set the example, but the time had not yet arrived for other boats to voyage out from Germany under their own power.

CHAPTER 10

THE *LUSITANIA* SEQUEL

WE had in 1915 a fair hint of what to expect in future from the enemy, for on April 29 the Harwich trawler, *Lord Roberts*, was very nearly incapacitated when a German "Taube" flew over near the Galloper in the North Sea and dropped bombs. That, however, was rather an isolated incident, and the continuous pressure of U-boats in the North Sea off the Scottish and Northumbrian coasts remained a perpetual threat to our trawlers.

Towards the end of April the apparent increase in the number of U-boats passing by the Orkneys and Hebrides was noticeable. Such areas as the Butt of Lewis and Cape Wrath especially needed patrolling, for the Admiralty collier *Mobile* was stopped by a submarine 25 miles NW. of the former and sunk by gunfire. But this was indicative of the extended voyages, which submarines now undertook: they were going regularly not merely round England, Scotland, and Wales, but even to the west of Ireland. For on April 30 the S.S. *Fulgent* was fired at by a submarine when 20 miles WNW. of the Blaskets, and afterwards sunk by bombs, killing one A.B. and mortally wounding the captain. On the same day the U-boat by gunfire sank the Russian S.S. *Svorno* 14 miles west of the Blaskets: Irish waters would soon be included in the regular sphere of German operations.

The Western Approaches of the British Isles were to become now of increasingly great importance. Transatlantic traffic from North America and other streams of commerce from the Mediterranean, Africa, and South America must converge before making for the English Channel, and that is why such areas as Cornwall and the southwest of Ireland came prominently into the picture.

Take, for instance, the reports of U-boats for the span of May 3–6, this period being intentionally selected as immediately working up to the memorable May 7. It was on May 3 that the S.S. *Minterne* was torpedoed 50 miles SW. of the Wolf Rock: that definitely established the submarine danger near Land's End. But next day a torpedo was also fired at the S.S. *Cayo Romano* near the Fastnet, whilst the schooner *Earl of Lathom* was sunk by gunfire 8 miles SSW. from the Old Head of Kinsale on May 5, but a U-boat was operating off southern Ireland on May 6, for the S.S. *Candidate*, at 10 a.m., was torpedoed 13 miles S. by E. of Coninbeg Lightship, and three hours later the S.S. *Centurion* 15 miles south of the Barrels Lightship. If there were two submarines co-operating, then the most notable was U-20, in command of which was Lieut.-Commander Schwieger, who had succeeded an officer named Droescher.

We know, of course, that occasionally off eastern England smaller submarines had luck, as for instance on May 1, when during the forenoon Lieut. Hacker in UB-6, near the Galloper Lightship, torpedoed H.M.S. *Recruit* (Commander W. C. Wrightson, R.N.), but that was the first time a Flanders submarine had sunk a warship. Admittedly this destroyer was not in the first flush of youth, but it showed what could be effected by even the smallest submarine when given a fair chance.

Schwieger, with a good craft under him, was out for something ambitious. He set out from Borkum Roads on the morning of April 30 and was off the south coast of Ireland by May 7, if not slightly earlier, viz. May 6. He thus covered the distance from Germany within a week, and this length of time became normal for a U-boat's passage. Now to-night the Admiral at Queenstown sent a wireless message to the homeward-bound *Lusitania* which had left New York on May 1 : she was advised to avoid headlands, pass harbours at full speed and keep in mid-Channel, being warned that submarines were off the Fastnet. This signal the *Lusitania* received.

Although economizing in fuel and labour and in restricting the use of her boilers by six, she could still do her 21 knots. Unarmed, with boats swung out, bulkhead doors and portholes closed, lookouts doubled, she made the Irish land, but at 8 a.m., May 7, eased down to 18 knots : otherwise she would be ahead of her tide into Liverpool. The Bar into the Mersey would not be capable of being crossed until 4 a.m. of May 8, and obviously it would not be safe for a 30,000-ton ship to wait about in Liverpool Bay, where already there had occurred sinkings by submarines. But May is a month when fog settles down, and the *Lusitania*, on making the coast of SW. Ireland, was there compelled to ease from 18 to 15 knots.

I have often found, when navigating a vessel off that south-western approach to Ireland, that in May the fog might suddenly come on very densely, but about noon with the rising of the warm sun, the land would break forth and all thickness vanish.

So, on May 7, it happened to *Lusitania*. Brow Head showed up, a course could be laid parallel with the coast and the speed again accelerated to 18 knots. At 1.50 p.m. it was full clear, and the passengers were below at lunch for the last time : to-morrow would see them breakfasting in the quietude of the Mersey.

Suddenly came the great climax. The Second Officer sighted a torpedo rushing towards the ship's starboard side. It struck her between the third and fourth funnels, the inrush of water disabled the engines, but the wireless operator was able to send out an S O S signal giving *Lusitania's* position as 10 miles south from the Old Head of Kinsale : time, 2.15 p.m., when the startling news reached Admiral Coke in Queenstown. Instantly he despatched to her assistance the few patrols of the steam trawlers, tugs, steam yachts, drifters, torpedoboats, and small motor yachts available on this station.

The plain fact emerges that at the moment of the disaster when Schwieger fired his torpedo at this conspicuous hull of a great liner with four prominent funnels, the sea was calm, the weather sunny and clear, and no patrol near at hand. So the *Lusitania* listed by the head and to starboard, disappearing beneath the sea at 2.30 p.m., with the appalling loss of 1198 men, women, and children.

What result did this contribute to the U-boat service?

Grand-Admiral Tirpitz remarked that submarine warfare had "no effect in securing the ultimate victory of the German people," yet still possessed "material enough to create incidents and quarrels with the Americans." On May 12 the United States despatched a Note to Germany pointing out that it was practically impossible for U-boats to carry out a blockade with due regard for humanity, and though this protest had no immediate effect it focused American opinion which was finally to lead to the United States entering the war on our side and giving her invaluable aid against the German enemy.

It is perfectly true that the *Lusitania* episode did not till two years later create that unity of purpose, but to any mind (other than that of a German) the trend of future political movement was becoming obvious. Sooner or later America would feel it her duty to come in.

And meanwhile we busied ourselves with anti-submarine patrols on a large scale : drifters based at Fleetwood in case of further attacks on Walney Island, other ex-fishing vessels patrolling the southern Irish Sea, nets laid off the Welsh coast and in the Bristol Channel, six steam yachts based on Milford. But every night from 6 p.m. to 10.30 p.m., before the departure of the Dublin to Holyhead steamer, one lot of trawlers cruised about the track whenever troops were crossing to England.

By the end of May there were one hundred and fifty net drifters based on Larne for protecting the North Channel : then, four days after the *Lusitania* incident, eight Scottish drifters were commissioned to be based on Queenstown with a view to their being sent off any required headland with their nets, or in some suspected bay. There can be no doubt that U-boats now had begun to extend their campaign farther westward, for apart from the loss of the big Cunarder there was further evidence.

Thus, at 10.30 p.m., four days after Schwieger's crime, one

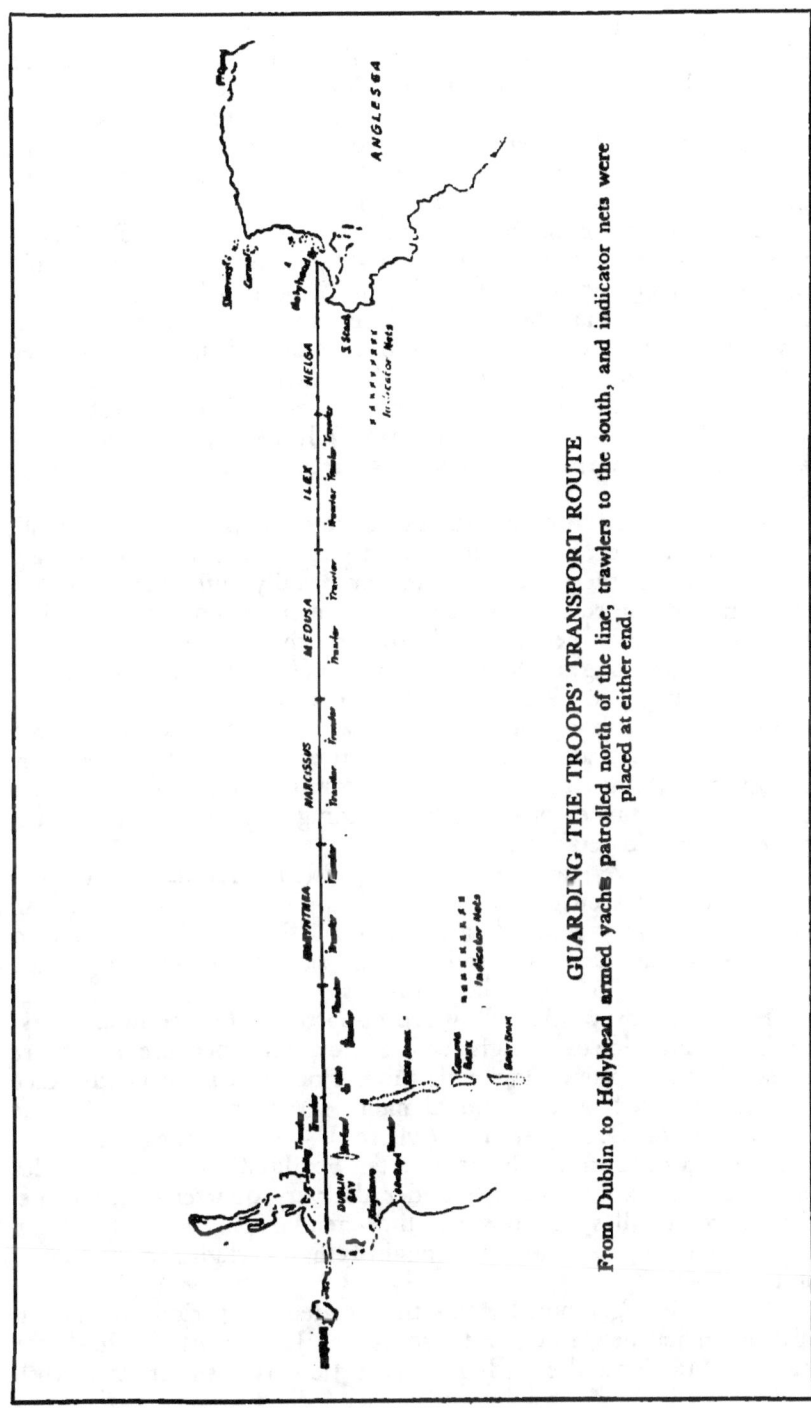

GUARDING THE TROOPS' TRANSPORT ROUTE

From Dublin to Holyhead armed yachts patrolled north of the line, trawlers to the south, and indicator nets were placed at either end.

U-boat showed her conning tower and wash some 4 miles southwest of Daunt's Rock Lightship where she was observed by Lieut. Cannel, R.N.R., in H.M. Trawler *Brock*. Two submarines were sighted after another three days—one in Tramore Bay (Waterford) and Ballycotton Bay, whilst the other motored near the Fastnet. Thus, at either end of the southern Irish coast, the Germans were prowling about to entrap other vessels.

So it was easy enough when the 1968-ton sailing vessel *Glenholm* was torpedoed on May 21 16 miles WSW. of the Fastnet. A submarine was sighted a day later in that neighbourhood, which still further confirms that these U-boats were hanging around to waylay inward or outward shipping off the extremity of the Western Isles. Then on the evening of May 25 the American S.S. *Nebraskan* of 2824 tons, one day out from Liverpool, was 48 miles west of the Fastnet when a submarine was seen, followed by a violent shock and explosion, hurling the steamer's cargo-derrick 30 feet into the air.

Luckily she still floated and her engines continued to go round, but she bleated on her wireless and a patrol vessel came to her aid followed by another armed yacht. Eventually with such an escort she rounded the south Irish coast, met a nasty northeast wind in the Irish Channel, became well down by the head in the breaking seas, but after hugging the weather shore of the Welsh coast gained Liverpool at 9 p.m. This was not the first American steamer to be torpedoed, for already on May 1, the S.S. *Gulflight* was thus injured off the Scillies, and she too was taken into port; but here, by choosing out neutral vessels for assault, Germany gave two undoubted instances of clumsily offending a great country which some day would retaliate.

And, moreover, were there not aboard the *Lusitania* a number of United States citizens wilfully sent to death? Some American passengers barely escaped, and from one I was given a detailed account which makes one admire the self-control of the United States President in not declaring war.

But Germany would still afford opportunity for the final break.

The submarine campaign persisted down here because there were a few—but only a few—fairly big submarines of large fuel endurance and commanded by exceptional men. It was on May 24, at the north side of County Mayo (where U-boats coming out from Germany would make the land after Scotland), that the trawler *Norbreck* sighted a submarine under the very quarter of a barque. Steaming at full speed towards the enemy, firing shots to which the German replied, the latter sought refuge in flight, so the sailing ship escaped.

Now Schwieger had by this time ended his period and begun his return journey, but there also off the Irish coasts in the latter part of May and the earlier half of June two smart craft with able captains : U-35 (Lieut.-Commander Kophamel) and U-34 (Lieut.-Commander Rücker). It is not always possible to define which of the two captains sank which ships, and which sank the rest when each was working the same area at the same time ; but both were pioneers, and the latter concluded his adventurous career as a British prisoner of war much later.

Two days after the *Norbreck* rescue, was sunk the British S.S. *Morwenna* south of the Fastnet, and then the White Star liner *Megantic* (14,878 tons) was chased, but got away from the submarine by superior speed. So, too, the 11,000-ton S.S. *Demerara*, on the last day of May, only saved herself by using her gun, but three ships in the adjacent St. George's and Bristol Channels also had narrow shaves. Having just arrived from the north, Kophamel in U-35 sank the sailing vessel *George and May* off the Mayo coast, and eventually shifted to the Scillies area.

At this time Rücker, in U-34, was also off the SW. Irish shore, and both these boats received some hard knocks when the patrol trawler *Ina Williams* attacked with her gun on two occasions this June. Rücker, to the very end, had a typically Hun reputation, but it was difficult to say whether his men or his prisoners hated him most. Brutal to his enemies, he captured the steam trawler *Victoria* to the southeast of Cape Clear, killing the British skipper and six hands, although they were fishermen and non-combatants. In the same district he sank the unarmed Cardiff fishing steam trawler *Hirose*, and after these ten men had been prisoners with four survivors from the *Victoria*, he cast the whole lot adrift in a crowded boat and an ugly sea, with a bit of canvas cover for sail and an oar as mast, till after twenty-four horrible hours the men were picked up by the S.S. *Ballater*. Soaked with the sea, exhausted for food and rest, they were landed at Milford.

Now during the next fortnight followed an alarming series of sinking sailing and steam ships in the area between the Fastnet and Lundy Island. British, Russian, Norwegian barques ; schooners ; cargo carriers of all sorts ; swelled the list, the enemy by the employment of the fewest submarines sufficiently indicated that this fresh sphere especially of southern Ireland, was likely to become even more important than the North Sea. Why ? Because it was the very highway along which passed valuable freights from the New to the Old World. Had our authorities, then, sufficiently appreciated all that Ireland meant ? Its harbours ? Its long and lonely indentations likely to be used for submarines ? The possibilities of Queenstown, Berehaven, Buncrana as naval bases ?

Just at this time, May 22, the veteran Lord Fisher resigned his appointment as First Sea Lord, and Mr. Winston Churchill gave up his appointment as First Lord of the Admiralty. The alteration was due to differences concerned with the Dardanelles policy.

After two days Mr. Churchill was succeeded by Mr. Arthur Balfour, and Admiral Sir Henry Jackson carried out the duties which had been Lord Fisher's, but as a practical detail there followed in this summer a great change which would link up the past with the future. Vice-Admiral Sir Lewis Bayly, after the *Formidable* torpedoing, found himself appointed as President of the Royal Naval College at Greenwich. Mr. Balfour now sent for him, invited him to accept the Queenstown command : the protection to ships reaching the Western Approaches from America with munitions, guns, machinery, and so on, demanded very particular qualities.

Admiral Bayly requested a fast cruiser be given him, and that was granted. So on July 20 he hauled down his flag at Greenwich, went aboard H.M.S. *Adventure* (of 2940 tons and 25 knots) at Gravesend that day, and on July 22 landed at Queenstown to begin a remarkable four years at Admiralty House in succession to Vice-Admiral Sir Charles Coke, whose regime had been interrupted by the *Lusitania* incident.

A new chapter in Irish sea history now began.

CHAPTER II

NORTH SEA STRATEGY

I HAVE specially mentioned U-34 and U-35 because these were two of Germany's much esteemed submarines, but another specially chosen was U-39 (Lieut.-Commander Forstmann), who was working the North Sea and attained dual distinction this May. Firstly, he attacked a ship in the 3rd Battle Squadron, 100 miles ENE. of the Forth, and achieved a wireless record in communicating over a distance of 340 miles. According to Gayer, U-9 (Weddigen's old boat which had sunk the *Cressys*) and U-16 (which rescued the "war pilot" Völckner), and U-36 were also in the North Sea this month. But we began to identify various callsigns, and could usually fix the positions of submarines passing up and down the North Sea.

On May 17 the German surface ships were most certainly engaged on North Sea enterprise since to-day was captured and sunk near the NW. corner of the Dogger Bank the trawler *King Charles*, and on the next day the three trawlers *Euclid, Duke of Wellington, Titania*; the crews being taken prisoner by enemy torpedoboats. For the enemy was laying the Dogger Bank minefield, which was meant to entrap our Grand Fleet, but this area of hidden danger was revealed on May 18 when the trawler *Reverto* discovered the first of these mines and newly painted. It was a lucky find because the Grand Fleet had left Scapa on the evening of May 17 for a sweep down the North Sea, and next day were approaching this dangerous area when they were ordered back home.

Gayer[1] confirms the theory that the Dogger Bank minefield was laid on the night of May 17–18 and that the two submarines, U-19 and U-25, with their leader G-137 and the cruiser leader *Hamburg*, were ordered to take up their position between the battle-cruisers (sent on ahead) and the main fleet. They afterwards returned to the Jahde. In other words the minelaying had been carried out under such strong protection of the High Sea Fleet that the arrival of the Grand Fleet during these operations was anticipated.

Laid at a depth of 16 feet below surface (low water ordinary springs), the mines were intended to entrap deep-draught capital

[1] *The German Submarines*, volume II.

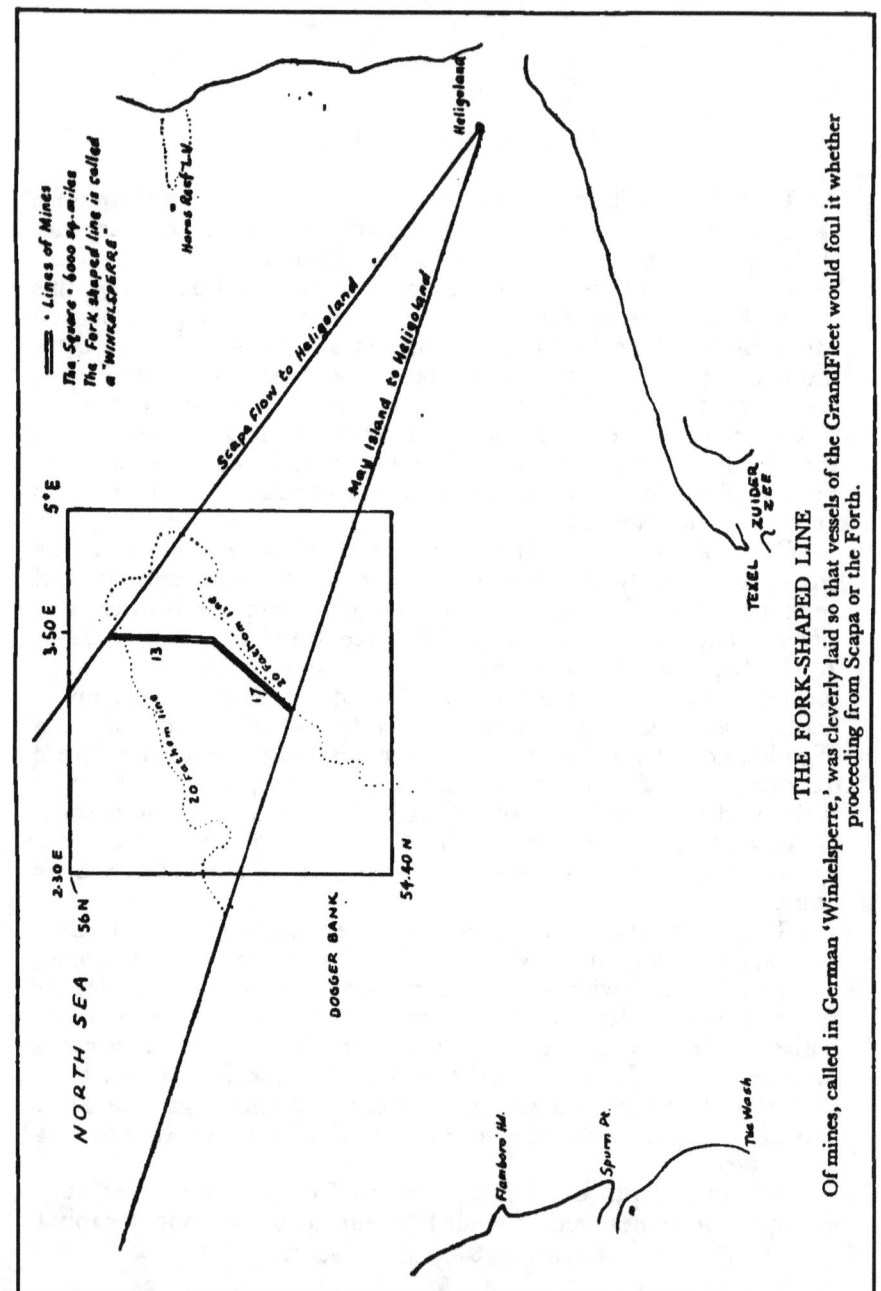

THE FORK-SHAPED LINE

Of mines, called in German 'Winkelsperre,' was cleverly laid so that vessels of the GrandFleet would foul it whether proceeding from Scapa or the Forth.

ships (such as cruisers and battleships), but not to be discovered by light-draught destroyers and sweepers. The first mercantile loss occurred on May 20 when the 6960 tons *Maricopa* with a cargo of oil was on her way from Port Arthur for Amsterdam, but this tanker, though striking a mine in Lat. 55 N., Long. 3.20 E., managed to reach the Tyne, and the fishing trawler by foundering also located something of the position. In order more precisely to ascertain the mined area, half a dozen paddlers and four sweeping trawlers came out from Grimsby, whilst Fleet sweepers left Scapa for a similar purpose. The Grimsby vessels obtained direction of the southern leg which ran for 8 miles in a northeast direction, and fifty-three mines were destroyed, followed by a further sixteen which were found in 1915. We never revealed any more here during hostilities, but five others were discovered afterwards in the Mine Clearance—laid on a direct line between Scapa Flow and Wilhelmshaven.

Actually this Dogger Bank obstruction did not avail much : it was hardly worth such meticulous care, for the best detectors were still the fishing vessels. Dutch and Danish trawlers doubtless dragged mines in their nets from the original locations, and our own fishermen did the same. In fact the fouled area did not incommode the Grand Fleet against whom it had been laid, but U-boats crossing the North Sea had to be careful of their navigation lest they should dive into danger. U-19 will be remembered as the submarine which collided off the Dutch coast one night when rammed by the destroyer *Badger*, and U-25 next month when continuing to watch the North Sea, was rammed in submergence and had to return home. It may be mentioned that groups of disguised British trawlers were at work now on the Dogger Bank to catch German submarines.

So frequent have been the assaults from the air against our North Sea trawlers in the Second War with Germany that we sometimes forget these were not wholly unheard of in 1915. When, for instance, Commodore Tyrwhitt in the *Arethusa* with destroyers was this May supporting the Dogger Bank minesweepers, a seaplane with two Germans on board was discovered on the water broken down. Of course, the men were taken prisoners and the 'plane sunk. Another German seaplane flew over to investigate the Dover Straits net barrage. It was of great importance that the enemy should learn how soon they might again send their submarines down Channel instead of round the north of Scotland.

As an instance of the way in which the highly trained German naval officers were being fought by hearty fishermen in the North Sea, we may relate the affair of May 24. The position was Lat. 59.30 N., Long. 1.53 W. The armed trawler *Ontario* (Skipper G. Garland) whilst steering to the southwest suddenly sighted a U-boat some 4 miles to the NNW. The trawler immediately put on full speed, and when about 3000 yards away opened fire with her starboard gun. The second shot was a misfire, so the helm was ported to bring the gun to bear. Then the shells appeared to fall all round the submarine, the eighth and eleventh shots exploding very near the hull. The light, slate-grey, U-boat was in no mood to remain and have a stand-up fight with the fishermen, especially as twenty-one rounds were fired at her, so she went "all out" (nearly 18 knots) on the surface, got well away from the scene, and sought safety in diving.

But trawlermen of other nations were bound in unseen unity by their hatred of the bullying Hun wherever found. On May 26 we had an excellent instance of this after the British S.S. *Morwenna* had been torpedoed some 160 miles west of St. Ann's Head (Lat. 50.27 N., Long. 8.44 W.). She was bound from Cardiff for Sydney, Cape Breton (Canada), when the steamer caught sight of a conning tower. What to do? Alter a course to bring the submarine well astern.

The *Morwenna* still hoped to elude the enemy, extra firemen were sent below, the engineer was doing his best to get full pressure out of a slow-moving ship, but the German on the surface was able to reach quite 18 knots and decrease the range. This now came down to ¾-mile, several shots from the deck gun were aimed at *Morwenna* and a signal was hoisted for the Briton to stop immediately. One man was killed, and two others wounded. The submarine was seen coming along hand over hand. Speed and gun versus an unarmed slow steamer!

It was useless to continue the uneven fight, the engines were stopped, boats were lowered and the crew stepped in. But in the meantime a vessel was noted on the starboard bow making straight for *Morwenna*, evidently anxious to render help. She turned out to be the *Jacqueline*—yes a trawler, right enough, but a Belgian. Some of these at the invasion had escaped their country and sought safety and fishing livelihood out of Milford or other port. Thinking to frighten off the *Jacqueline*, the German fired at her a couple of shots, but the Ostende skipper, Arsene Eugene Blonde, bravely and defiantly hoisted his national colours and led the German to suppose that the trawler was armed: in fact, when the *Jacqueline's* stem got within 200 yards, the submarine thought it was time to break off firing and scurry off.

The Belgian held to his bluff, chased the submarine and picked up the steamer's crew, but presently the submarine dived out of sight and disappeared, Meanwhile the *Morwenna*, mortally wounded, settled down to founder, and the *Jacqueline*, with the survivors, went back to land the men at Milford. Skipper Blonde was disappointed that he had not destroyed the German, but there had been a pretty vigorous effort. "I regret," said he, "that I had no gun on board my ship: otherwise the submarine had been sunk without doubt—our speed being insufficient to ram her." Admiral Dare

(Senior Naval Officer at Milford) was so impressed by Blonde's initiative and courage, that he obtained for the skipper a silver medal for gallantry in saving life at sea, whilst the sum of £2 was awarded each member of the crew.

It was to Milford the six steam yachts[1] *Marynthea, Sapphire, Medusa, Narcissus, Jeannette,* and *Valiant* were now ordered for the purpose of attacking submarines in the neighbourhood of St. George's Channel and Bristol Channel. Impressive as they looked, painted a navy grey, and not inelegant, it is, however, doubtful whether these expensive craft really justified the expense of manning, coaling, and fitting them out. Not built for heavy cruising, it is doubtful if they could be suitable for patrolling in almost any weather, and I have seen them compelled to bear many a hard knock unsuited for pleasure vessels. Some of them were too lightly built for carrying guns. During the period when troops of the Xth Division were being brought across from Dublin to Holyhead, one unit of trawlers was patrolling between Dublin and the Kish Lightship between 6 pm. and 10.30 p.m., but all the way from Ireland to Anglesey there would be a chain of these yachts, and trawlers and drifters with their indicator nets watching to the southward at the shore ends. They used to tow these nets at about 2 knots but there was always a good deal of trouble.

Ordinarily the yachts spent six days at sea and two in harbour, their armament consisting of two 12-pounders, but the *Valiant* carried four of this calibre. It was their aim to prevent any particular locality being used as the lurking place for submarines which should rather be kept on the move. Of course the mistake was made of supposing that these underwater boats could afford such a waste of time : records show rather that they arrived in an area, did their sinkings strenuously during the fortnight, and then moved on.

Much more valuable than patrolling like a sentry was the employment of a trawler for use in some surprise or ingenuity. What exactly do we mean by this?

Well, we shall presently adduce instances of using brains instead of maintaining a beat along the coast, but even by the end of May had been introduced the practice of a trawler—apparently quite innocent—working with the Aberdeen fishing fleet, resembling any of them with the wire aft leading (at first glance) to her trawl. But actually this wire led down to one of our C-class submarines, who during her period of forty-eight hours' stalking, might have the good chance to come across a German U-boat, for it had been realised this month that such fishing vessels would be found anywhere from 14 to 70 miles east of Aberdeen or Peterhead. Our submarines from May 21 thus commenced an ingenious project.

At the same time a vast anti-mine and anti-submarine organiza-

[1] Cp. the yachts in the accompanying illustration.

tion had been built up during the first ten months of war, so that by the end of May we had working 77 yachts, 632 trawlers or drifters, 630 net drifters, 258 minesweeping trawlers, 150 motor boats, and very soon the depth charge would gradually make the glass-ball floats and indicator buoys obsolete. The fight against the U-boat was thus beginning to pass from the stage of experimentalism.

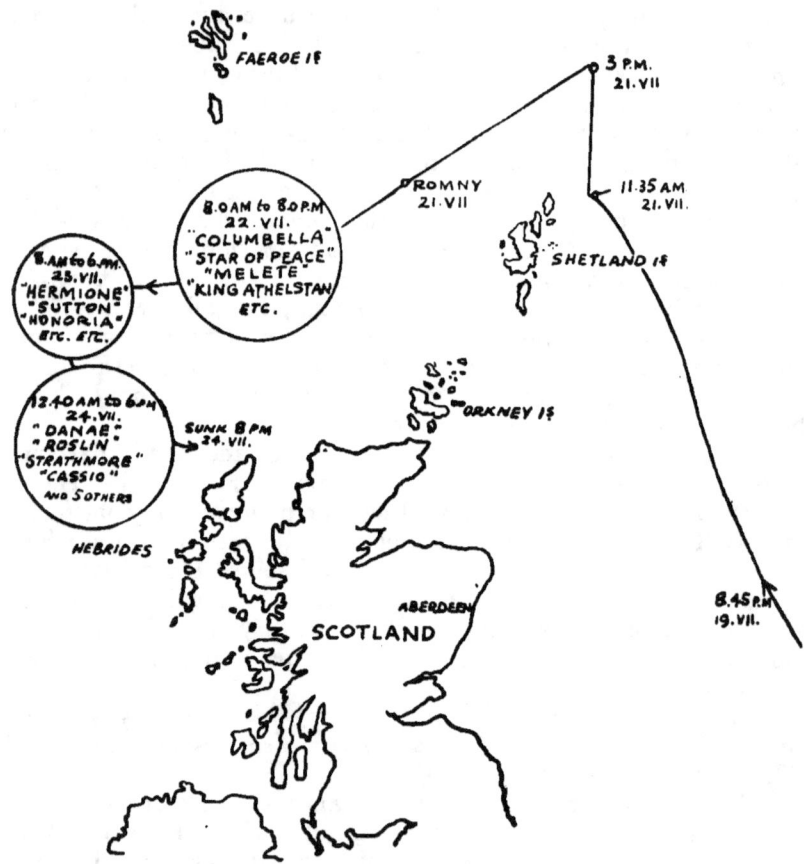

SUBMARINE DESTINY

The above shows part of U-36's cruise off Scotland in July 1915, roughly indicating her positions and shipping sunk.

The Germans, however, still stuck to their renewed zeal for minelaying—not by submarines, not (as in the Second German War started in 1939) dropped from aeroplanes—but by vessels of the Fleet. For, having made a sweep, as we have seen on May 17, to lay the Dogger Bank ambush, they made another sweep on May 30 to create a new mined area near the Silver Pit. They had great hopes that explosives near this North Sea bank would be of solid success, but it turned out otherwise. Several U-boats lay ready to co-operate with the High Sea Fleet, but a storm from the west which piped up in the course of the morning caused the fleet to return. Looked at through German eyes, these mined areas of 1915 were of the slenderest success only: those British and Dutch trawlers almost immediately "dug up these tares", and at the request of the German head of submarines, Admiral von Pohl finally abandoned this method of minelaying before the year ended and the submarine was able to do the work with greater stealth and right up the selected channel, though not on so ambitious a scale. It seems curious that the enemy had not yet thought of the magnetic mine, for we have instanced the use of German 'planes in the last war, and even on May 31 at 9.30 p.m. a Zeppelin was seen and fired at by armed drifters of the Downs patrol.

When, with the beginning of June, the Germans began to send out the UC-minelaying submarines, they selected well-used navigation marks, or lightships, as likely to be traversed by traffic. Thus Lieut. Walter Schmidt, in UC-11, came across from Flanders to lay her "eggs" off the South Goodwins lightship. Thanks to the investigation by himself and also from the air, the German authorities revised their previous attitude: whereas the passage of the Dover–Calais defile had been forbidden by Germany to all except the small UB's and UC's, this obstruction had now been examined and the gaps definitely ascertained. The submarine commanders were protesting that the round-about route via Scotland, and the prevailing bad weather round stormy headlands, should not really be necessary.

U-23, who had sunk several craft at the end of April in the south-west of Ireland (the collier *Fulgent* and the Russian S.S. *Svorono*), had also established the fact when off the East coast of England between May 10-25, that certain numerous areas which we had announced as "strewn with mines" were, in fact, not so. So said her captain, H. Schulthess, but this young man spoke a little too easily of North Sea dangers. As will be related presently, we sank U-23 on July 20 and took him prisoner.

That by the way. It may be asserted this prevailing confidence finally overcame the head of the Flanders Submarine Flotilla, so that after June 21 the ban was removed, and it was decided to let UB-6 prove that the Dover Straits were really quite easy. Well, this experimentalist—Lieut. Hacker, whom the reader will remember as having sunk H.M.S. *Recruit*—did manage to get through the Dover Straits by night, and on the surface. This so satisfied the head that on June 27 he allowed four boats to make the attempt so as to get across and operate on the Dover–Boulogne steamer track.

Now of these four the first and second safely negotiated the Straits, but on account of fog, bad weather, and "energetic countermeasures", they were unable to fire. Then the third submarine found herself baulked by a new obstruction between the Colbart Bank and Gris Nez; for the new Folkestone–Grisnez Channel Boom had not been suspected: so she turned back. As to the fourth boat? No: she didn't succeed either. For she developed engine trouble and after eleven days' absence from home had to be towed back from the Ruytingen neighbourhood. That was enough for the Flanders head, who stopped any more of these expeditions west of Dover, so the boats out of Zeebrugge and Ostend concentrated their efforts against commerce off the east and southeast coasts once more by mines and torpedoes.

It is convenient to anticipate the strictly historical order by remarking that UC-1 laid mines in the Downs, but that UC-2 was sunk by a British steamer off the east coast on July 2 (see below), and that UB-10 found how our Dover trawlers and destroyers were very much alive both by night and day. Nor could the enemy forget that in April U-32 had found these Dover drifter nets so awkward that she preferred the round-Scotland route; and there were plenty of instances where the U-boat was lucky to extricate herself from difficulties. As, for example, on May 30, when a periscope was most certainly seen *towing nets*. This entanglement was observed by H.M. Drifter *Galilean*, $1\frac{1}{2}$ miles west of the No. 2 Buoy (Dover Area), but presently the submarine got clear.

So let us relate the exciting venture of UC-3 (Lieut. Kreysern), which was energetic in laying mines off our southeast coast though next year (April 23, 1916), was sunk by us off the Norfolk littoral by fishermen and their nets. She was really fortunate to have survived so long, since frequently on negotiating Dover Straits she was menaced by the nets. On one occasion when running, not submerged, but with her conning tower showing well above the surface, she was abreast of Grisnez when she sighted two drifters ahead. She therefore dived, but ran clean into these nets which, of course, wound themselves round the submarine's hull. Kreysern, therefore, flooded his tanks, and by sheer weight tore the net away and eventually hit the bottom.

She was found to be apparently undamaged, but when they tried to go ahead with the engines, the fuses of the main motors gave out and it was concluded that the meshes of netting had fouled the propellers. The boat was brought to the surface by blowing all tanks, and the oil engines now started, so that the propeller was freed, and thus they were enabled to limp back into Zeebrugge. Here an examination showed that the submarine was still covered with net from conning tower to stern. One part had become jammed between the rudder and one of the hydroplanes, the bight having wound itself so tightly that the motors were brought up standing. It was only through the greater power of the oil engines that the wire netting had been parted.

On the other hand, these smaller Flanders submarines were very active in June. UB-6 has been mentioned, but we shall refer to her again as sinking the S.S. *Saidieh* on June 1 ; on June 3 and 4 UB-16 also sank three British fishing craft off the North Hinder Lightship, though before the war ended she was torpedoed off Harwich by our submarine E-34. So also, UB-10 and UB-13 sank shipping in the southern part of the North Sea, but it was this UB-13 which we sank a year later off the Belgian coast, and UB-10 which the Germans blew up before quitting Belgium as the war ended. So regularly indeed were these small minelayers in making their voyages across the North Sea to deposit their cargoes that UC-1 and UC-2 became steady visitors to the Thames Estuary.

At the same time, the U-boats were not quite as free to fight as they could wish. Nor could it be said that the Dover obstructions were the sole factors. Early in June a secret order was issued to German commanders that they were forbidden any longer from attacking *passenger* ships. From the view of a German naval officer this was an impracticable regulation and could not long be maintained, but for the present it existed as a reply to the world indignation, and especially American anger, after the sinking of the *Lusitania*. It thus took a month of protesting and Note exchanging before something definite accrued : but if Germany's self-pride would not allow her publicly to state this modification, it did not prevent some U-boats from being extremely successful.

Thus, for instance, U-19 (Lieut.-Commander Kolbe) and U-25 (Lieut.-Commander Wünsche) sank respectively nineteen steam trawlers and eight trawlers : so we note that the North Sea fishermen had to bear the brunt of German venom.

Chapter 12

THE MINELAYERS

Of course some of these smaller UB-boats were more successful than others, but UB-6, apart from Lieut. Hacker's general enterprise, and the sinking of *Recruit* in particular, was decidedly prosperous until later on in the war he was destined to be interned by the Dutch.

It was on June 1 that the British S.S. *Saidieh*, of 1984 registered tons, was bound from Alexandria to Hull when, at 2 p.m., she was torpedoed just as she was passing through British waters. She drew $23\frac{1}{2}$ feet forward and 24 feet aft, so would be an easy target whether for mine or torpedo. Up from the Downs she had come with a pilot on board, and was almost past the chalk cliffs into the North Sea, going at full speed, when, about 6 miles to the NE. of the Elbow Buoy, just beyond Broadstairs, she was hit by a torpedo. At that precise moment the captain had been in his cabin only a couple of minutes, and the first thing felt was a concussion on the starboard side whilst the cabin became "full of sulphur". Rushing out on deck, he found his ship sinking, and in six minutes the *Saidieh* had foundered.

Now H.M. Trawler *Eske* (Lieut. Green, R.N.R.) was at the time on patrol and steering for the Elbow Buoy, when the steamer passed $\frac{1}{4}$-mile distant on Green's port beam. He, too, felt a terrible shock, noticed the steamer was beginning to settle down, and the crew taking to the boats. Had she been torpedoed? Or had she struck a mine? At once the trawler made towards her, lowered a boat and signalled another trawler, *Strathalladale* (patrolling not far off), to do the same thing.

By this time the *Saidieh* had disappeared till only her two topmasts appeared above water, and whilst the trawler's boats were picking up survivors several of the crew shouted:

"Submarine on the port bow!"

And the steamer's captain, with his officer, called attention to the periscope 500 yards off.

Lieut. Green shouted down to his engineer:

"Give her all the steam you can," he urged, and proceeding on starboard helm, hoped that even if it were not possible to ram,

THE MINELAYERS

at least it might be practicable to get a shot in with the gun which, unfortunately, was mounted on the starboard side.

This was a pity : had the gun been placed in a position for all-round fire, the weather was so calm and the sea so smooth, that the trawler would hardly have missed the target, but Hacker did not waste time in delaying, and made off. He would soon be on his way back to Zeebrugge.

It was a sorrowful affair, since in answer to a wireless summons, there quickly arrived destroyers on the scene, but the trawler had picked up forty-six survivors, including a woman who died from shock, and *Strathalladale* rescued two others : but seven more had no time to get away and were drowned in the stokehold, whilst the first boat launched from the steamer capsized before reaching the water and all its occupants were thrown out. The old story! One of the crew had bungled letting go the falls—he cut the forward ones with a hatchet, and the boat was poised at a dangerous angle till the people were shot out.

I have previously stressed the brutal behaviour of Lieut.-Commander Rücker, who commanded U-34, but he ingloriously celebrated the Glorious First of June by bullying the men on board the steam trawler *Victoria*, which had set out from Milford Haven to fish on the Labadie Bank, some 145 miles west of St. Ann's Head. It was 5 p.m. when firing on June 1 was heard and, on looking round, the trawler-men sighted a U-boat a long way off. Painted grey, U-34 had a mizzen set : in fact she seemed at first sight to resemble a drifter. I am not sure that Rücker invented this employment of a mizzen as hoisted sometimes from a slender mast at the after end of submarine, but this is the first recorded instance of a practice which became universal when circumstances demanded.

Off-hand, I can mention the hoisting of a mizzen by U-boats in such localities as far separated as the West of Ireland, the coast of Italy, the west coast of Africa, and the North Sea. The idea was certainly to make the submarine, in a widely scattered area containing drifters or trawlers using a similar sail, look inconspicuous. But it is permitted to add how in the year 1917—when the standard of prudent German seamanship had considerably deteriorated—I recollect one foolish young German who wanted to explore the entrance of a certain bay. He had been outside, where certainly the steadying canvas did keep the craft from rolling violently, and whilst waiting about she could economize in fuel and let the submarine ride comfortably. But he forgot that the wind was blowing directly out of the bay, and as he steered up the inlet the mizzen was very much on the shake, very conspicuous in sound and sight, but horribly unseamanlike, too.

Rücker, on seeing the *Victoria* doing her best to steam away, began firing rapidly : the enemy was consistently ruthless and heartless. Human life was recklessly valued, when it was other than his own.[1] A shell flopped on board and killed a boy named Jones who had come to sea with the skipper for pleasure, and been sent up to the bridge. The *Victoria* stopped engines, but U-34 continued to close from a distance of 1½ miles and maintain a rapid fire. Thus were now slain both Skipper and Chief Engineer by one shell, then came another shell which took life away from the Mate and a trimmer whilst a deck-hand was wounded.

When the submarine was only 200 yards off she continued to fire although five had been killed, and the trawler had surrendered. The rowing boat having been smashed by shells, the remaining survivors jumped overboard with planks, and then U-34 went alongside. She removed the wounded deckhand, placed explosive charges on board, and after firing these picked up the survivors: they had been one and a half hours in the water. Rücker began by asking them if they were in the Navy, whether any arms were on board, had they seen any patrol boats. The dripping men replied in the negative, and were afterwards sent below. But at 6 a.m. the next day U-34 arrived at a spot 130 miles W. by S. ½ S. from Lundy Island, and now sank another steam trawler, *Hirose*, by gunfire.

Owned by Messrs. Neale and West Ltd., of Hope St., Cardiff, this *Hirose* had been built that same year, and set out from Cardiff at 9 a.m. on June 1 for the fishing grounds. She was proceeding at full speed—9 knots—the third hand and boatswain having the watch.

Suddenly the former sang out to the skipper, Francis Ward. "Come up here, will you? There's shells flying around."

Without waiting, the request was obeyed, all hands were called, and the engines were rung down to be stopped. Then the shelling ceased, so Ward now went full speed. Again the shells resumed, so a second time the ship was stopped and the boat ordered out. Whereupon the submarine came by the stern, and Rücker called out from the conning tower:

"Leave your ship. I give you five minutes."

Tumbling into the boat, the trawler crew pulled to the U-boat where they discovered four fishermen of the *Victoria*. Thereupon Rücker sent three Germans aboard the *Hirose* and destroyed her, but Claus Rücker was well known for "collecting" souvenirs and possessed that reputation when he went to the Mediterranean. He now brought back from the *Hirose* the chartroom clock and a pair

---

[1] Claus Rücker, after serving later in the Mediterranean, was brought back north and given a newer submarine, U-103. In May, 1918, he was in the English Channel waiting for breakfast and the White Star *Olympic*, escorted by American destroyers. *Olympic* shelled and rammed her so heartily that many Germans and the submarine were lost. Some were saved, including Rücker, but his truculent manner on board did not favourably impress the officers of the U.S. destroyer *Davis*. Indeed, one American naval officer described Rücker to me as "a rat-faced bird that I wouldn't trust ten feet from me." Transference to a British camp for prisoners-of-war concluded his submarine experiences. He had been particularly anxious to be rescued when so many of his crew were lost.

of binoculars, and about 6.30 a.m. there were cast adrift in this boat *Hirose's* ten men plus the remaining four of *Victoria*.

These unfortunate fourteen had before them a depressing outlook. Alone they had little to hope for, a rough sea and a strong WSW. wind. But they rigged up a bit of sail by using the boat's cover, and an oar as mast : so did they run before the wind all that long day and throughout the night. Fourteen men in a crowded clumsy boat, hungry and thirsty, wet with spray and nerve-tried, they stuck it bravely till twenty-four hours had passed. Then, by good fortune, they sighted a steamer—the *Ballater* of Liverpool —who rescued them with great difficulty, owing to the heavy sea running, and at length utterly exhausted they were brought into Milford.

But it is not only the fishermen whose lot is uncertain and unenviable : the U-boat made a destroyer's existence liable to sudden change. The German submarine minelaying campaign caused a heavy strain in sweeping the approaches to Harwich, Lowestoft, and Dover. H.M.S. *Mohawk* struck the first minefield laid by the enemy in the English Channel, and got amid four floating mines whilst patrolling the NW. end of the net area near the South Foreland. Although she saw the mines, she was unable to clear them, but the remarkable thing is that she did not go up in dust : although severely holed, and her upper deck almost level with the water, she actually was brought into Dover harbour and salved.

The favourite spots for the UC-boats to lay their explosive cargoes were off the Sunk Lightship—for that fouled the traffic coming in or out of Harwich including such naval shipping as our own submarines, destroyers, minesweepers, Commodore Tyrwhitt's light cruisers—the Kentish Knock, and Elbow Buoy, for these were normally milestones in mercantile voyages. Gradually, during the summer of 1915, the minelaying situation became serious, so that hurried additions were made to our forces in these areas. Large number of paddlers were collected at Sheerness, since the mines discovered close to the Edinburgh Channel in the first half of August indicated how persistent were these small UC's which brought twelve mines on each trip that needed only a few hours coming from Zeebrugge.

It was quite a different method of tactics from the mode of the surface minelayers, and though the "eggs" were in numbers fewer, they could be carried right to the places where a surface ship would immediately reveal her presence. The first time submarine mines were found off Lowestoft was about the middle of September, 1915, to the eastward of the Newcombe Sands, but similar traps were also located off the Shipwash and South Goodwins lightships, abreast the South Foreland and off Folkestone. During October, November, and December these minelayers came over with such regularity to the Shipwash, Aldeburgh Napes,

Galloper; to Dungeness, the Varne, and Black Deep; that serious shipping losses accumulated and traffic was dislocated.

So marked was this determined UC effort that between Lowestoft and Dover during the second half of 1915 over one hundred vessels were lost by mines: destroyers, sweepers, patrol trawlers and drifters, transports, hospital ships, British and neutral commercial steamers, Trinity House vessels, fishing boats—the same kinds of victims were repeated in the sinkings list that followed twenty-five years later.

In the upper part of the North Sea fishing trawlers were deliberately sought out by the U-boats as enemies, because whether commissioned by the Admiralty or not they were under suspicion. But the bravery of trawler men sticking to their job and coming to sea far from the land, without any sort of gun or protection, is typical of these tough fellows. The steam trawler *Arctic*, for instance, was 77 miles southeast of the Spurn on June 5 and had just completed her fishing when the gear was being hauled for the last time before starting for home. All the men were at the ship's side stowing things for the trip back, when unexpectedly a few hundred yards off, rose to the surface a submarine, and without any warning opened fire. It was as instant as that.

The first shell struck the Skipper, who was leaning on the ship's rail, and he fell into the sea dead before the eyes of his son a little farther aft. The next shot struck two deck-hands who were engaged in dragging the net aboard: they were both killed. Since it was obvious that the German meant to slay them all, the rest of the crew raced aft to get the boat launched, but even while so endeavouring another shot arrived and instantly wiped out the Mate. It was almost miraculous that the other five got away in the boat, for the shells stilled rained on the *Arctic* till they saw her finally sink under this bombardment. Pulling hard at the oars, the five were glad to notice a misty fog over the water such as one often finds hereabouts when the warmer weather is coming. It was this curtain of concealment which enabled the boat to escape, and after twelve hours she was picked up by the S.S. *Jurassic*.

On that same day in the North Sea, but in Scottish waters, there was yet another brutal bullying. I mention this for the reprisals that quickly followed, but it would be possible to mention also on this same June 5 the Grimsby trawler, *Persimmon*, which was sunk by a submarine's shell-fire 50 miles ENE. of Peterhead at 10.15 a.m.; and of the trawlers *Curlew* and *Gazehound* of Sunderland, these two vessels being sent to the bottom at 5 p.m. in Lat. 57.37 N., Long. 0.34 W.

It was 11 p.m. on June 25 when 5 miles NE. of Kinnaird Head that a submarine decided to do his worst on one of those light, summer nights which will be remembered as prevailing in such latitudes. The fishing trawler *Japonica* had come out of Aberdeen,

ARMED DRIFTER
Many of these from Scotland were sent to the Ægean

ONE OF THE SLOOP CLASS
Going out on patrol

to which port her crew of nine belonged. Her skipper was William Henry Butler, they were just shifting watches and the mate had climbed on to the bridge when they heard a gun fire.

Looking to starboard, the shell could be seen exploding ahead. All hands went aft to get out the boat, and the submarine could be noticed tearing towards them at top speed. Then the German commanding officer sang out:

"Hurry up and leave your ship. I shall sink you."

So the crew jumped into the boat, and pulled towards the submarine.

"Ah, no," said the Teuton. "I do not want you here. Clear out!"

"Can we go back and get some food?" asked the skipper. "And some sails for the boat?"

"No," objected the commander firmly. "No—and clear to hell out of it."

Then at a distance of only 200 yards from the trawler the enemy fired two shots—and both missed. He fired a third, but that went through the trawler's cabin. The fourth he sent through the boiler: *Japonica* sank at 11.25 p.m. Through that night the unfortunate men rowed about until H.M.S. *Acacia* (one of the recently built Sloops) picked them up at 4 a.m. and took them into port where they were given railway passes to Aberdeen.

But June 5 was a day of contrasts. Based on Peterhead near by was a unit consisting of the five trawlers *Hawk*, *Oceanic II*, *Limewold*, *Vigilant*, and *Gull*. They were under the general command of Lieut. H. J. Ferguson, R.N.R., in the *Hawk*. Recollecting that the enemy had been sinking our fishing trawlers so readily, a ruse was planned to defeat the enemy by a cleverer subtlety. The principle was to use one of these five armed trawlers as a decoy duck, whilst the other four should keep ready at hand, so that they might quickly close when wanted.

Having come to sea and arrived in Lat. 57.17 N., Long. 0.23 E., Ferguson ordered *Oceanic II* to put out her trawl, steer ENE., act as "live bait", but arranged courses so that whilst separated the *Oceanic* should be kept in sight, notwithstanding that the day was overcast and hazy though calm. Like preparing for a drama, everything was now set, the actors all in their places, and they waited only the curtain raising.

It began at 6.55 a.m. when *Hawk* heard firing and observed the *Oceanic* on *Hawk's* starboard bow, 3 miles off, in action with a submarine—actually U-14 (Lieut. Hammerle). About this craft we know very little, but she was certainly one of the ten boats which had started out from Germany for an explorative cruise on August 6, 1914. *Hawk*, going to her consort's assistance, observed U-14 on the surface clearly noticeable 3000 yards to the westward. When the range came down to 2000 yards at 7.10 a.m., the *Hawk* opened fire with her gun and several shots were undoubted hits, but the remaining trawlers were now closing on the German and concentrating their fire.

At 7.15, however, Ferguson saw his chance, ceased fire, and very cleverly rammed the submarine between conning tower and bow : it was a most satisfactory piece of tactics, for we have previously emphasized how difficult it is for straight-keeled, comparatively slow, trawlers to strike a U-boat squarely. But so well had this effort been made, that the submarine was now in a bad way despite all her previous attempts to waylay trawlers : at 7.30 she was leaking so much that she must come to the surface and the German crew, crowding on deck, proceeded to leap in the water as U-14 began to sink for the last time.

With great promptness all trawlers lowered boats, rescuing twenty-seven German officers and men. Usually from a sinking U-boat the captain was the first man to seek safety, and the chief engineer was the last : but in this rare case all were saved with the exception of Hammerle. Some of the fishermen spectators even allege that Hammerle did not try to be rescued. Why? Possibly because his previous lack of success had placed him under a cloud, but this final failure showed an imprudent and incautious character.

At 8.10 a.m. everything was over, and *Hawk* with her surprised prisoners was steaming back towards Peterhead. There had never been a simpler instance of a foe overcome by superior tactics, but because Lieut. Ferguson carefully thought out his plan previously and every trawler knew exactly what to expect, the engagement was over almost before it began. Conversation with the Germans confirmed that the first three shells pierced U-14's outer skin, and one shot put the diving apparatus out of action. It was therefore an excellent specimen of that principle which in May, 1941, was noted at the sinking of the German battleship *Bismarck* : first put the enemy's steering gear and engines out of action, then you can deal with her in detail.

"I was in the engine-room and saw a big hole made by a shell," said the submarine's Chief Mechanic to his captors, "and by putting the engines to 15 knots we could have escaped on the surface, but another shell came and blew the hull wide open." U-14 had only just come across the North Sea, for she left Germany on May 31, and yesterday, off Peterhead (June 4), stopped at midnight to sink by torpedo the Swedish S.S. *Lappland* bound from Narvik with iron ore for Middlesbrough. She also sank the Russian schooner *Adolf*. It was learned that U-16 had been working in May off Aberdeen, and this was an interesting statement to be made to the skipper and first engineer of *Limewold*.

From Gayer[1] we do know that U-16 was operating in the North Sea during May, but from our fishermen it was learned that

[1] *Ut supra*, volume II.

about May 9 H.M. Trawler *Limewold* was patrolling 20 miles east of Peterhead in charge of Acting Skipper C. C. Bond, the usual officer being ashore sick. Bond was on duty in the wheelhouse, when suddenly a shell burst close to his bows, causing the water to splash aboard. He next saw the submarine from right astern overhauling *Limewold* fast, distant some 1½ miles, conning tower and bow well above water.

Manning his 6-pounder gun, Bond ported a little and engaged the enemy, but the submarine (U-16) quickly got into action, the second shot passing very near *Limewold*, the third falling between the trawler's bridge and mast. Still, the *Limewold's* first two or three shells flopped very near the target, and when U-16 sheered to starboard in order to keep astern of the trawler, it was the port side of the U-boat which presented itself. This the *Limewold* with a fifth shot hit : "fair on the water-line abreast the conning tower, the shell burst with a cloud of flame and black smoke," the range being 600 yards, but a few seconds later, just as *Limewold* fired her sixth shot, U-16 dived and disappeared. She was certainly not destroyed and her German commanding officer (Lieut.-Commander Hansen), though undistinguished, managed to escape. Their lordships at the Admiralty showed their appreciation by awarding Skipper Bond and crew £100 between them. It is, however possible that U-16 was hurt sufficiently to be repaired secretly, for the U-14 prisoners, after co-operating so closely in the North Sea this spring, had not seen Hansen's boat since May 9.

To clue up, then, Lieut. H. J. Ferguson of *Hawk*, and Skipper John Cowie of *Oceanic II*, were each awarded a D.S.C., whilst Mathieson (gunlayer of *Hawk*) and Petty Officer Fuller of *Oceanic II*, were given a D.S.M. The sum of £388 was divided between the crew of *Hawk*, *Vigilant* similarly awarded £133, *Limewold* £98, and *Gull* £83. Sounds a lot ? But a very neat job had been perfectly accomplished, and had the old prize allotment not been accomplished, these trawlers would have been entitled to the value of the enemy vessel sunk—£150,000.

CHAPTER 13

TRAPPING THE SUBMARINES

THIS Second War of 1939 has been in some respects the expansion, and carrying out to their logical conclusion, of certain principles laid down in the previous hostilities : the most obvious instance being the Germans' exploitation of the military tanks. But it is patent they did not in previous fighting fully make use of the air, as however they have done since. We earlier mentioned that at least from the sky they were investigating the Dover Straits obstructions, and noting whether the surface could be crossed there by U-boats : but the Zeppelin was not fully tried. Later on, for special occasions, the North Sea was divided into airship patrol areas—as for instance when on August 19, 1916, the Grand Fleet's advent might be expected—though so much misunderstanding by atmospheric conditions was caused, that Admiral Scheer found the German strategy hindered. But at least on June 6, 1915, our minesweepers sighted a Zeppelin above Bridlington, and opened fire at her for about half an hour before midnight. On this port, for some reason known best to themselves, the Germans have dropped many aerial bombs during the following war.

But afloat they still continued during the early summer of 1915 to divide their U-boat attention between Irish waters and the North Sea. A good instance of the former was when the biggish barque *Sunlight* was sunk 20 miles SW. of Galley Head on this same afternoon, or when, on June 7, Rücker (having worked so far distant) sank the Norwegian barque *Superb* 60 miles west of the Fastnet. It is indeed one of the calamities of history that the final years of square-riggers coincided with the 1914-1918 hostilities. It was thus the German mine and U-boat which gave the last kick of banishment to the windjammer, and from this shock there has been no recovery.

The submarine had indeed made the war so full of surprises that it became normal to expect unusual incidents during a normal day. It seems grotesque to relate that H.M.S. *Moy* (destroyer) was 3 miles east of the Longstone when in the course of her patrol she sighted a periscope, and so promptly rammed the submarine that the latter's bridge and guard-rails were afterwards found twined round the *Moy's* port propeller. This onslaught had occurred on June 8. Sixteen says later the destroyer was docked, when the following evidence substantiated this claim for damage : several deep scratches on the bottom, one bilge keel bent, one propeller shaft bent, one propeller likewise injured.

Yet that U-boat returned safely to her base. Ramming might be lucky, or unlucky : but no one could foretell, and any submarine might just brush near to death. Fights with trawlers were becoming very much more frequent, and certain captains of U-boats seemed to seek out attacks against sailing vessels. Let us tell the yarn of the barque *Crown of India*, which on June 11 left Barry Dock for Pernambuco with 3000 tons of coal. Owned in Liverpool, she did not hesitate to run a great risk, for the South Atlantic had been made perilous by German raiders as well for steamers as sailing vessels : but the *Crown of India* was unfortunate from the very first.

She had barely got outside the Bristol Channel when calms and light southerly winds alternated, and a strong southerly set to the northward was accompanied by misty weather. Next day she had gone no farther down the Irish Sea than 68 miles WSW. of St. Ann's Head, when a submarine appeared : it was U-35 once more, and Kophamel opened fire when half a mile off. Two boats were hoisted out, and the crew of twenty-three pulled away for their lives towards the Norwegian barque *Bellglade*, which was lying 3 miles away practically becalmed also.

Meanwhile U-35 fired again at the British barque and she sank inside half an hour, but then Kophamel came alongside the Norwegian and hailed the master.

"Where are you bound?"

"Sharpness," shouted the answer. "From Halifax, Nova Scotia, with timber."

"Come aboard, and you shall bring your papers."

The Norwegian skipper obeyed and after being cross-examined by an interpreter, one of the submarine's crew, the *Bellglade* was hit amidships by three shells and at the stern by a fourth. Owing to the cargo of timber she did not immediatrly sink, and the submarine would have spent a longer time at the job, but suddenly Kophamel desisted. One of the Germans for some while had been watching with his telescope a fishing craft approaching.

She was the drifter *Queen Alexandra*, but the enemy had taken her for one of our armed patrols, wherefore Kophamel preferred to hurry from the area. That same day at 11.30 a.m. the poor *Bellglade* was sighted by some of the Milford patrol vessels, still abandoned, but still afloat. The fishermen warriors climbed aboard, cleared up decks and furled the sails. Then three of the Milford drifters, *Cromorna* (Sub-Lieut. Prestridge, R.N.R.), *Ivy Green*, and *Marys* (all coming originally from Scotland), took her in hand, *Cromorna*, with *Marys* towing ahead from a 100-fathom tow-rope of 3-inch wire, whilst *Ivy Green* kept a look-out astern. In this fashion they maintained a speed of 4 knots.

But the flat calm changed into a fresh breeze and the wind came easterly. A rough sea got up and the barque in curtseying to the swell put rather a heavy strain on this rope : finally, at 5 a.m. on the 14th, the hawser could hold out no longer, and snapped. Efforts were at once taken again to tow the *Bellgrade*, but her stern already was 4 feet below water, and now in the sea's trough she gave a heavy lurch, went right over, and turned keel uppermost.

The party of men which had been toiling at the job just managed to scramble off and were all picked up, one fellow being bruised by an iron cathead striking him as the vessel capsized. What next? It seemed pretty hopeless for these little ships to try again, so now they steamed into Milford Haven, leaving the bigger and more powerful armed trawler *Wistaria* to stand by the wreck and warn passing ships. At this time the derelict was situated in Lat. 51.32 N., Long. 6.24 W., but daily for the next week was the barque continuously watched by some of Admiral Dare's vessels until on June 21 she was towed into St. Bride's Bay and there brought to anchor.

Thus the alien was snatched from death only by ten days' pluck and hard work. The fishermen had fought fate splendidly, and at a time when the country could not afford to sacrifice this imported timber. The cargo was worth about £50,000, so they had not toiled in vain.

But the attacks on these two barques opened up more widely the problem (of which we have already given some hint) concerning sailing ships as possessing a national importance. They might load their cargo somewhere overseas and weeks later make the Irish land in safety ; but, having evaded the ocean raider, the sailing vessel might yet be boxing about the Welsh coast through frail or contrary winds. Owners therefore suggested the desirability of the Admiralty providing free towage into Liverpool, Falmouth, or wherever bound. The demand for these sailing ships was now keen because so many steamers had been sunk, yet between June 1 and 15 alone there had been destroyed by enemy action in the southwest approaches 5 British, 3 Allied, and 2 neutral sail-driven vessels. A spell of easterly winds exposed the home-comers to great risks, which could be mitigated by providing tugs at Queenstown and Falmouth as well as at Liverpool and the ports of the northeast coast, to which at present they were restricted.

But whilst this very suggestion was being considered, the sailing vessel *Dumfriesshire* was torpedoed at 10.15 a.m. on June 28 25 miles SW. of the Smalls, the crew being picked up by H.M. trawler *Weymouth II* and taken into Milford. Was this not the *Bellgrade* incident again? The *Dumfriesshire* of Glasgow was more than a great sentimental loss, for she had left San Francisco with 4100 tons of barley, and after rounding Cape Horn had reached Falmouth safely on June 25 : that is to say, she had come right through the danger zones both of high sea raiders and the more restricted submarines. Ordered from Falmouth to Dublin, she had to pass through waters much frequented by U-boats, and it was pathetic that these losses should happen so close to home.

We spoke just now of the many which were victims. Actually in the three months between March 31 and July 2, 1915, there were 43 sailing vessels sunk round our coasts, whilst 138 were still at sea bound to the United Kingdom with such valuable cargoes as nitrate, timber, or grain. The only procedure, therefore, was to keep west of the 100-fathom line until a favourable wind enabled them to head direct for a western port if possible, or else provide necessary tugs where practicable.

But why were even such experts as Rücker and Kophamel so apprehensive whenever they sighted any kind of trawler? The answer was made by the *Vossische Zeitung* of June 15, which published an article by Rear-Admiral Kalan von Hofe on the destruction of British fishing craft by German submarines. The idea (he said) widely current in Germany that these trawlers were harmless vessels and not worth a U-boat's while to destroy is quite wrong.

"These trawlers are a very important auxiliary arm of the British Navy," emphasized the German Admiral, "not only in the laying of mines, but also in attacking German submarines." He reminded his readers that most of the 2000 British steam trawlers were in the Admiralty's service. The incident of June 16 might well be quoted as showing how precisely these patrol vessels by their presence frightened U-boats.

Late in the afternoon of June 15 the S.S. *Turnwell* (2788 net tons; Master, A. E. Humby) left Liverpool in ballast for New York. At 1.40 the next day she had rounded the Tuskar and got 34 miles to the WSW. when the second officer reported a periscope 200 yards off the port quarter, and by the time that Captain Humby arrived from his cabin, the submarine was plainly visible with her crew on deck. The U-boat fired a shell which missed the merchantman, then a second projectile burst close alongside amidships, and anyone could have wagered that the end was coming, especially as the British crew of thirty-two were now ordered to leave the ship in three boats. Four German seamen then came aboard, shortly afterwards an explosion followed, and she took a heavy list.

Then was an interruption caused by the coming of the S.S. *Trafford* (82 tons) on her way from Cork, and at once the submarine made for this coaster, but the latter's master, Captain A. Hughes, at once gave orders to go hard aport, intending to ram the enemy. The German, however, when about 130 yards away submerged and came to the surface $1\frac{1}{2}$ miles off, but starting to fire. Seventeen shots boomed forth, six of them hitting the *Trafford* at such places as the foot of the foremast, the hull, and penetrating to the boiler.

No good! After about an hour's duelling the *Trafford* had no alternative but to yield: she was stopped, and finally sank.

The enemy then resumed her attention against the *Turnwell*, and determined to use the injured vessel as cover, wherefore she lay close under the Liverpool ship's quarter and hidden from passing traffic: so good a position did she occupy that the motor craft could quickly emerge and pounce upon some bigger steamer coming round the corner.

But the best-laid schemes of submarines often go wrong. Three patrol trawlers were approaching—*Good Luck*, *Loch Shiel*, and *Osprey II*—having previously sighted the U-boat that morning, and now they were beginning a fresh search. The sight of these patrols, however, alarmed the German who foresaw trouble, so quickly dived and then rose again to the surface heading off to the westward. That left the sea clear, so Captain Humby with his officers and men went back to the *Turnwell*, which was afloat all right, though one hold was full of water and another leaking badly. But the engines were still found to be in good order, the pumps were set to work, and under the escort of *Loch Shiel* with *Osprey II*, the *Turnwell* proceeded at 10 knots, arriving in Milford Haven on the early morn of June 17.

Once more the trawlers had put fear into a big submarine, and most probably it was again U-35, for she was certainly in the neighbourhood.

And now matters were working towards the grand climax that had to come. There was determination on either side, and ambitious U-boat captains saw (or at least hoped) that they might rival the man who sank the *Cressys*. On the other hand, even a trawler skipper might look forward to sinking an enemy, thereby winning a decoration and monetary reward. First, let us mention U-40, in command of which was Lieut.-Commander G. Fürbringer—not to be confused with Lieut.-Commander W. Fürbringer of the much later UB-110. Both, however, were destined to be captured, but the latter not till July 19, 1918.[1]

On June 20 the 3rd Cruiser Squadron was making a sweep across the North Sea when the neighbourhood seemed to be alive with submarines: the positions will indicate the ubiquitous resolve of the Germans. Thus at 7.50 a.m. when in Lat. 56.48 N., Long. 2.28 E., a torpedo was fired at H.M.S. *Argyll* by U-40, but the missile broke surface. He did not have the power of prevision, but in three days G. Fürbringer's craft would be sunk. On June 20 also when in Lat. 56.14 N., Long. 2.35 E., a torpedo was aimed at H.M.S. *Birmingham*, though she, too, escaped and the periscope was seen. The time was 8.10 a.m., but fifty minutes later when in Lat. 57.9 N., Long. 1.51 E. two torpedoes were aimed at H.M.S. *Roxburgh*. Still no hits, yet after an interval of twenty-four minutes

---

[1] How UB-110 met with her fate will be related in our subsequent volume.

H.M.S. *Devonshire*, in Lat. 57.8 N., Long. 1.53 E., sighted a periscope and tried unsuccessfully to ram.

Nothing further happened till 1.33 p.m., and this time *Roxburgh* was struck by a torpedo when steaming through Lat. 56.50 N., Long. 0.32 E. It happened at the time when she had been detached with a destroyer to overhaul a suspected vessel. No question that *Roxburgh* on this occasion received a fair hit, for the torpedo holed and flooded one of her compartments. And it was fired by Lieut.-Commander Max Valentiner from U-38. I would ask the reader to bear this officer in mind, for he was later destined to become as famous as Hersing, Schwieger, Rücker, and Kophamel.

At 3.10 p.m. H.M.S. *Nottingham* had two torpedoes fired at her in Lat. 56.23 N., Long. 0.38 W., but *Roxburgh*, despite her serious injuries, got safely into Rosyth, and we were fortunate that the squadron had so lightly escaped, though the enemy had shown by his disposition of several U-boats in a limited area that the greatest effort of attack would be taken. In the neighbourhood there was a large fleet of Dutch fishing vessels, of whom many certainly were not at work with their trawls down. But, as we saw in an earlier chapter, the Hollandish fisherman was always unlucky : if he were not suspected by the British Admiral, then at least the Germans doubted his genuineness.

And still the primitive aircraft persisted : four of our trawlers being attacked in roughly Lat. 52 N., Long. 43, by two German seaplanes which dropped several bombs and injured a sailor. That was on June 20, but five days later H.M. Submarine D-4, which[1] had set out from Great Yarmouth to patrol north of Nordeney Gat, after being bombed by a biplane, later attacked a German seaplane on the water. It continued risky life in those days for every kind of craft, and it seemed ludicrous that vessels which had been constructed entirely for pleasure should find themselves men-of-war and having remarkable escapes.

In one and the same day H.M. Yacht *Portia* (Lat. 56.20 N., Long. 1.0 E.) sighted a U-boat at 9.45 a.m. making for a Swedish schooner and was evidently intending an attack, but the yacht intervened with a long shot and undoubtedly saved the Swede, for the submarine was compelled to dive. That evening, being about 8 p.m., H.M. Yacht *Salvator* was passing through Lat. 54.4 N., Long. 1.10 W., when a torpedo nearly struck. Commander O. U. Coates, R.N., was then in command, and presently saw a submarine. He told me that though the missile had narrowly evaded the yacht's stern, he was quite convinced the *Salvator* passed right over the submarine, and examination in dry dock strengthened this claim. They found the starboard side marked in a very distinct manner from about 27 feet from the stern, and the gash was $\frac{3}{4}$-inch. wide.

[1] It was this craft which on May 12, 1918, cleverly destroyed UB-72 in the English Channel.

Still, in spite of this shock and the nearest of fatal collisions, that submarine did afterwards get right home, but so thrilling an account of deliverance from death could not fail to make German submarine personnel nervous in the future.

Meanwhile, at Leith, many things were being planned. Young naval officers rode their motor cycles up and down the quays, read magazines, wrote home and became very bored that they could not go out in their C-class submarines to torpedo the enemy. Then, one day, an idea came to Lieut.-Commander Harrington D. Edwards, R.N., senior officer of this flotilla. Quiet, reserved, serious at his job, he discussed his scheme with superiors and juniors. Crews began their special training, secrecy sealed everybody's lips.

By May 24 everything was worked out. But would the plan succeed?

The trawler *Taranaki* was to make for the fishing grounds, and offer herself as live bait to the enemy. Astern would be seen a thick wire-hawser as if she were normally towing her trawl, but at the end of that wire would be a C-class submarine invisible below the surface. For means of communication between the two a light telephone-cable ran down the hawser. Not till the ripe moment would the trawler give the signal, when submarine would be cast off and allowed to operate.

The first full-dress attempt was made on June 8 out in the North Sea. Along came the U-boat, C-27, and she manœuvred for position, yet things somehow went wrong. The enemy was too close—in fact, she passed right over the British submarine, and got away.

Fifteen days later, *Taranaki* came out again, this time with Lieut.-Commander Edwards in charge. Leaving Aberdeen at 1 a.m. on June 23, she steamed about 50 miles southeast and took C-24 in tow. It was a lovely summer's day, with excellent visibility, a slight swell, and gentle northeast wind. Commanding the submarine was Lieut. F. H. Taylor, R.N., keen and expectant. He took her down to 30 feet, whilst Edwards kept a careful look-out.

At 9.30 a.m. nothing in sight!

Suddenly, some 50 miles SE. by S. of Girle Ness, a black object rose not far away, shaped itself into a conning tower, then a 4-inch gun showed immediately in front. Next, the whale-like creature resolved itself into a 210-feet U-boat. Men came tumbling out of the hatch, pointed the gun, and a shell burst about 20 yards ahead of *Taranaki*. Unfortunately Taylor (not knowing of the enemy's presence) assumed this to be an explosive signal from the trawler summoning him to show periscope and read a semaphore signal. Still, to make sure, he first telephoned, waited . . . and received this message:

"Submarine 1500 yards away port bow," A pause. Then: "Submarine 1000 yards astern."

The exact moment had come, he gave orders for the hawser to be slipped, but . . .

"Leggo!" he ordered again.

The confounded hawser had jammed! Three men tussled with it, but nothing could be done. Taylor telephoned the bad news to Edwards, then something else happened. The telephone ceased to function.

Meanwhile, on the surface, the German had stopped 1000 yards off the trawler's starboard beam, trimmed ready for instant diving, slightly suspicious and smelling a trap.

In order to encourage the enemy, and to simulate panic, Edwards made his men pretend to abandon ship, and to exhibit the kind of bungling likely when a trawler's boat has to be shoved over the side in desperate hurry. The ruse was acting nicely, the German had evidently been properly impressed, everything working out as hoped. Tense seconds sped by. Then Edwards looked, saw a torpedo with a feathery wake rushing across the water, and a deafening explosion followed immediately.

It had all occurred so quickly. After the telephone failed, Taylor went ahead with his engines, helm hard a starboard, and found that *Taranaki* had evidently slipped hawser and cable from the trawler's end. Good!

But C-24 was behaving strangely, became unhandy, took a dive to 38 feet. Taylor did his best to bring her under control and by immense effort adjusted her trim. She was still not herself, still most awkward. Thanks to the cleverness and persistence of Coxswain Petty Officer A. Ribbons and Second Coxswain McCadden, the steering and trimming were being carried out so ably that the British submarine never once broke surface to give herself away.

Taylor, badly handicapped, kept raising his periscope and glancing over the swell, took a good "look-see", spotted the U-boat, closed her till within about 500 yards—then a touch of the helm—and he was ready for a beam shot. Time, now, 9.55 a.m.

It was a British torpedo which the *Taranaki*'s people watched. Beautifully directed, the silver fish ran perfectly, smote the U-boat under the conning tower, and simultaneously with a flash came the end. Clean, cool revenge on a dangerous foe before there could be time to sink the first trawler!

U-40 simply disappeared into non-existence, *Taranaki* went full-speed ahead towards the scene, C-24 rose to the surface and sought for survivors. He picked up Kapitan-Leutnant G. Fürbringer, transferred him aboard the trawler, then looked about for any other survivors, being fortunate in rescuing one more officer and one petty officer.

Of that long submarine nothing whatsoever remained, except an odd bucket and a life-buoy. And the Royal Navy was not sorry. U-40 chanced to be on her maiden voyage, having left

Germany only five days previously, yet on June 19 she almost had beginner's luck. Making a sweep across the North Sea, our 3rd Cruiser Squadron passed quite near to U-40 : so near, in fact, that the latter (as we have observed) fired a torpedo at H.M.S. *Argyll*, and it only just missed. But on that day U-38 was about also, and hit H.M.S. *Roxburgh* in the same squadron.

Taylor had done more than bring about a great success : he had triumphed over most tantalizing troubles. For, having completed his purpose, and delivered all prisoners to Edwards' safe keeping, C-24 tried to go astern. She refused to move, the propeller stopped dead ; and when his crew proceeded to investigate they found that about twenty turns of telephone-cable had wound themselves round the shaft. In addition, some 100 fathoms (200 yards) of $3\frac{1}{2}$-inch towing wire, and 3-inch hawser, plus most of 100 fathoms more telephone-cable, were still hanging from the bows. No wonder she had seemed so unmanageable ! No wonder she yawed about from side to side, trying to dive deep and then break surface !

Fortunately the crisis had not developed till victory was won, but it needed a whole hour before the trouble could be untangled and she was taken in tow back to Aberdeen. On the way home Harrington Edwards and Fürbringer had the opportunity for a plain conversation as one sailor to another, and it was learned how utterly *Taranaki* had deceived the German, though U-40 was watching her long before contact took place. Fürbringer was certainly no impetuous fool, and already had been careful to avoid three other armed trawlers with a fish-carrier cruising together.

Great rejoicing spread through the seaports after this successful and novel method of trapping the U-boats. Harrington Edwards has since passed away, but not before receiving a D.S.O. for the *Taranaki* incident, whilst Taylor was awarded the D.S.C., and each of the two coxwains got a D.S.M. The sum of £1000 allotted between the two craft followed as further encouragement to those adventuring dangerously against a ruthless slayer of fishermen.

Chapter 14

WHAT A SUBMARINE CAN DO

THERE can be no doubt that this combination of the "mystery ship" idea with the use of a British submarine was a most excellent method for catching the enemy off his guard. We who in such entertaining days, were daily meeting these C-class naval officers, knew that so well-matched was the most astute German submarine captain by our own experts that our ruse having proved its worth, might again indicate fullest success.

Of course the idea is so subtle, the chances of some mistake so manifold, the possibilities of things mechanical failing at the most awkward moment so often experienced, that the whole thing might be ruined by the least accident or some stupid bungling. The incident just related deceived the enemy, however, on two accounts: the nature of the trawler which really was armed, and the presence of the submarine.

In fact, with a kind of professional pride, the captured Fürbringer admitted that he had been deceived entirely, for he had been watching the *Taranaki* all the morning. That U-40 should have been fooled was still more remarkable when German submarines were carrying men like Völckner, supposed to be more than familiar with trawlers and their ways.

Fürbringer that morning had kept his eyes open, sighted three armed trawlers and a fish-carrier cruising in company. He knew them for what they were, and very naturally avoided them. Combined short-range gunnery would almost certainly bring disaster to a submarine. Even this German believed that in such circumstances the safest place for a U-boat was when hiding below water, and the most dangerous was to remain on the surface while shells poured in his direction. That may be regarded generally as a perfectly true statement, but we may add that it is just possible a submarine may get into the most awkward predicament from which she can save herself only by amazing self-resource and good fortune. U-40 was sunk on June 23 by a trawler's perfect aid. Now see how on practically the same date a British submarine in German waters was able by means of an enemy trawler to do something not less wonderful than C-24. It is a great example of stoicism.

The Heligoland Bight, with its blustery weather most of the days and nights every year, its heavy seas and prevailing northwest wind, has always been an unpleasant area for small vessels. But what with minefields, and all sorts of German patrols on the alert, British submarines have never found it exactly a home-from-home.

Yet those brilliant achievements in this present war by such officers as Lieut.-Commander G. C. Phillips in the *Ursula*, and Lieut.-Commander E. O. B. Bickford in the *Salmon*, have reminded us that neither the enemy's mines nor destroyers and light cruisers can prevent our submersibles from torpedoing Nazi men-of-war well within Hitler's territorial waters.

Not less daring were some of the British exploits during the first German war, even when things seemed to be going as badly as ill-luck could possibly contrive, but the triumph of patient pluck, despite all discouragement, was in itself the finest sort of victory.

His Majesty's Submarine S-1 in the latter half of June, 1915, had been sent to patrol the Bight. Anything, of course, might happen and if fortune favoured she might possibly bag one of the High Sea Fleet bound out of Wilhelmshaven. Contrariwise, the watchful Germans might harry the visitor into death.

Now, on June 21, S-1 (Lieut.-Commander Kellett) was so-to-say just outside the enemy's garden gate. Precisely 10 miles to the north of Heligoland. Not altogether too near, provided nothing should go wrong.

But this turned out to be no easy day, for the Germans kept her continuously on the defensive. First of all, a Zeppelin made her dive into hiding, then a seaplane annoyed her, next steamed out nineteen trawlers sweeping the locality, and finally appeared that deadliest of submarine's foes—a destroyer. At the latter Kellett fired a torpedo, but missed. This was anything but Kellet's jolliest experience.

For, that evening, the port engine of S-1 became temperamental and declined to do any more work. Why it had chosen for its strange behaviour this risky neighbourhood, instead of Home Waters and the vicinity of a friendly dockyard, needs no discussing. She switched over to the starboard engine, kept on patrolling, whilst her engine-room staff toiled away at the defect even whilst the hull was below surface.

So the time passed, and during the 22nd she had worked up towards Horn's Reef Lightship, sometimes surfacing, but when airships floated through the sky, down she descended again to obscurity, making use of her electric batteries for that purpose. A hard tussle the artificers were having in trying to coax the port engine back to life, but it was a sad, losing, fight. Next day—will you believe it?—the starboard engine died on them, too. As if to complete the captain's anxiety a Zeppelin was seen to be patrolling aloft, and determined not to leave.

At all costs the airship must not perceive what doubtless she was looking for: else the bombs would begin to fall, and a wireless summons would soon fetch half a dozen destroyers with their depth charges on to the scene. S-1 lay inert on the sea-bed, as a great drama within was being fought by desperate men. Bad enough for one engine to have "conked". But *both*. . . . Fate was not acting quite fairly.

Ingenious and resourceful as these submarines showed themselves hour after hour, they finally found all their efforts defeated. So there they were, in hostile waters, above which moved German sea vessels, whilst higher still were the faster airships. And the batteries of S-1 fast exhausting the electric "juice". Moreover, since the engines would not revolve, no hope of recharging batteries could be entertained.

What a situation ! What a tragedy for any playwright or novelist !

But this was real life, with death definitely approaching . . . or else some miracle of the sea.

One of two alternatives. Either remain on the bottom till everybody breathed his last ; or, with the final supply of electricity, rise to the surface and there remain impotent till the first bomb fell from the sky or the first destroyer's guns shelled them to annihilation.

It was now June 24, Lieut.-Commander Kellet blew his tanks, brought his boat to sea-level, looked round, sighted a German trawler, had another look, saw she had no gun and, instead of displaying any sudden eagerness for attack, the steamer remained with trawl down quietly fishing.

This extraordinary state of things persisted all the afternoon, the two craft being so near that there could be no question of the German having failed to observe S-1. So the summer's day was drawing to its close, the airships had gone home, no destroyer or anything else was visible on that lonely sea. And now Kellett took destiny in his hands.

There still remained a modicum of electricity, he went slowly towards the trawler, read her name *Ost*, hailed the Skipper to launch his rowing boat and come alongside. Herr Schafer, a man of forty, obeyed without demur just as British fishermen had been compelled to do when U-boat officers ordered. Back to *Ost* that boat carried Lieut. Kennedy (the second-in-command of S-1) together with a prize crew of five British sailors, who sent aboard the submarine every German save two who were needed down below at the engines. Then a rope was passed from trawler to submarine's bows, and the voyage across the North Sea began.

To say that Skipper Schafer and his nine men were surprised would be less true than to remark that they could scarce credit this amazing development. Yes : they had been aware of the submarine throughout this afternoon, but supposed her to be German. And all the while she was lying there broken down . . . ! Never had there been such a piece of bluff.

But the first and uppermost desire of S-1's commander was to get away from Heligoland Bight with all possible speed, ere the short June night should end and German forces overtake them. Much might happen before sighting the east coast of England. More than likely a German U-boat coming back from minelaying off Norfolk, or sinking our own trawlers, would find S-1 nicely framed in the periscope as a sitting shot.

The night vanished, dawn broke, Schafer and his crew were well cared for, and most valuable information their tongues provided: news such as Whitehall would be glad to receive. Yes: the German Admiralty had already commissioned so many trawlers from Geestemunde, which was *Ost's* home port, whence she had set out on June 22. At least fifty of these fishing steamers, most of them mounting a 15-pounder gun with naval personnel entirely, now flew the German white ensign.

Aboard the *Ost* Lieut. Kennedy was to have no trouble with his two captives, the towing further presented no difficulties, not one U-boat or patrol came upon them nor had heavy seas constantly carried away the rope. It looked like an easy passage towards England.

Then, ludicrous and incredible though it may seem, within twenty-four hours of quitting the Bight, *Ost's* steam engines broke down. As if the submarine people had not suffered enough disappointment of this sort, they now went aboard the trawler; overhauled the high-pressure piston, cross heads, crank head bearings, and a few fancy bits of that nature, then started off again.

Not too pleasant a delay on the open sea. Thus did the 25th fade into night, the cavalcade proceeded at a miserable 4 knots, and now at last no more trouble could assail these weary men.

On the contrary, there must have been a Jonah somewhere about. The *Ost* had been steaming moderately well for about a day, when she once more followed S-1's unfortunate example, and this time it was the low-pressure cylinder which needed the artificers' attention. Luckily that ended the week of suspense, and never were returning seafarers more pleased to pick up the East Anglian coast. Off Cromer they spoke H.M.S. *Firedrake* (destroyer), and on June 27 this destroyer towed S-1 safely into Harwich, whilst Lieut. Kennedy steamed *Ost* between Great Yarmouth piers proudly as a well-earned prize.

Another coincidence. For at Great Yarmouth in the year 1875 Skipper Schafer had been born of German parentage, and as a youngster used to go out fishing in British trawlers. By the time he was aged twenty-three he left England, returned to Germany, and continued trawling, but never forgot how to speak English.

As to the *Ost*, she was duly condemned to change her nationality, and on September 23 appropriated by the Royal Navy who altered her name to *Cromsit*. Nor was this by any means the last of such captures, for on September 5 H.M. Submarine E-4 went across the North Sea, captured the trawler *Esterburg* and brought her into Harwich. On the last day of that month Commodore Tyrwhitt's Harwich light cruisers were making an incursion towards Heligoland Bight when they took no fewer than nine German trawlers, followed a week later by sixteen more (of which one was sunk).

Thus, in some measure, did we make the enemy pay up for that list of British trawlers destroyed by U-boats. What happened to these small German steamers? Well, they also were taken over by the Royal Navy for such duties as patrolling and minesweeping, and after being refitted at Lowestoft were sent to serve in the Mediterranean.

CHAPTER 15

WHAT THE RAM DOES

JUNE had been an anxious month for our fishing fleets round the coast, and fifty-eight of such vessels were this month sent to the bottom. The principal localities were off the N.E. Scottish coast, the Dogger Bank, 50 miles E. by S. of Lowestoft, 40 miles S.W. of the Lizard, in the Irish Sea, off the Scillies, 30 miles W.S.W. of the Tuskar, and the southern coast of Ireland generally. Schwieger, in U-20 in the latter locality, sank the Russian four-masted barque *Marion Lightbody* on the 8th of the following month, so the *Lusitania* recollection did little to depress his spirits, and there was also Lieut.-Commander Forstmann in U-39 who was specializing in this district of the Western Approaches. The latter came down via the North Sea, Fair Island Channel, St. Kilda, Valencia, south Irish coast, even till he reached the Scillies section. Such a route unquestionably meant that U-boats were called upon to exercise great endurance even in the short nights of the summer months.

There were landmarks for guidance such as Fair Island off the Orkneys, thence the Butt of Lewis at the northern end of the Hebrides, the lonely Flannan Isles (with their lighthouse), St. Kilda, and thence they could make the coast of Ireland at its northwest. They could fix their position down the west and southwest Irish coasts, afterwards take their departure anywhere between Cape Clear and Daunt's Rock (off the entrance to Queenstown Harbour) to bring them to the western entrance of the English Channel where steamers of all sorts could be found arriving from foreign for home ports. In that, the first war, there existed the German drawback that a whole week was thus spent on the way from the Heligoland Bight: after June, 1940, however, when U-boats were based on Lorient, or other French ports, they could save this week by using it to start the voyage of destruction at once and utilize their fuel endurance further out in the Atlantic.

Personal originality had its full scope in the U-boats. Not merely were masts erected for sending wireless messages, and the after mast also for hoisting the mizzen sail ; but the submarine would sometimes disguise herself on the high seas with two funnels and heavy smoke be emitted therefrom. At a distance, hull-down, the submarine would not be taken for what she was, and surprise in attack might be carried out with remarkable ease. For instance, let us take the 1st of July in just the one southwestern sphere between the Fastnet and the Scillies : no fewer than seven ships were then sunk. There were the sailing-vessel (schooner) *L. C. Tower*, 30 miles south of the Fastnet ; the S.S. *Gadsby* 33 miles SSW. of the Wolf Rock ; the S.S. *Caucasian* 50 miles north of Ushant ; the S.S. *Inglemoor* in the latter locality ; the S.S. *Welbury* 40 miles west of the Fastnet ; and a couple of steamers—*Craigard* and *Richmond*—about 50 miles SW. by S. of the Wolf Rock.

The *Caucasian's* master averred that it was U-39 who waylaid his ship (an oil-tanker), and that Forstmann said he was expecting her at this time. The previous master of *Caucasian* was a naturalized Prussian who had served in the German Navy, lived (when ashore) opposite Sheerness, and his sympathies were openly German. The *L. C. Towers*, though set on fire, was owned in the United States and afterwards towed into Berehaven by our armed patrol trawler *Ina Williams*. On this same day an eighth disaster happened 20 miles SW. of the Mizzen Head (Ireland) when the Italian barque *Sardomene* was making the land from West Australia with a cargo of timber. Although escorted by the armed trawler *Bempton*, which carried one of the ablest of our skippers, the submarine managed to get in a shot between *Bempton* (steaming 1000 yards ahead) and the ship under sail. A terrible explosion ensued and although *Bempton* launched a boat she could only rescue seven survivors in good health, two injured, with two corpses. There were missing ten men.

It is not claimed that U-39 herself sank more than *Caucasian*, *Inglemoor*, and *Gadsby*, but it is pretty certain that the rest were wiped out by Schwieger in U-20. On the other hand Germany, too, was having her losses. We remember U-30 which on Christmas Day, 1914, was sent out against the British aerial attack on Cuxhaven ; we recollect also that at the inauguration of the German Submarine Blockade U-30 in February after reaching the Irish Sea sank the S.S. *Downshire* and *Cambank* though she was unlucky enough to foul the *Alex Hastie's* fishing nets.

Get home safely U-30 certainly did, but on June 22 when in Borkum Roads she foundered and only three men were saved whilst ten times that number suffered terrible deaths. Three months she lay on the bottom, washed by the North Sea, scoured by the sand-laden tides until at length she was salved, taken into port and given a thorough refit : yet her engines never became quite reliable and in November, 1916, U-30 was again the sharer of trouble.

July brought about three disasters to U-boats. Staggering was the nature of these incidents, but though the first was accidental it was as real as the other two were deliberate. For it happened on July 2 that UC-2, a small minelayer which had arrived in Flanders on June 29, loaded up her cargo, and then left for the East Anglian coast to deposit these explosives near Lowestoft. Thus she was quite new and this happened to be her first voyage across the North Sea, her commanding officer being a junior lieutenant named Mey.

Novelists before to-day have instanced certain events happening quite independently, then uniting to bring about one great drama. Few people could have suspected that when the British S.S. *Cottingham* started out from Calais bound for Leith she was destined—with the width of the North Sea available—to be drawn to that exact spot through which UC-2 would pass at a certain tick of the clock. Unseen fate however was drawing the two together, the clock went round to 2.50 p.m., the steamer was passing through Yarmouth Roads. All of a sudden there came a violent contact, yet there was visible no sort of obstruction.

The *Cottingham* was a coaster of 512 tons and she felt as if there had been a sudden contact with some object first on the starboard quarter, then on the port side, next ahead. A considerable disturbance of water followed as if a strong blast of air had been released from below, and a powerful smell of gas came up, followed by oil on the water. The master felt convinced that he had hit a submarine getting into position to attack a large steamer that happened to be near.

The collision was quite accidental, but on reaching port it was decided that *Cottingham* should be docked, and the evidence seemed to prove that under the starboard quarter she certainly did hit something. In consequence of her master (Captain Colin Mitchell) reporting this incident to a patrol vessel, and also to the Senior Naval Officer at Leith on arrival, the matter was carefully investigated. The position was swept carefully by a couple of minesweepers, nets were laid to entrap the submarine should it move, and a continuous watch placed.

Suddenly, without further argument, the submarine UC-2 at 9.40 p.m. blew up, evidence pointing to the fact that one of her mines had gone off. Later it was ascertained that she was fitted with six chutes each containing two mines, so the explosion had made a thorough job of it and every one of the German crew became a corpse. The Admiralty awarded the steamer the sum of £200.

Yet the proceeding did not end here. The months went by, summer changed to winter, the S.S. *Cottingham* was coming along towards port but this time not in the North Sea. It was the day after Christmas and the position 16 miles SW½W. of Lundy Island. Suddenly a U-boat appeared, and by means of gunfire succeeded in sinking the *Cottingham*. Thus in the most curious manner an accident had been followed by revenge before that year could end.

When old sailormen of lengthy memories learned that the famous and historic *Fiery Cross*[1] had survived the sailing-ship age,

---

[1] The *Fiery Cross*, which was sunk by Forstmann in U-39 during the summer of 1915 off the Scillies, was then owned by the Norwegians, but years previously she was one of the most famous vessels which Britain ever constructed and sailed. She will always be remembered as the historic China clipper, which came out in 1860. For consistent pre-eminence in making fast passages *Fiery Cross* was remarkable, and the famous race of 1866 up the English Channel in the company of other tea-carriers is familiar to all collectors of sea-prints.

it was with gladness and pride : but when they learned that this vessel (now owned in Norway) was sunk off the Scillies by Forstmann of U-39 after giving the captain a receipt to say he had thus acted, old shellbacks could only bewail that the Germans could still feel pleasure in robbing the world of something which would never be replaced.

But there was humour associated even with tragedy. A Norwegian steamer, named the *Peik*, was blown up in the North Sea on July 5 about a mile NW. of the Long Sand Lightship, and we who now understand the work of the UC-boats can quite well appreciate their usual practice in laying mines off the Long Sand. When a Trinity House vessel was sent to destroy the wreck, a persistent rumour got around that the hull was full of mines, therefore she could not be a genuine Norwegian but a ship disguised for minelaying. Actually, however, it was eventually realized that she was a perfectly innocent victim : she carried no mines whatsoever, but the creatures of suspicion were merely bundles of Indian grass mats floating in the holds with air beneath ! It was all the same, significant that on the next day a German seaplane was observed in this vicinity : doubtless it had flown over to make sure that the minelaying had been effective.

Gradually the tactics of the U-boat were becoming apparent. We learned to know, for instance, that the submarine about to attack would usually first get into position about 500 yards on either the starboard or port bow of her enemy. Abaft the beam was less likely to be successful because the target would be retreating rather than advancing, and the wash of the propeller might interfere with the torpedo's direction. There was pretty good evidence that U-boats after coming round Scotland to NW. Ireland and making their first contact at Eagle Island, thence struck across to pick up the Blaskets. The latter are wild, primitive islands, but the inhabitants with their skin boats that put to sea even over a heavy Atlantic swell are not less primitive. These home-made, oared, craft are handled with a brave seamanship, and after being brought finally to the beach are capsized by a couple of men who on their backs carry the simply-fashioned hull up the mountain-side.

Fishing vessel owners of the Humber rather felt aggrieved that so many trawlers were being taken up by the Government, but when so much work had to be done round our coasts against mines and submarines this was inevitable and increased. The minesweeping trawler *Agamemnon* was typical of the hard-working responsibility which such vessels received, and their duties were rendered even more trying by the new activity of the UC-boats. She was near the Shipwash Lightship, had just finished sweeping, and the gear being hauled aboard, when a terrific explosion happened killing nine men. Yet some of the trawlermen, such as this crew deemed themselves, were not badly off serving under the White Ensign. In peace time they were accustomed to keep the seas through all weathers, all latitudes, and all seasons, for periods of fourteen days in the North Sea to even six weeks in Icelandic and other high latitudes.

Now it is strange and wonderful how the chain of submarine events linked itself up till one long cable was formed. Romance and adventure in such are the results proceeding from this mighty strength.

Let me without further metaphor introduce Lieut.-Commander Claus Hansen, who in command of U-41 fought British seafarers of all sorts: fishermen, Mercantile Marine, Royal Navy. The Atlantic, the English Channel, and North Sea, were to be the various backgrounds but they looked the same even if his rivals varied from time to time. Hansen bluntly was a rapacious enemy, but true-to-German type; by which I mean that he did the most foolish thing in the biggest crisis of all and, after narrow escapes through his life, failed badly. Hansen left Germany on July 14 bound for the west coast of Great Britain there to attack commercial ships, but on the way he must pass near those keen Peterhead patrol trawlers that always were on the lookout for U-boats as a sheep-dog watches the unpenned sheep.

It was early in the morning of July 16 when the three armed trawlers *Searanger*, *Eastward Ho!* and *Cameo* off the Scottish coast were steaming in line-ahead on a NW. course about 2 miles apart in a NW. direction. Roughly in about Lat. 57.20 N., Long. 0.40 E. *Searanger* observed a steamer steering in an erratic manner, closed her, and found she was picking up floating timber. *Cameo* also altered course to the south to examine another ship and then sighted on the surface a submarine fast approaching. This was U-41.

At once *Cameo's* crew were sent to quarters, and the other two trawlers flew the "Submarine in sight" signal. Hansen opened fire at *Cameo* but the shot fell short, then four more shells followed but they too were ineffectual. The submarine decided to get nearer, and when about 2000 yards away, U-41 motored round *Cameo's* stern and opened fire with two guns. The trawler was smart enough to follow the German round, and kept the latter on the starboard bow.

But though the German mounted two guns more powerful than the *Cameo's* one small 3-pounder, the trawler did not hesitate to blaze away. A shot whizzed across from the submarine, struck in the fore part of the wheel house, went through the steel plating, smashed the upper part of the steering-wheel, and then passed out through the open door on the after side. The Skipper (Albert Sayers) had a narrow escape, being wounded by splinters slightly in the right side and in the right eye: still this brave man continued to steer with the remainder of the wheel and never made a remark.

A second shot struck *Cameo* on the starboard quarter just above the upper deck and pierced the side plating, whilst a third entered the galley and wrecked this compartment. Still the most incredible thing is that though the engagement lasted fifteen minutes and U-41 fired about twenty-five shots against eleven of the *Cameo*, not one man aboard the latter was even hit. But they had time to notice this submarine was large and painted a light grey.

The *Cameo* blew hard on her steam whistle though the other two trawlers did not hear, owing to the wind's direction. This may seem extraordinary, but myself I once had the same experience when overhauling a vessel that for a time even did not hear my shells falling around. When *Eastward Ho!* saw the splash of a shot near the U-boat, it was time enough to hurry up the engines and make straight with her stem against this newly arrived enemy.

That was Hansen's cue and he ceased fire, making for the westward at high speed (18 knots) along the surface. The incident thus suddenly ended, and *Cameo* proceeded into port much damaged. Sayer was afterwards awarded the D.S.C. for his gallantry, Leading Seaman C. Buttons (captain of the gun) got a D.S.M., whilst the sum of £150 was divided among the crew.

The submarine continued north and that light day at 9.45 p.m. was in Lat. 64.43 N., Long. 0.30 W., when H.M.S. *Speedwell* (gunboat) sighted her only 250 yards away on the port bow, worked up to full speed both engines, tried to ram, and steered for the periscope. At 9.52 p.m. there was a mighty collision, the blow being sufficient to raise the bow of the gunboat from the water, send a heavy jar vibrating through the ship, and cause her to heel right over to starboard even though travelling at 15 knots. Seven minutes later the masthead look-out reported patches of oil on the water, and next day when *Speedwell* arrived at Lerwick to coal she was examined by divers who reported both scratches and a bulge in the bottom plating and the port bulge keel burred up.

Hansen was therefore getting close to death, and death was approaching nearer to him. Admiral Jellicoe thought that the submarine had been struck near the conning tower, but not holed. Years passed by, the war ended, and Gayer in his narrative of this ramming said that "three cruisers of the 'Pelorus' class" were met with north of the Shetlands, that U-41 "fired at the middle cruiser" and missed; that at this moment the submarine was rammed by the *Speedwell*, rendering both periscopes useless, and obliging the German to return home, and she reached Germany on July 19.

The moral effect on the crew can be guessed: such a shaking up would be calculated to unnerve the roughest men, yet Hansen was of the strongest fibre that is undeterred by danger. Gayer even described him as "one of the most thorough-going among our submarine commanders". U-41 was quickly repaired, crossed the North Sea again, and got round Scotland even to the southern end of the

Hebrides near Barra Head by the early morning of July 27 : so she started west from her German port probably on July 24, and this repair job had needed less than a week.

Hansen was indeed a glutton for adventure. But much more was coming to him.

At 4 a.m. on July 27 the armed trawler *Pearl* (commanded by Sub-Lieut. A. C. Allman, R.N.R., and based on Stornoway) was patrolling off Barra Head. The wind was freshening from the southeast with thickness which at times grew into rain, and there was a moderate SW. swell. Any mariner could have foretold the approach of a gale. At 4.15 a.m. a small object was sighted on the starboard bow and with the strengthening light a submarine shaped itself, distant 5280 yards. Oh, yes : this was U-41, right enough, though the surprising news was not learned till later.

Hansen was out for blood, but the *Pearl* wanted a fight even at this hour of the morn. It was obvious that U-41 was on the surface heading south, and the trawler was cleared for action ready for any German : all hands at their stations, officer expectant, skipper at the wheel, full-speed on the engines. The enemy altered course to the SSW., but Sub-Lieut. Allman instructed the Petty Officer not to fire with his gun—for it was only a 3-pounder—until the range came down to 1000 yards. In other words, make it a sitting shot !

At 4.25 a.m. the *Pearl* altered course to ram, at the same time bringing the gun to bear. The submarine, travelling at high speed, fired across the trawler's bows at a distance of 500 yards, and then the trawler opened fire. Her range from the first was correct, the first two shots dropping close under the submarine's stern. The fifth and sixth shots were excellent, and Hansen's craft received damage amidships. Excitement became keen, the shooting still good, and the *Pearl's* men so enthusiastic that they worked quickly ; but at 4.30 a.m. the enemy began to submerge close to the trawler's bows.

What, then, now ?

Put the helm hard aport, dash ahead ? This was done, but the ramming missed by 40 feet. U-41 was now under water, one periscope showing, but the British Petty Officer took careful aim with his gun and at the second shot broke off the periscope. Thus once more Hansen was annoyed and headed southwest at 7 knots below surface. Keeping parallel with, but off the submarine's bow, gun bearing and waiting for an opportunity to ram when once the German should emerge to the surface, Allman held on to his rival, continually closing him with the desire to ram.

It was now 6.30 a.m., day wide awake, but unfortunately it was coming on thick with rain, and the German could not indefinitely continue submerged, but must surface soon or run out of electric power, and Hansen knew things were shaping for a crisis. At

9.15 a.m. the submarine came near to the surface, but did not show herself. The *Pearl* was kept steaming at full speed (about 9 knots), continuously getting nearer, but the enemy in his underwater condition could do no better than a rate of 5 knots for 80 miles. Say sixteen hours at the most. Thus by the time it was 10 p.m. the German would certainly be done for and must rise to fight it out on the water.

Eleven o'clock!

The contest between Allman and Hansen was as fierce as in any dog-fight. *Pearl* had no intention of letting her assailant go, so endeavoured to fire an explosive sweep 500 feet well ahead: Hansen would certainly steer straight for the explosion—and destruction? But this venturesome German seemed fated never to die, for there was an accident to the electric cable in getting the sweep overboard, and the thing refused to fire! All right, then. As before—be ready with the gun, and ram.

Believe it or not, as the *Pearl* was still chasing, the chief engineer sent up unhappy news. It was just about midday.

"What's that you say?" asked the Sub-Lieutenant.

"The air-pump's out of order, sir."

"Air-pump? How long to put it right? We can't stop now."

"In an hour's time we'll certainly have to stop. Can't do the job under three hours."

After all these hectic moments and the thrill of chase, it was grievous to hear that announcement. By this time the *Pearl* was 38 miles SW. by W. of St. Kilda, and Hansen must be getting anxious about the electricity endurance: the man would surely want to charge his batteries soon, and that must mean coming up on the surface?

But the trawler had no alternative as to what could be done. Reluctantly the chase had to be given up, and with great difficulty the trawler made her way into the lonely St. Kilda miles out in the Atlantic. There she arrived at 4.30 p.m. with scarcely any water in her boiler. Nevertheless, Allman continued to do the right thing even now, for he sent a wireless to all adjacent patrols of what had happened and this was picked up by H.M. Yacht *Vanessa*.

The latter now took up the duty, being farther to the north, and immediately altered course to cut the enemy off, for there could be no more diving just yet awhile. U-41 had been again too damaged not to return home, and Hansen dared not risk submergence just yet awhile. At 9.10 p.m. the *Vanessa* sighted the submarine and chased her for nearly an hour, but no maritime reader needs any convincing that over so wide a space as the Atlantic the submarine managed at $16\frac{1}{2}$ knots along the surface in the uncertain light to get right away and obtain invisibility. Next morning at four o'clock H.M. Trawler *Stanley Weyman* picked up from a distance the track, so did H.M. Yacht *Maid of Honour* and H.M. Trawler *Swan*, and thus they kept her in sight until 5.40 a.m., but lost final sight of her.

For the second successive time U-41 was compelled to shorten her voyage and return home. Hansen had indeed been favoured by the most extraordinary luck that any man of his calibre could dare to contemplate.

Yes: but that was not the final act in this moving drama. We shall come to that presently and witness the grand climax in September, but it must not be omitted that Hansen made a mistake about *Pearl* from the very first. In the misty morning he did not realize she was on patrol, then he omitted to take full notice of her gun, with the result that she jammed his control gear, then pierced his conning tower and mortally wounded Lieut. Schmidt, the third officer. When *Pearl* tried to ram, the submarine dived barely in time, yet now it was a race in U-41 between leaks and the ejecting pumps: in any case the German craft dared not submerge deeply because of the pressure.

And Schmidt was laid in his bunk with his body maimed and bleeding from a shell. The extraordinary thing was that a mere 3-pounder had so far defeated this submarine and the *Pearl* could not be shaken off: she was very much there on the surface, impressing the Germans with her presence, increasing the suspense almost to breaking point.

"It's all over with us now!"

Even Hansen felt himself up against fate at last, but he did not realize just then that later, when the depth charges became practically universal, U-41 would not have had a remote chance. As it was, the air became offensively foul after so much hermetically sealed activity, the batteries were running out, and from Schmidt life, too, was draining. Race against time!

But then *Pearl's* pump ended the suspense and pursuit, the perforated steel hull could be brought up to navigate above the surface, though the oil still seeped out as a tell-tale. Schmidt passed away about the time when *Pearl* was anchoring off St. Kilda, men's nerves barely held out: but after a terrifying interlude U-41 once more got back to her German port.

Hansen did not realize that two months later he, himself, was to experience that crossing of the bridge which joins life with death. As to Allman, the Admiralty was so pleased with his resource that they promoted him to lieutenant with seniority of July 27, and awarded the sum of £150 to the crew. Does not this pertinacity of the trawler with a 3-pounder gun show that even the smartest modern submarine, with two guns and plenty of torpedoes, can be sent home wounded by British pluck and determination?

Chapter 16

TRAPPING THE U-BOAT

LIEUT.-COMMANDER SCHULTHESS, an officer of great skill, was operating in U-23 up the Baltic, whence they sent him to attack shipping off southwest Ireland.

She returned home, had a refit, and on July 17 left Borkum with a total of thirty-four officers and men, bound for the Irish Atlantic coast as usual, but via the Fair Island Channel off Scotland. Just before eight o'clock on the morning of the 20th a sea-gull might have noted impending trouble. In that same locality were the trawler *Princess Louise* towing the British submarine C-27 (Lieut.-Commander C. C. Dobson, R.N.).

In charge of the trawler was Lieut. L. Morton, R.N.R., Lieut. A. M. Tarver, R.N.R. as his assistant, whilst Lieut. Colin Cantlie, R.N. (from Harrington Edwards' flotilla), acted as *liaison* officer. U-23 hove in sight, steered at right angles to the trawler's bows, and began shelling her, though not before Cantlie had 'phoned down to Dobson. The latter then slipped his tow at 8.3 a.m., four minutes later found himself well situated, got a little closer, and at 8.12 released a torpedo.

Almost simultaneously Schulthess—his boat being not submerged but on the surface—sighted Dobson's periscope and the torpedo's track.

"Full speed ahead!"

The U-boat answered, and the torpedo passed clear of her stern by 10 yards. Immediately C-27 acted again, Dobson fired a second torpedo, heard a fierce explosion, rose to sea-level, and was satisfied: his "fish" had struck U-23 just abaft the conning tower abreast the engine-room, starboard side. When the 80-foot column of water and dark yellow-black smoke subsided, only part of the enemy's bow remained and in half a minute that too had gone, leaving large quantities of oil-fuel on the waves. Three survivors were picked up by the trawler's boat. Dazed, helpless, their lungs full of oil and sea-water, their ears plugged with cotton-wool wads, they had to be lifted aboard *Taranaki*, but sleep and good food soon revived them.

Dobson was able to rescue Schulthess, Prince Ernst von Ratibor, Prince Zu Hohenlohe-Schillingsfurst (her three officers), besides four of the crew, furnished them with clothing and food, and that night brought them into harbour. More decorations were awarded, another £1000 to be divided between two plucky craft. Four years later Dobson won the Victoria Cross. To-day Cantlie is an admiral: otherwise I doubt if he would be alive.

For, till the coming of the Second German War, he was Captain of H.M.S. *Royal Oak* which sank in Scapa Flow. It was by a torpedo from a German U-boat.

The sinking of U-23 had a most regrettable sequel. Lieut.-Commander Schulthess was kept a prisoner of war until December 4, 1916, when he was transferred to Switzerland. From there he was able to inform the German Admiralty of this *Taranaki* and *Princess Louise* ingenuity which had led to the loss of two submarines: he added that the British were kept well informed regarding the U-boats and their movements. From that date this stratagem was worked out, and even before that date the secret somehow got about: by mingling with interned alien civilians and mutual conversation the secrecy of our trap was made known, but in the next chapter we shall relate another incident, though it was not until October 24, 1915, that the British Admiralty stopped this method for a while of employing submarines. For C-33 failed to return home, having (it was believed) hit a North Sea mine. In those days we were prepared for many an emergency, as for instance when U-boat or Zeppelin might surprise some fisherman at work off the East Coast. As it was not practicable always to instal wireless, carrier pigeons were released from aboard, but by the time these reached land and the decoded message came into the office, the news had become so late as to pass into history, and the enemy had gone far out of sight.

Sometimes, however, curious U-boat incidents arose because a foreign neutral after being intercepted off Scotland by one of our Blockade armed liners would be sent into Lerwick, or other port of examination, with an armed guard, and it could be a risky affair. Thus, in 1915, H.M.S. *Motagua* found it necessary to stop the Norwegian S.S. *Fimreite*, and as an armed guard went Mr. P. B. Clarke with four men. Course was now altered for Kirkwall, and an hour before sunrise when NW. of the Hebrides on July 23, they sighted U-36 off the port bow, approaching along the surface at high speed.

This submarine was under Lieut.-Commander E. Graeff, who had set out from Heligoland on the 19th, crossed the North Sea, then on the 22nd being now west of the Orkneys sank no fewer than nine trawlers and one steamer. Still pursuing his heartless tactics, Graeff, at 4 a.m. next day, fired a gun as signal to *Fimreite* that she would be next victim on the list.

"Lower a boat and come alongside."

The Norwegian Master proceeded to obey, but whilst he was being rowed across the waves, some serious thinking had to be done by Clarke who happened to be only a midshipman R.N.R. What, in this difficult and sudden dilemma, should he do?

He decided that his first duty would be to save the lives of his four men, and under no circumstances let them be made German prisoners. So, whilst the Master was away, the young midshipman ordered his quartet to remove their uniforms, disguise themselves as best they could, put revolvers in their pockets, and assist the Norwegian crew in lowering the other boats.

When, presently, the Master's boat returned it was to announce the following conversation which had taken place with Graeff.

"Where are you bound?" demanded the latter.

"For Hull," came the answer.

"Oh! Hull? Going there direct?"

"Well . . . not quite. Calling at Kirkwall."

That obviously told its own story.

"I see. You go to Kirkwall? You have then a Prize Crew on board, yes?"

"One British officer and four men."

"So? Then I shall sink your ship for trading with the English. Get your crew into the boats, but the Englishmen . . . ah, no! They shall go down in the *Fimreite*."

Clarke, however, had other ideas on the subject, and the five Britons, no longer wearing uniform, joined the Norwegians in the boats quite inconspicuously. They pulled away from their doomed steamer, U-36 fired fifteen shells, of which one penetrated to the boilers, down disappeared the steamer bows first and Graeff, after watching the disaster with gloating satisfaction, dived below surface on a westerly course. Doubtless some more victims would come along presently.

It was a cruel, typically German act to leave those boats rolling about the lonely Atlantic with no expectation other than death by cold and starvation, or that madness which follows when thirsty men yield to drinking sea-water. The bitter hours dragged on, the sun rose over their heads, afternoon set in, but how many British or Norwegians would be able to last out? A million-to-one chance of being sighted by some hurrying steamer. Every man realized that too well. How many other poor mariners had suffered that same fate at the hands of U-boat captains!

But that same afternoon at 3.30 a miracle of the sea happened —a coincidence, if you like to call it, and such as no fiction writer would dare to invent. Something was coming along over the water. Tall, conspicuous, but not a steamer. She turned out to be one of the survivors of the sailing-ship age, and an historic example too. Stately and picturesque as ever under her cloud of canvas, leaning over from the wind, here showed up that famous old barque the *Springbank*, once a famous ocean traveller known all over the world.

I

But, with the advent of mechanical propulsion, she had been sold by British owners and now flew the Norwegian flag.

Did ever fellow nationals meet more strangely on the high seas? Luckily, too, she was homeward bound. So all hands were picked up, and the five Britons, likewise, found themselves in luck; for, after a while, the *Springbank* sighted the S.S. *Caliban*, to which Clarke's party were transferred, who thus reached Stornoway in safety.

Lucky? Perhaps even now, years afterwards, these men have not realized their narrow escape. U-36 was not far away, still doing her dirty work. At 6 a.m. on July 24 she sank a British trawler and a steamer. Twelve hours later, at 6 p.m. of this same 24th, Graeff was molesting the Danish S.S. *Louise* when he sighted the somewhat unattractive 373-ton collier *Prince Charles*. That steamer, being British, somehow seemed to the German, just then, the most luscious morsel, impudently daring to hoist her Red Ensign. Graeff would speedily send her to where he believed Clarke and the four men had gone.

So, forsaking *Louise*, U-36 began shelling the collier which obeyed the bully, stopped engines, and awaited the next instruction. Another shell passed so closely between funnel and foremast that evidently the submarine was going to waste no time. And now only 600 yards separated smart U-boat from smoke-begrimed steamer.

Then, all of a sudden, the latter's roughly clad crew seemed to develop intense activity, guns actually barked, missiles came whizzing from her deck, the German gunners darted panic-stricken down the conning tower, ugly holes were torn in U-36, two of Graeff's men were killed, and she began sinking by the stern with bows standing up in the air. Soon the sea became black with Germans swimming for their lives, then one final lurch and U-36 went down in her final plunge. She was paying her penalty at last.

For this was the day when the most dramatic thing ever happened to a U-boat. This was the first time a Q-ship had surprised a German submarine. But since it became possible to save only fifteen of the thirty-three German lives, and a prison camp was now to become the former's new address, Britain's new "secret weapon" remained unsuspected until another Q-ship in another locality was to repeat this initial success.

"What is the Navy doing?"

Some people used to ask this quite unnecessary question even during the last war. Had they but known at the time! Only three days after we sank U-36, H.M.S. *Hildebrand*, which also was one of the Blockading Squadron, on July 27 spoke the Norwegian S.S. *Trondhjemfjord*. Since the latter was carrying general cargo from New York for Bergen, and so much contraband had been indirectly finding its way to Germany, the *Hildebrand's* commanding officer decided that the Norwegian must be sent for examination into Kirkwall under Lieut. Crawford, R.N.R., and armed guard.

Captain Bang was *Trondhjemfjord's* Master, and a very fine, kindly mariner he proved himself. Next day, just before 12.30 p.m., the usual tragedy began when a U-boat appeared from nowhere and began shelling mercilessly. Captain Bang altered course to bring the enemy astern, whacked up to full speed, and a great race ensued. But the Norwegians' efforts could not prevail, at the end of half an hour the German had overhauled the escaper and resumed shelling, wherefore there was no other alternative than to stop.

Now *Trondhjemfjord's* Master had brought his wife with him on this voyage and well enough he now realized the danger which threatened. The German was signalling to fetch the ship's papers aboard and to waste no time ; but, before so proceeding, Captain Bang, with most considerate and unselfish forethought, arranged that Crawford and the guard should not be betrayed. Mrs. Bang selected enough of her husband's clothing to go round, then packed the officer's uniform among her own effects, whilst rifles and other gear were concealed in the steamer's forepeak.

Scarcely had Bang reached the submarine than the following questions were put to him :

"Has any British patrol boarded your ship ?"

"Not yet," lied the old skipper heroically.

"Then no armed guard is there ?"

"No," insisted the Master, fully conscious that his guests would be shot. He was glad to have saved their lives.

"I shall now sink your steamer", said the U-boat commander, "so it would be well for you to go back and abandon her immediately."

Thus, within an hour of this meeting, everyone took to the boats, the submarine approached to within 130 yards, a torpedo dashed forth and gashed a hole amidships. Over she listed to port, then a large quantity of sulphuric acid in her cargo exploded violently, sending debris high as the mastheads, and finally the *Trondhjemfjord* vanished beneath the water.

It was now that another scarcely credible coincidence followed. Believe it or not, these shipless people were picked up by another Norwegian, and a barque she likewise happened to be. Named the *Glance*, this vessel unfortunately was outward-bound, but within a short while she sighted and signalled the S.S. *Orlando* flying the Swedish flag and on her way for Sweden. So to her were transferred Captain Bang and his people, whilst the armed guard were again transhipped—this time to the trawler *Princess Juliana* which landed them, after many adventures, in Thurso.

So that summer passed, and with September began the long succession of gales which made the work of boarding no easier. It was the 16th of this month, and the scene that cold lonesome area northeast of Iceland, when H.M.S. *Orcoma*, having intercepted the Swedish topsail schooner *Valand*, decided the latter must go into Lerwick. As armed guard she was given Mr. Cyril A. Bamford, Midshipman, R.N.R., two seamen, and a stoker. They guessed that life in such regions, at such a season, in a sailing ship would be no yachting cruise, but not one of the four suspected what an adventure they were beginning.

During the first three days, apart from discomfort, there was little of which to complain, though the fair wind fell so light as to render progress deadly slow. During afternoon of the 18th the breeze came easterly, but not till 9.30 the next morning did they sight the Faroes, that rugged group of twenty-one precipitous islands which lie between Iceland and the Shetlands.

A shift of weather was indicated, the wind backed to the southeast, and by the 20th increased to a gale which compelled *Valand* to heave-to. Worse and worse it blew, the seas rose so monstrously that Bamford decided to uphelm and run off to the northward. So they sighted the Faroes for a second time. One anxiety after another. In the night of the 21st *Valand's* steering gear broke down and it looked as if she would be driven across towards Greenland's icy mountains.

But next day was followed by one of those ominous calms with an ugly swell which made the schooner roll and wallow like a drunken thing, straining her rigging, and jolting ropes and canvas, whilst spars creaked protesting and blocks whined mournfully: yet the toiling crew managed to get the wheel repaired, and course for Lerwick, in the Shetlands, was again attempted.

Alas! The fickle wind now changed to SSE., which meant right ahead, and dense banks of fog accentuated everybody's anxiety, since fog usually foretells a gale. Sure enough on the 25th a northeaster, whilst dispersing the thickness, developed into another gale shortly after sunset.

Matters were looking not too good. Ten days of boxing about had practically exhausted the crew's provisions and those of the armed guard. Starvation would have been the next threat, but fortunately the *Valand's* cargo consisted of salted herrings, and on this fare all hands must subsist. Optimism returned at 8 p.m., when Muckle Flugga was seen to the southwest, and weary men promised themselves a good long drink when once ashore at Lerwick.

Again hope descended with a bump. Owing to the violent storm blowing on a lee shore, the absence of all lights along the Shetlands, the improbability of sighting any Lerwick patrols on such a wild night, Bamford, with seamanlike prudence, decided to stand right away from the land than risk piling up on the rocks. Yet even now the conditions grew more alarming.

For at 1 a.m. of the 26th the battered *Valand* showed that she could not carry on much longer. Away snapped the fore-rigging, and the foremast seemed destined to crash over the side. The wind howled, seas smashed themselves against the sides with continuous hammering, whilst Norwegians and British toiled to save their ship and selves from destruction. Strange responsibility for a young midshipman in these days of steam to be commanding a primitive old sailer, ill-found and leaking! Yet what a glorious experience for his future career when he should return after war to serve in liners!

An odd situation, too, for the stoker to find himself doing the job of able-bodied seaman aboard a real sailing-vessel instead of shovelling coal into furnaces. Truly a war does odd things to a man's routine of life!

By much effort, knocking away the schooner's port bulwarks, passing wire strops round her hull, setting up temporary stays, that mast was rendered secure before dawn. Then one wave, more powerful than the rest, picked up the starboard anchor, hurled it against the hull, threatening to create a good-sized hole; but after making nothing worse than an ugly dent, the heavy creature was recovered.

Twelve days having passed, and this northeasterly gale still giving no sign of easing, Bamford had to make one more decision which would have worried the most experienced of shellbacks. Here they were, about midway between the Shetlands to the north and Orkneys to the south; but if Lerwick had been a lee shore, so was Kirkwall. It would be foolish to attempt the latter, especially as ropes and canvas in their rotten state kept carrying away. Indeed the lower topsail was the only sound bit of stuff in the ship.

Bamford, therefore, could but disobey orders, run down Scotland's east coast before a wind which at least was fair. He would make for the Firth of Forth, whose wide entrance should be of some help.

Land was sighted on the 29th, then a town, which the Swedish Master assumed to be Aberdeen, though actually Montrose. At 6 p.m. two lots of flashing lights were descried which the Master took to be from fishing craft, but the Midshipman was not satisfied, ordered the ship to be hove-to for the night, and morning justified Bamford's cautious wisdom. There, abaft the port beam, rose May Island lighthouse. On the other side was Bell Rock. Course up the Forth was now easy. After a fortnight's anxious voyage he brought *Valand* to anchor off Leith despite lack of charts, navigational instruments, or the sun's visibility.

No wonder the Admiralty sent this young seafarer their congratulations, and the King awarded him the Distinguished Service Cross.

CHAPTER 17

THE ENEMY DELUDED

HOW slight was the difference between success and failure may be related in the narrative of the incident concerning U-16. Be it mentioned that it was not Lieut.-Commander Hansen who was in command : we remind ourselves that the latter now was captain of U-41, though formerly he did skipper U-16 and, according to Gayer, Lieut.-Commander Hillebrand had taken his place.

It was July 26, the disguised-trawler-plus-submarine idea intended to be employed when to-day the *Taranaki* (Lieut. F. H. Peterson, R.N.R.) was at sea in company with H.M. Submarine C-24 (Lieut. F. H. Taylor, R.N.), who was taken in tow from Lat. 56.43 N., Long. 0.55 E. At 6.17 a.m. they were heading SE. by E. when *Taranaki* reported that a submarine was on the horizon to the north-northeast. The scene was such as often presented itself to the enemy when fishing vessels off the east coast of Scotland were sunk : the summer's day presented a sight of twenty sailing drifters, a couple of steam drifters, and two steamers making for port. Hillebrand well knew why he had been sent.

First he went up to the sailing drifters, cruised around them, and having fully inspected their appearance went after a more valuable ship. At this time *Taranaki* was carefully watching the movements and telephoning each development down to the invisible C-24.

"Submarine coming down fast," was the latest announcement, so at 7 a.m. the British craft slipped her towing-wire and the two separated, yet now it became difficult. The German was hurrying to the southward making for a timber-laden steamer that had come across the North Sea. At the end of twenty minutes U-16 allowed her to proceed, for doubtless he realized that a vessel laden with a cargo of planks would float for hours after being holed.

Taranaki gradually altered course to keep the enemy on the starboard beam and close the German slightly, as it was most necessary not to let the latter become too far away. Why? Because the atmosphere to-day possessed such an effect that it became difficult to distinguish the barely noticeable U-16 from the skyline.

The latter decided to examine the *Taranaki*, but was emitting from the exhaust-pipe a thick yellow, oil, smoke. It was just after 9 a.m. and the German would not come nearer than about 1500 yards, so *Taranaki* hoisted Danish colours and after a pause the naval White Ensign instead, opening fire with her starboard 3-pounder. That was a perfectly legitimate declaration, the first shell fell exactly in line with the conning tower though 200 yards short, but the fourth shot hit this tower fair and square, most of the next shells coming in a similar manner.

Hillebrand was taken off his guard, but that first bang so surprised him to full consciousness, he hastened into submergence and disappeared in a cloud of white smoke. The German had prepared for this: he had done his best to make his craft inconspicuous and create no suspicion. The reader will recollect what we said about the disguise in mizzen, of mast, and so on. Well, U-16 had come from Germany cleverly feigning another fisherman, with dummy funnel painted yellow with black top. *Taranaki* thought the disguise excellent—but as usual the enemy just failed by neglect of detail. If only she had remembered to hoist the mast, she would have resembled a steamer absolutely.

The struggle, then, was broken off, and most certainly taught him in future to be ultracautious.[1] From German sources we know that U-16 was within an ace of falling a victim to *Taranaki*—let alone to C-24—that the German opened fire at 1200 metres and *Taranaki* hauled down the Danish Ensign before hoisting "the English war flag". It also is admitted that U-16 was hit several times, but on trying to dive found that her diving gear had been seriously damaged: at first, therefore, Hillebrand went to an excessive depth, rose again to the surface whereupon he was hit and once more disappeared below surface to 76 metres. Finally, with a list of 10 degrees, this submarine got away on her return voyage to Heligoland, where she arrived the next day.

This inconclusive contest, besides alarming the enemy and causing him to be on the defensive in the presence of our fishing fleets—which was much to be desired—rather "queered the pitch" of any disguise-and-sink proposition: yet subsequent events proved that these U-boat commanders had still a very great deal to learn and were remarkably reluctant to acquire information from others' mistakes. A little more humility, and less personal confidence, would have made a wonderful difference to what may be termed the "Trap Ship" era.

Thus had been our practice first inaugurated on June 23 when C-24 fooled U-40; it was repeated on July 20 when U-23 was defeated by C-27; and on July 24 the "innocent" steamer *Prince Charles* sank U-36. Cleverness rather than brute force! There were three similar sinkings by ingenuity during August and September, for a new phase had begun and the enemy had not guessed right until it leaked out from internment that the trawler co-operating

---

[1] After obtaining command of U-46, Hillebrand was more cautious in his tactics, but this did not prevent his sinking obvious targets.

with one of our small-class submarines was too well known. On the other hand the disguised, yet armed, steamer evidently contained mighty possibilities that even the smartest German officer could not yet grasp. *Prince Charles* had succeeded almost instantaneously, though Lieut.-Commander Herbert, after all his eagerness in the *Antwerp*, and weeks of patient cruising, had failed to have any luck.

Yes, this novel Q-ship idea was going to be tried further.

After *Antwerp* had, in March, just failed to make contact off the Scillies with Weddigen in U-29, Herbert felt there was something wrong and hurried up to the Admiralty where he saw the blunt old Lord Fisher—at that time still First Sea Lord. Pointing out that a Great Eastern steamer accustomed to the Harwich–Holland route was an obvious anomaly off Land's End in war time, and that therefore any U-boat officer would "smell a rat", the younger mariner won his case and the ancient mariner agreed. In five minutes the former was permitted to take over a certain "three-island" cargo vessel of about 4000 tons.

Chartered from the Ellerman Line, a typical "tramp", and able to steam at 12 knots, she had a single funnel and was now sent round to Pembroke Dockyard where *Antwerp's* guns were placed in her and a third 12-pounder as well. As second-in-command to Herbert was Sub-Lieut. G. C. Steele, son of a naval officer, grandson of an officer in the Royal Marines. Steele had already seen submarine service in the D-8 (to-day he is the holder of the V.C., and commands his old training-ship *Worcester*). Thus with a hand-picked crew and a better type of ship, Herbert began afresh in April to seek out submarines, and though he had steamed 12,000 miles by the middle of August he never saw a U-boat again, and the outlook was not hopeful—unless indeed things were going to be entirely different and *Prince Charles* had changed the whole submarine outlook.

The new decoy, then, was named the *Baralong*.

Simulation! That was the idea: normal-looking vessels, yet performing the most extraordinary feats. Perhaps Hansen, in U-41, might be caught again in this manner? Perhaps by the *Baralong*? Perhaps even off the Scillies?

Meanwhile this sinking of fishing vessels in the North Sea was a most annoying menace, and if the *Taranaki* notion was to-day no longer convenient, then another stratagem must be substituted. In the Lowestoft area those UB-boats made themselves such a menace to sailing smacks that the only thing was to send out other smacks secretly armed, stiffened with a few people from the Navy, but otherwise going about their business with trawl towing from the stern. It was a particular way of using the decoy.

On Friday, August 13, UB-4, commanded by Lieut. Carl Gross, set out from Flanders for the fruitful Smith's Knoll region and was off there by Saturday night. She measured 90 feet long, displaced 127 tons on the surface and 142 when submerged. In the latter condition these submarines were good for 5 to 6 knots, but only during one hour. In surface trim their speed was about a knot faster.

It is quite evident, therefore, that against a strong tide (such as in the Dover Straits), or when trying to chase a steamer, their ability was limited. Sailing smacks were their objectives, bombs their chief weapons; one machine-gun, and a couple of torpedoes being employed as required.

Now at 8.20 this summer's night UB-4 was 3 or 4 miles NNE. of the buoy, alert for plunder, when she espied what looked like the ripest gift. But this smack *Inverlyon* belied the true character. Usual skipper and his three hands, of course. But that disguised Gunner, Mr. E. M. Jehan, R.N. (lent by H.M.S. *Dryad*), and his four naval ratings were aboard, not for the purpose of fishing. Certainly everything looked normal, the 3-pounder was concealed from sight, and anybody could notice *Inverlyon* to be at work with trawl down.

Wherefore, Herr Gross, with perfect confidence, motored till 30 yards distant, broke out the German Ensign, and shouted something from the conning tower. What he ordered was the customary "Get into your boat." All that the Englishmen could hear was the last word. And it sufficed.

Firing his revolver at the Ober-Leutnant, Mr. Jehan used this as a signal for the fun to begin. Up went the White Ensign, 3-pounder swung round smartly, and there was some mighty quick shooting.

One, two, three shots, of which the first and third pierced the conning tower's centre and exploded inside, the second shell demolishing the tower's after side, ensign and all. Not merely that, but Carl Gross fell dead into the "ditch".

Caught by the tide, UB-4 was carried round the smack's stern to within *10* yards. A gunner's dream of Heaven! Ten yards?

Fast as the shells could be inserted bang went the 3-pounder again. Six times. The first smote the conning tower, second and fourth falling over, but third, fifth, and sixth, going right into the hull itself.

That did it. No escaping, this time.

At an angle of 80 degrees the submarine disappeared gurgling to the depths. It was getting dusk now, about half a dozen rounds had been eased off by the enemy from rifle, revolver, or Maxim gun. Pretty bad aiming, too! Not one Englishman wounded, though six Germans on the submarine's deck seemed near enough for doing damage.

The North Sea gave a convulsion, much water and oil were thrown up, three bodies too, one having enough vitality to shout.

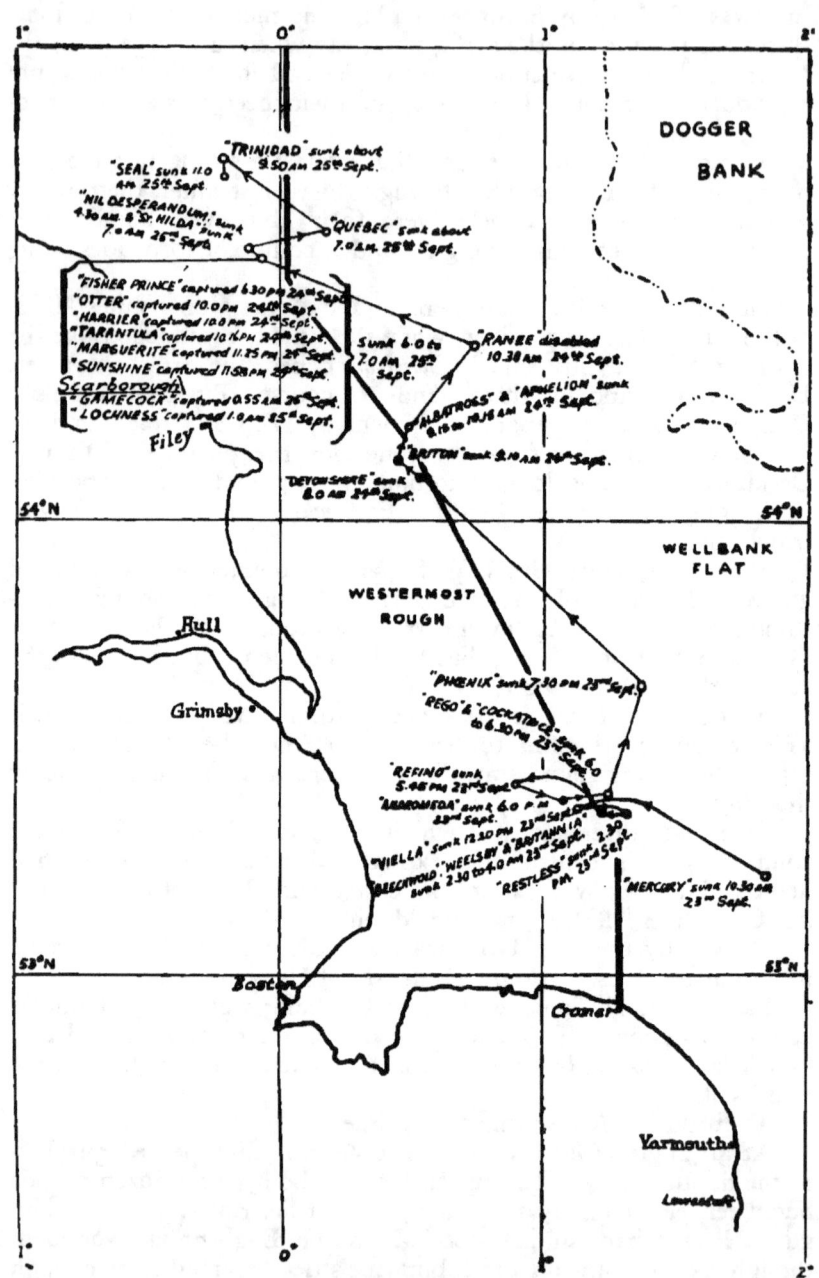

N.E. COAST SINKINGS

The above gives some idea of the progress of U-boats up the N.E. coast in September 1916 with their attacks on fishing craft.

Gallantly Skipper Phillips threw his own clothing aside, swam with a lifebuoy, made a bold effort to save the raider, but the German sank too soon. Darkness settled over the sea.

Despite wind in the sails, *Inverlyon* was not going ahead. She had been brought up, all "standing", for her trawl had caught the 142-ton UB-boat like an anchor, until released. But it was all over, no survivors went back home. German authorities in Flanders waited till the end of August before giving her up for lost, though not till long after the war did they learn the reason.

The King bestowed on Mr. Jehan the D.S.C., and great was the joy in Lowestoft over *Inverlyon's* victory.

"The fortune of war." How often we read that expression! But how true it is! Even during present hostilities we learn of one man being among the very few survivors from a sunken ship, then being appointed to another vessel and being among the very few to succumb when she foundered. Neither logic, law of average, nor any other explanation can provide the why and wherefore.

There is some little doubt concerning what happened to U-26 up the Baltic. She certainly torpedoed the Russian cruiser *Pallada* early in the war and the Russian minelayer *Yenesei* in June, but some time during this summer U-26 did not return. History will never be able to reveal such details as how, when, and where she foundered, but it is practically certain that one day she encountered a Russian minefield and blew up with all hands. It has also been claimed that during the summer of 1915 UB-1 passed directly into the navy of Austria-Hungary and became therein Submarine XI.

Several submarines which were under construction in Germany for Austria at the outbreak of war were put into the German service by the month of August. Of these we can trace the movements, when U-66, U-67, and U-68 made noted sinkings of ships off the west of Ireland and the Western Approaches. The destruction by gunfire when 70 miles south from the Scillies of the S.S. *Portia* by U-69 on August 2 is thought to have been done by U-69: so also that of S.S. *Costello* by U-68 at eight o'clock on the morning of August 3 when 95 miles WbyS. of the Bishop. This submarine was painted with black-and-white checks.

The UC minelayers during August became very busy, UC-1, 3, 5, 6, and 7 were thus employed off the east and southeast English coasts, and during this month no fewer than sixteen minelaying trips were made off our shores by these five boats. It was a nuisance and there was still a shortage of guns, but we had to compromise by removing sixty-five 12-pounders from merchant ships and replacing them by 3-pounders: an excellent decision, because recent events had shown that many of our patrols were under-armed.

According to the official shipping losses, enemy submarines during this August sank 135,153 tons: a high figure and one never reached again until October, 1916. Thus was August, 1915, one of the most important submarine months of the war, and one of the most notable incidents was on August 8 after U-22 had left Borkum five days before and sank H.M.S. *India* off the Vestfjord stopping the German ore-laden steamers coming down with Narvik cargoes.

But much more important was Germany's decision to transform the Mediterranean into a sphere of U-boat campaigning. Had not Hersing shown both that the outward voyage was practicable, and the sinking of merchantmen very much within the limitations of those men who in northern Europe had proved their ability? But there was a deeper reason for this change of scene.

Ever since the torpedoing of *Lusitania* there had been considerable feeling in the United States against Germany's U-boats. Notes had been exchanged and diplomatic pressure in Washington exerted, that for a time it looked as if a crisis was coming. America did not enter the war, however, until 1917, but all the same these U-boats were gradually doing the Germans irreparable harm diplomatically, so that from September 24, 1915, until March 1, 1916 (excepting the brief period within December 20-28), all torpedoing of merchantmen around the British Isles was stopped. Thus the declaration in the previous February of a Submarine Blockade was considerably modified.

We find that from the high figure in August and the great activity also in September we suddenly pass in northern Europe to a different standard. There could be no risk of offending in the Mediterranean any of America's susceptibilities: all ships there sunk would be either pure warships, or cargo-carriers, or military transports. So in August began that gradual southern voyaging which Hersing three months earlier had initiated, and was not to be discarded till the war ended.

On August 4, then, this neo-pioneering began when U-34 (Lieut.-Commander Rücker) and U-35 (Lieut.-Commander Kophamel) started out from Heligoland. Their instructions were to reach the Adriatic, but not to do anything hostile beyond the latitude of the English Channel until they started in the Mediterranean and Aegean. Two days after leaving Germany Admiral von Tirpitz (at whose suggestion they had been sent) wrote somewhat apprehensively. "I hope all will come right if Turkey can be kept going. Our two new submarines are on the way. May the Lord protect them! I don't know whether England has got wind of them."

This pair had a good voyage, and reached Cattaro on August 23. Such arrival gave satisfaction to the German Admiralty that on August 27 U-39 (Lieut.-Commander Forstmann) started from home and next day U-33 (Lieut.-Commander Gansser) followed him. Like the predecessors, these went round the north of Scotland. Forstmann got through Gibraltar Straits and on September 8 was sighted at 5.30 p.m. when about 130 miles east of Cartagena heading to the southeast. He sank two French and one British vessel on the 9th, and came into Cattaro on the 13th. Gansser after leaving Borkum sank a British vessel 95 miles north of Cape Wrath (which shows how wide a berth the submarine was giving the land), sank another 29 miles west of the Fastnet, a third when 137 miles southwest of the Fastnet, then a Norwegian in the Bay of Biscay, passed the Gibraltar Straits, and came into Cattaro on the 16th, that is three days after Forstmann.

In November came also Max Valentiner in U-38, and with these six boats (including Hersing) we thus have six of Germany's "star-turn", well-tried experts, from the north to extend the Submarine Campaign in the Mediterranean, Aegean, and Adriatic. The destruction of cargo and passenger vessels ; ships laden with khaki soldiers or munitions ; men-of-war and (subsequently also) Q-ships ; were all the targets for these visitors, and as time went on so the submarines came south in greater numbers, and the ships sunk grew more numerous.

The destruction of German submarines by us after mid-August, 1915, until mid-March of the following year consists solely in northern Europe of two sunk by a Q-ship, one torpedoed by a British submarine ; the remainder finding their fate by mines or by stranding, and these seven months seem to exhibit a strange lull. But Germans got to use submarines for other purposes than sinking ships. When the *Meteor* was sent under command of Captain von Knorr to lay on August 8 a big minefield (374 mines) off Moray Firth he was escorted on the outer voyage by U-17. When he was returning to Germany and had to sink his surface ship rather than fall into Admiral Tyrwhitt's hands, he and his men were taken by U-28 from commandeered fishing vessels. So, at a later date, when an outward bound raider was about to steam through our Blockade often enough she would be escorted by a U-boat.

CHAPTER 18

DECOYS AND DESTINY

GERMANY still had the desire to do harm from the sky. On August 9 she dropped over Lowestoft a couple of bombs from a Zeppelin at 10.15 p.m. and the next night over Dover Harbour some more: one exploding on striking the water and damaging H.M. Armed Trawler *Equinox* in forty-three places, shaking the compass out of its gimbals and wounding three of the crew who lay in their bunks asleep. The Second German War in principle (though not in detail) thus became largely akin to the First War.

We related earlier how East Coast fishing smacks were being secretly commissioned and sent out from Lowestoft to trap the UB and UC boats off the Smith's Knoll Buoy area. The Admiralty gave permission for as many as four of these vessels to be armed, but they were definitely sailing smacks and not steam trawlers, since the latter would fail to be peculiar in the place. We saw also how the first smack to win success was the *Inverlyon*, when she sank UB-4 on August 15.

But the first unsuccessful attempt was by the smack *G. and E.* on August 11. She had been taken up for service on July 26 under Lieut. C. E. Hamond, R.N., of H.M.S. *Halcyon*. The object she especially noticed on the August date was 5 miles south of the Smith's Knoll Buoy when a submarine of the UB-class surfaced 600 yards from the smack *Leader*, ordered the crew into their boat and to go alongside the German. The enemy then used this boat to place a bomb in the *Leader* which was blown up, the fishermen being now again given use of the boat but cast adrift.

The submarine next closed the *G. and E.*—looking like any other smack with all the crew dressed in fishermen's "rig" and the 3-pounder well concealed—but at 200 yards the German bully fired a rifle shot. The *G. and E.*, following the practice of Q-ships so recently inaugurated and presently to become the stereotyped drill in decoy vessels, made a pretence of the panic party bungling their rowing boat into the sea. This gave time for the submarine to approach parallel, and only 40 yards away.

Then action was ordered, the White Ensign hoisted, five shells fired from the gun, and three penetrated the base of the conning tower, one also going through the tower's lower portion. Utterly startled by this, the enemy waited no longer than he could disappear with great rapidity at a steep-angle nose first. Nothing further was seen, the boat went home licking her wounds, and the smack sailed back into Lowestoft. The incident was all over quickly and it showed—as other fights with submarines taught us—that with a 12-pounder the enemy might have been blown to fatality, yet in four days the submarine UB-4 we assuredly know to have become a loss.

Meanwhile the sum of £1000 was erroneously awarded *G. and E.*, whilst Lieut. Hamond was given a D.S.C. But the claim to have sunk the enemy to-day is not substantiated.

And this August 11 became memorable further up the North Sea because of a very difficult, but somewhat tragic, further attempt to catch the enemy by that previously outlined submarine-and-trawler strategem. The story begins on the evening of August 10 when H.M. Submarine C-23 (Lieut.-Commander Harrington D. Edwards, R.N., previously mentioned in connection with his patience on this work) came out of Leith and proceeded in company of the trawler *Ratapiko*. Down the Firth of Forth they sped, passed Inchkeith Island, and at 10.15 that night were off May Island.

About 2 a.m. both vessels being now well out in the North Sea, stopped engines and the *Ratapiko* (Lieut.-Commander B. Acworth, R.N.) proceeded to take C-23 in tow. Unfortunately the coil rope, whilst being paid out fouled the trawler's propeller, but after two hours' nocturnal work a new one was used and the tow continued. Then one quarter of an hour later an enemy submarine was seen some 30 miles east of May Island, only 4000 yards away and approaching from WSW. on the surface at 13 knots. So far, so good.

It was a few minutes after 4 a.m. when the enemy opened fire. To Edwards in the submarine Acworth was able to give all details down the telephone, and they both agreed to maintain their course awhile. The German was resolved on the trawler's destruction and began to fire continuously, but the shots fell short. Steering to starboard, the enemy had now closed to 3000 yards and came parallel with *Ratapiko*. This being 'phoned down, Edwards slipped, but unfortunately the telephone cable parted in the trawler instead of in C-23 so that 250 yards of wire still unfortunately dangled attached to her bow. For the second time this morning there had been an awkward contretemps, and this was sheer bad luck since both Acworth and Edwards was each full of zest and a keen submarine enthusiast. But it is the nature of mechanical things, highly developed, that some item will go wrong at the least convenient moment.

At just over $6\frac{1}{2}$ knots C-23 headed SSW., stopping only to raise the periscope and have a look-see when at a depth of 18 feet. The German, however, and we were now on opposite courses, but after starboarding helm Edwards found himself well within the minimum firing range and diving under her. Finally, however, on again rising C-23 observed that the German had disappeared and the trawler was heading full speed to the northeast, so Edwards followed the latter. Then whilst C-23, was travelling at nearly 7 knots along the surface, one of our armed trawlers appeared at 8.35 a.m. and chased the chaser into obscurity for an hour.

This was often the case with our submarines, and one of the C-class captains coming home after a North Sea cruise told me that they always dreaded making the land, for our vigilant trawlers were ever more keen to sink a submarine than first verify her nationality. Finally, Edwards surfaced, hoisted a large White Ensign, and spoke a minesweeping trawler who escorted him up the Forth to Leith where it was discovered that the telephone cable had actually jammed in the bow cap.

As to *Ratapiko*, she had conducted an engagement on her own, sending spare hands to do the "panic party" with the ship's boat, pretending to get excited and doff lifebelts. Just before 5 a.m. Acworth, seeing no sign of C-23 and the range being now only 1500 yards, deemed it time to engage the German. Going full speed, he therefore fired a dozen rounds from the 6-pounder, whereupon the submarine dived and the trawler tried to ram.

But as so frequently came to be realized, the trawler was too slow for that manœuvre and by 5.30 a.m. *Ratapiko* made towards a patrol steam yacht who reported the proceedings by wireless. It turned out an unfortunate day, good luck had been within their very reach, but that broken telephone cable had ruined what promised to be an excellent occasion.

It will be apparent to the reader that often enough the difference between success and failure in destroying an enemy submarine was not so much as even the thickness of paper. It was therefore scarcely surprising that originally the Admiralty was wrong in presuming that the smack *G. and E.* had sunk a German submarine. Actually we know that it was only the same day (August 13) that UB-4 had slowly sailed from Flanders for East Anglia. Gayer admits that it was not known to the Germans how UB-4 came to be sunk and only after this month did they finally give her up. That three German bodies had risen to the surface, and that *Inverlyon's* trawl-net located the submarine's hull, may be taken as confirmatory evidence of the sinking and the *Inverlyon* (which had been taken up on August 2) was subsequently awarded £1000.[1]

German submarine commanders had to think up every kind of trickery. When on August 14 the fishing trawler *Gloria* was sunk

---

[1] How useful were these disguised smacks working off Lowestoft may be ascertained by the loss of the fishing smack *Amethyst* on the morning of August 13 some 7 miles ESE. from that port. This time the enemy was UC-5 which we shall later find being captured off the coast of Suffolk on April 27, 1916.

at breakfast-time 55 miles east of Aberdeen, the culprit was found painted light grey at one side and dark the other, and the same day our Peterhead patrols noticed that submarines still set a mizzen. But the Teutonic mind was capable of doing many things which surprise us. U-24 (Schneider) we remember well as the craft which sank the *Formidable* on New Year's Day, 1915, yet it is difficult to appreciate a certain event which followed nearly nine months later.

For on August 5 Schneider having left Borkum, proceeded round the north of Scotland, west and south coasts of Ireland, then up the Irish Sea and bombarded a benzoline factory at daybreak on August 16 at Lowca near Harrington (Cumberland) before coming home the opposite way. What was the cause of this bombardment? Superior orders? Yes. But, we may ask, *cui bono?* Frankly, it was to nobody's benefit. These are the facts.

Lowca is a village lying half-way between Workington and Whitehaven, consisting chiefly of small works producing naphtha, benzol, and coke. Sunrise on the 16th was at 4.53, the weather being fine and calm, with a slight haze ; and at 4.50, moving to the southeast about a mile from the coke ovens, the submarine (which mounted one gun forward and one aft) opened fire. The first dozen shots did little damage, but the next thirty were all direct hits on the works, the bombardment lasting twenty-five minutes, after which the submarine moved away. There were no casualties, just as there were no military features in the neighbourhood. The damage done amounted to only £800 although the firing was more deliberate than by U-21 off Walney on January 29, and the works had to stop for not more than four days.

To every Englishman this incident seems motiveless. Admittedly the Germans possessed full plans of the works down to the most minute details, for in 1913 one hundred coke ovens had all been erected by a German company, and the crude naphtha plants by another German firm with German labour. Such enthusiastic photographers were these labourers from across the North Sea, that before installation of this job they actually took snapshots of the works *from the sea.*

One can only assume that jealousy, vindictiveness, or similar vice, was the motive for this completely useless gunfire.

But Schneider committed a more grievous delinquency. After going south down the Irish Channel to the Irish south coast he molested the wounded S.S. *Dunslay* (4930 tons) on the 19th about 48 miles SbyW. from the Old Head of Kinsale (near the *Lusitania* area) and would have sunk the steamer, but at that moment appeared a large vessel of 15,801 tons. Against her he fired a torpedo at close range, fortunately most of four hundred persons were saved, but forty-four people went to their doom including several American citizens. So the man who had sunk the *Formidable* now rivalled him who had sunk the Cunarder: for this was the White Star liner *Arabic* and the sensation roused not merely Britain but the United States.

Co-operating with Schneider in this area was Lieut.-Commander B. Wegener in U-27: that very afternoon he happened to be only 25 miles away and at three o'clock captured the S.S. *Nicosian* (6369 tons). The reader will bear in mind that it was he who earlier in the war had torpedoed our submarine E-3 off Borkum, and later sank the armed merchant cruiser *Bayano* off southern Scotland. Now had fate destined that on this August 19 was to be brought about the most remarkable contest between a U-boat and a Q-ship. Still more, after all these months and miles of cruising, at last Lieut.-Commander Godfrey Herbert was to have his chance in the *Baralong*.

Let us recollect that everyone aboard *Baralong* from the captain downwards was quietly, but deeply, angered by the news which had reached them of the loss that ended *Arabic* and forty-four lives. Our Q-ship men could not conceive that German sailormen should send children, women, and men passengers to death unwarned, even though the *Lusitania* case of May was still quoted.

Imagine this August afternoon calm, sunny, and pleasant: the sea at 3 p.m. looking so bright and restful as to suggest anything but war. *Baralong* was in Lat. 50.22 N., Long. 8.7 W., steering east, being then 80 miles west of the Scillies. Suddenly one of the wireless operators rushed up to Lieut.-Commander Herbert on the bridge. An S O S signal from a steamer had just been intercepted.

"Captured by enemy submarine. Crew ready to leave. Lat. 50.22 N., Long. 8.12 W."

From the very loud bleating it was reckoned that this cry for help came from less than 20 miles away, and on scanning the horizon there could be seen the topmasts of a large ship. The *Baralong* at 3.10 wirelessed back:

"Steer NE. (Mag.)."

At 3.20 the stricken steamer called:

"For God's sake, help."

Course was altered towards the distant topmasts, and at length the *Baralong* perceived the 6369-ton S.S. *Nicosian* stopped, and with a feather of steam blowing off. At her stern was evidently something resembling a submarine, then boats lowered from the ship were sighted through the binoculars also.

Nearer came *Baralong* to the *Nicosian*. The former hoisted the International Code signal:

"To save life only."

The submarine was espied lying on the *Nicosian's* port quarter and the Q-ship approached from the starboard beam, then turned eight points to starboard. At the same time the U-boat went ahead along her victim's port side, being for a minute or two obscured from the gaze of *Baralong* who (with perfect respect for international law) was flying American colours whilst over the ship's sides were let down two big signboards with the Stars and Stripes painted thereon. Presently the enemy having started her *electric* motors, being

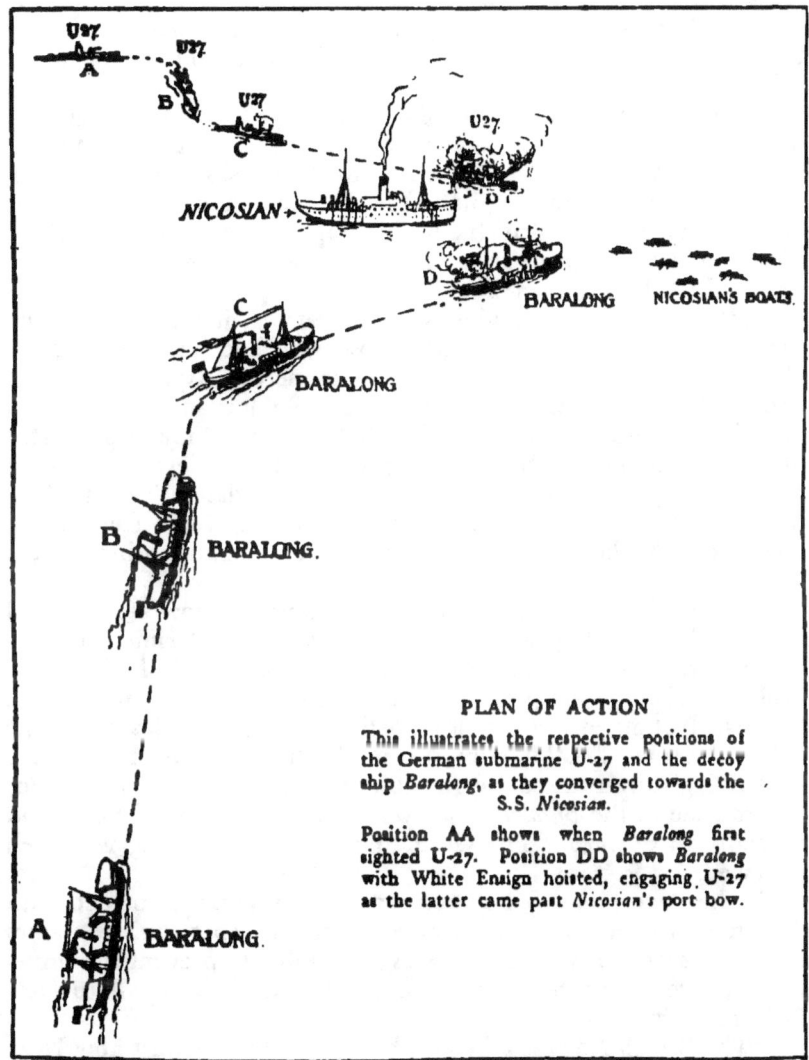

PLAN OF ACTION

This illustrates the respective positions of the German submarine U-27 and the decoy ship *Baralong*, as they converged towards the S.S. *Nicosian*.

Position AA shows when *Baralong* first sighted U-27. Position DD shows *Baralong* with White Ensign hoisted, engaging U-27 as the latter came past *Nicosian's* port bow.

trimmed light and ready for quick submergence, began shelling the *Nicosian* from the deck guns.

But the British steamer had time to lower false colours and hoist the White Ensign, opening fire with rifles and 12-pounders as the submarine's nose just opened clear of the *Nicosian*. As clever tactics and an expression of dramatic surprise, it would be difficult to over-estimate the perfect synchronization of this meeting. The second shell from *Baralong* hit the German at the conning tower's base, but at least another thirty-four shells came also with such remarkable and instant effect that the submarine was completely doomed, heeled over after firing only one shot—and that fell short—then went down and down to the depths, a terrible escape of air being noticeable.

Such then in almost the twinkling of an eye U-27, with Wegener, disappeared for the last time in a fair and just fight. Now the scattered boats of the *Nicosian* were called alongside and her master (Captain C. H. Manning) joined Lieut.-Commander Herbert on the latter's bridge. The British rescued ship belonged to the Leyland Line, and was bringing across from America a cargo of 700 mules for the British Government.

Just as these two captains were conversing, it was noticed that some of the Germans (evidently those who had been serving the U-boat's deck guns) were saving themselves, trying to climb aboard *Nicosian* by means of ropes and the pilot ladder which had been left hanging down. Fearing that these men might set alight the large amount of the mule-ship's fodder, Herbert ordered his riflemen to do their duty : six reached the Leylander's deck alive, the rest flopped back, but presently not one survived. Refusing to surrender, the last of these Germans were found hiding in the propeller-shaft alley.

By 6.20 that evening *Baralong* took *Nicosian* in tow after several holes had been plugged-up below the latter's waterline, and she arrived with her valuable cargo at Avonmouth. It had been a brilliant victory—simple and complete—but there was more besides. Not merely did it restore belief in the Q-ship idea, not alone did to-day's remarkable triumph justify the faith which had been kept living during these days of disappointment : but every sailor and marine in the *Baralong* was roused to believe that U-boats had no reply to Q-ships. The German menace to shipping was itself menaced.

If there were to-day no survivors, it thoroughly coincided with the anger which all seafarers entertained on repeating the names of *Lusitania* and *Arabic*. But it was impossible to prevent the mule-teers, on returning home, from unburdening their minds to New Orleans journalists.

"The British Navy is all right, but let me tell you just how U-27 was . . ."

The German Consul gathered sworn statements from eye-witnesses, pamphlets were circulated in neutral countries, Germany was in a frenzy. "Captain William McBride"—as they imagined was Herbert's name—must be obtained alive or dead, but his identity was unrevealed for years, he had been rewarded with the

THE FIGHT WITH U-27

From a sketch made at the time aboard the *Baralong* by Commander G. C. Steele, V.C., R.N.

D.S.O. and soon came promotion to Commander also. On the other hand the Germans behaved disgracefully this self-same August 19. It happened that Lieut.-Commander Layton was taking his submarine E-13 from England via Danish waters into the Baltic, and had the bad luck to get ashore on the Danish island of Saltholm. Whilst still on the rocks in territorial waters, she was attacked by German destroyers with the loss of fifteen British officers and men. Layton, however, was among the survivors, was treated with every kindness by the Danes who interned him, and they (not altogether unsympathetic) allowed him to escape so that he managed to reach England safely.

This officer was a marked man in other senses than this. He won more than ordinary approbation, his career had barely begun, and even four years before the Second German War he was promoted to flag rank. As every one knows who reads the daily papers, Admiral Layton was destined for future command of our Navy on the China station.

The *Baralong* sinking of U-27 avenged the losses of *Lusitania*, *Arabic*, and E-13, but unknown to the public and unsuspected by Germany, "Captain William McBride" went back to his original service among submarines and took over command of E-22, being succeeded in *Baralong* by Lieut.-Commander A. Wilmot-Smith, R.N. Meanwhile the sinking of *Arabic* caused the fiercest quarrels at German Headquarters : this repetition of a *Lusitania* incident, and the fear of complications with the U.S.A., resulted finally in an order that henceforth no passenger ships were to be sunk without warning and saving of the crews.

It was that decision which we have noted as shifting the centre of submarine effort this summer from northern to southern Europe, and the most distinguished German Admirals began to realize their own folly. Let me quote only two spokesmen.

"I fear that the *Arabic* incident will raise a fresh storm against the submarines," foretold Admiral von Tirpitz on August 22 with undoubted accuracy.

"The sinking of the *Arabic*," affirmed Admiral von Pohl on September 1, "has given Bethmann the opportunity of openly opposing the submarine war, and as a consequence I have recently received orders which so restrict Commanding Officers of Submarines as to make it impossible for them to gain any success." And four days later in referring to the United States he remarked : "We are giving up the weapon with which we injured our chief enemy in the most vital spot."

The Kaiser decided in favour of Bethmann Hollweg, the German Government informed the U.S.A. that the American demands for limitation of U-boat activity are accepted. Thus the wail went up in Germany that no submarine officer could discriminate between freighter and small passenger steamer.

CHAPTER 19

THE COMING CHANGE

WEGENER was regarded by the Germans as "one of the very best submarine commanders". He had left Germany on August 4, so his death after about a fortnight happened promptly. Off the south Irish Sea he had spoken to Lieut.-Commander Max Valentiner of U-38 and it shows the latter's prowess, because in five days during this month he sank no less than thirty ships solely in the southwest approaches. German naval historians regard this as the greatest submarine success achieved in the waters of Great Britain throughout the whole war. Valentiner's tactics were to rely principally on his 8.8-cm. gun and thick weather, but it was not till November that he set out for the Mediterranean.

When Admiral Bacon on August 22 left Dover with seventy-nine miscellaneous craft to attack the harbour and defences of Zeebrugge, it was a successful operation because monitors, destroyers, gunboats, paddlers, drifters, all contributed their share; but though monitors bombarded at 16,000 yards for two and a half hours, firing some seventy shells, it was rather the implication of what these operations suggested that really caused the enemy anxiety. The Germans could only assume from the impressive cavalcade that a landing was imminent. Advance patrols seemed continually to disturb the Flanders coast, so that UC-boats were sent out to mine the Flemish banks and thus render the work of these shallow monitors difficult. But UB-boats by reason of the trepidation and uncertainty were in great demand.

In practice the newly justified use of disguise (such as fishing smacks and tramp-like decoys) was hard to beat, and the Admiralty was backed by the enthusiasm of Admiral Sir Lewis Bayly now at Queenstown. Whilst some more very ordinary-looking steamers were being taken up to follow the *Baralong* tradition, Lowestoft was pursuing its policy with the decoy smacks, and we have given two instances.

The third event belongs to August 23 and the sailing smack *Pet*.

Again it was when 6 miles south of Smith's Knoll that at 9.40 a.m., not far from the Spar Buoy, she sighted carrying a lug-sail either a UB or UC craft. The German fired from her machine-gun to which the smack replied with nine rounds, registering three hits on the conning tower. The submarine reappeared at 10.20

a.m. after having hurriedly submerged for about half an hour, now appearing slightly further off and with pole hoisted for transmitting a wireless message : evidently warning Flemish headquarters that British sailing smacks would be on the defensive. *Pet* fired another four rounds, and one shell was a hit, so the submarine again dived but soon reappeared only 100 yards off. Why? She wanted to fire a torpedo at the smack, but the missile fell short by 12 feet. The smack contested the matter by firing six rounds from the gun and four of these were hits, but the submarine heeled forty-five degrees to starboard and then sank nose downwards.

Then was this truly a kill? The *Pet* was commanded by Petty Officer G. M. Lee and he had with him three R.N. ratings besides the smack's fishing skipper and crew of three men. Lee was awarded the D.S.M., and this vessel (which had been taken up on August 2) was after the incident awarded £1000. Nevertheless, in spite of the fact that sweeping was carried out to locate the hull and an obstruction was found and two charges of T.N.T. were exploded upon it), the Admiralty did not in the end believe the enemy had been sunk. The truth is that in this area the ground had become so foul that the mere discovery of unseen wreckage was not in itself convincing. There is reason to suppose that though this undoubtedly was a shattered submarine, it was that UC-2, sunk accidentally by the S.S. *Cottingham* on July 2 and already narrated.

Off Ireland, whilst the success of *Baralong* gave enormous hope, yet we very much needed that support seeing the risks which had to be endured. The increased number of munition ships coming over the Atlantic from America, the munition ships which we were sending to Archangel—these were of many kinds and I remember seeing one famous vessel which had been built as an exploration ship—the need for escorts in the Grand Fleet, the protecting valuable units such as the bullion carriers ; required the use of many anti-submarine craft just now. Trawlers were all very well for hunting U-boats, and their fighting spirit was wonderful, but they were deficient in speed. Therefore the Q-ships by their mysterious character possessed the element of surprise and would undoubtedly make the attacker very cautious.

The withdrawal of four Q-ships to the Mediterranean, and the defensive alertness off the Flemish coast by the UB-boats expectant of some attack by Admiral Bacon ; then the order issued by "the All Highest" both to the Northeast U-boats and the Flanders Submarines that war against shipping must stop, came as the plainest yielding to the U.S.A. intervention. An examination of the Merchant Shipping Losses reveals that (except by mines off the British Isles and in the White Sea) no sinkings occurred by U-boats after September 24 for several months in the waters north of the Mediterranean. The only disasters were during that sharp interlude of December 20-28, 1915, when U-boats on passage to the

Dardanelles snatched victories off the southwest of Ireland, and it is true also that on February 1, 1916, a ship was sunk by a Zeppelin. Otherwise the resumed U-boat activity did not begin again till March 1, 1916, and finish on the following May 8, yet once more was resumed on July 5, 1916. This is the explanation of those uneventful periods, which at that time were incomprehensible to our patrols.

Careless and inaccurate talk grossly exaggerated the enemy's potentialities by the end of this first submarine phase at the end of September, 1915. Altogether not more than forty-four boats were available, viz. :

    North Sea : 9 U-boats plus 1 UC-boat, total 10.
    Flanders : 8 UB's and 7 UC's, total 15.
    Pola and Cattaro : 5 U-boats, 2 UB's, and 2 UC's, total 9.
    Constantinople : 3 UB's and 2 UC's, total 5.
    Baltic : a miscellaneous collection of not the first rank, total 5.

In other words these forty-four boats represented the strength of the Submarine Blockade, but owing to the time spent on passage between bases and operation areas ; on periods required for resting crews and refitting boats ; it is doubtful if more than a dozen were at any given moment available for active service. On the other hand we were making incursions to the Heligoland Bight, and H.M. Submarine E-4 on September 5, was another of our craft which captured a German trawler by cool enterprise. This was the *Esterburg* which the submarine brought into Harwich.

A few days later (September 10) H.M.S. *Nimrod*, during one of Commodore Tyrwhitt's visits to the German waters in strength, sank the trawler *Fichandel* of Altona. It was learned from the captain and mate that only a dozen trawlers were now fishing out of Hamburg, the rest having been taken over by the German Navy and based on Cuxhaven or Wilhelmshaven.

Whilst the Germans in Flanders were still nervous of what Admiral Bacon's activities might attain, they kept two submarines as a permanent look-out off the coast, viz. off Middelkerke and the Thornton Ridge Buoy. By the end of September our flying men were making such severe attacks on the outgoing and returning submarines that even the Germans admitted "some damage" to UB-6 and UC-1. Conversely a couple of our trawlers off East Anglia fired at a Zeppelin 2 miles from the Haisborough Lightship, and she appeared to be steering west, but promptly rose at a sharp angle, and then followed a second airship. This incident occurred at 7 p.m.

German minelaying by surface ships was resumed in the North Sea when light cruisers, on September 11-12, laid 281 mines in six rows off the eastern flank of the Swarte Bank minefield, which had been laid earlier that summer. The object, among others, was to entrap Commodore Tyrwhitt's forces if bound north to join the

Grand Fleet anywhere between the Dogger Bank and Harwich.

More than twelve months had passed since the outbreak of war, but on September 14 the first of those M.L.'s to be assembled in Canada reached Portsmouth aboard the S.S. *Statesman*, and four more left Montreal two days later. Thus was initiated that long-planned scheme which grew up as a patrol force against U-boats, and did good though monotonous work till the end of war. The M.L.'s on more than one occasion were directly responsible for destruction of a U-boat, but as already emphasized what at present we still needed was some sort of subtle surprise; and this was the case on September 15. Occasionally British submarines used to lie in ambush near Udsire (Norway) in the trust that a U-boat might be waylaid on the voyage along that coast to or from Germany. At least some ore-steamer might be sighted coming south from Narvik.

Now, on February 28, 1915, a small collier named the *Thordis* was battering her way round Beachy Head in heavy weather, when she rammed a German submarine. At the time it was believed that the U-boat had been thus sunk and this was recognized by granting of an award: but in truth the submarine was not destroyed. By an accident U-6 did get under the steamer's bows which damaged the German badly, so that only with difficulty, and after a terrible experience, the submarine limped back home.

On the following September 15, H.M. Submarine E-14 was 4 miles SW. from the southern end of Karmo when at 12.32 p.m. the former sighted U-6 coming along the surface from dead astern. Eleven minutes later, when the range was only 500 yards, both British bow tubes were fired: one torpedo hit just in front of the conning tower, and when the smoke had cleared there were found two German officers and three men. These—out of a total numbering twenty-nine—were rescued and brought back to Aberdeen. Commander C. P. Talbot, D.S.O., R.N., one of our most experienced officers, was in command. In U-6 Lieut. Lepsius, the captain, had been killed. The normal complement amounted to thirty-three, but the boat was four men short, though one junior lieutenant and an engineer were among five survivors. She had been out from Germany only five days.

The reader, however, is still waiting to learn more about Hansen's[1] U-41 which, after narrow escapes and near-death episodes from our patrols, managed to survive ramming and get home for repairs. In September this tough fellow was again at sea, having come out of Wilhelmshaven on the 12th. It was her fourth trip, the first having been begun on April 15. Picture September 23 as a day of great activity, for between 9.45 a.m. and 7.20 p.m. he sank no fewer than three steamers within 86 miles of the Fastnet, when Admiral Bayly ordered the Q-ship *Baralong* to leave Falmouth and steer for this area.

[1] See Chapter 15.

Actually she had already put to sea, though now she was under Lieut.-Commander A. Wilmot-Smith, R.N. In order to simplify matters, *Baralong* became known as the *Wyandra* : the possibility of repeating her previous success did not seem likely, but she could remain at sea for one month at a time. The autumn night soon passed, the *Wyandra* rounded the Lizard and at 9.45 the next forenoon sighted 8 miles ahead, the S.S. *Urbino* stopped and blowing, off steam, to-day's weather being very fine and clear.

The *Urbino* was 67 miles SW. by W. of the Bishop Rock, and the cleverness of Wilmot-Smith was to entice U-41 within gun range. Presently, after approaching still nearer, the Q-ship could make out the submarine's conning tower, but at 5 miles' distance the enemy dived. *Wyandra* then altered course to the southward, to compel her—should Hansen still mean to attack—to surface and use her engines. Let us remind ourselves that the German was far from inexperienced and knew all the tricks : yet he obligingly did as wanted. Shortly afterwards she rose up and proceeded at full speed to head off her opponent.

Wyandra hoisted neutral colours, whereupon U-41 hoisted, "Stop instantly".

Wilmot-Smith obeyed, Hansen came nearer still and signalled "Bring your ship's papers aboard", being now $2\frac{1}{2}$ miles away. Under easy steam *Baralong* approached and began also to lower a boat on the side visible to the German. Having got the submarine about two points on the starboard bow, it was *Wyandra's* intention to keep her there, so by clever shiphandling the distance was firmly but almost unnoticeably reduced to 700 yards when, helm being put hard over, the steamer apparently meant to give a lee to the boat being lowered.

The real reason, however, was not to assist the panic-party, but to bring the starboard and stern guns to bear. Then instantly the command to open fire followed, and the dramatic moment had arrived.

Five hundred yards barely separated the two, the marine's rifles were the first to rattle, followed by a round from the German's gun ; but both as to line and range it was a long way off the mark. Then *Wyandra's* 12-pounders very quickly got into action, and with the second round scored a direct hit at the base of the conning tower. The enemy made no further reply, but on the upper deck appeared panic-stricken Germans who forsook their guns and sought shelter within the conning-tower hatch. Did they succeed in so gaining protection ? Not much : for whilst thus retreating another British shell struck the conning tower, blowing the captain and six men to tiny fragments.

At least five more direct hits struck the pressure hull, so that three minutes later U-41, that had been so ruthless towards others, now took a violent list to port and a big inclination by the stern. There

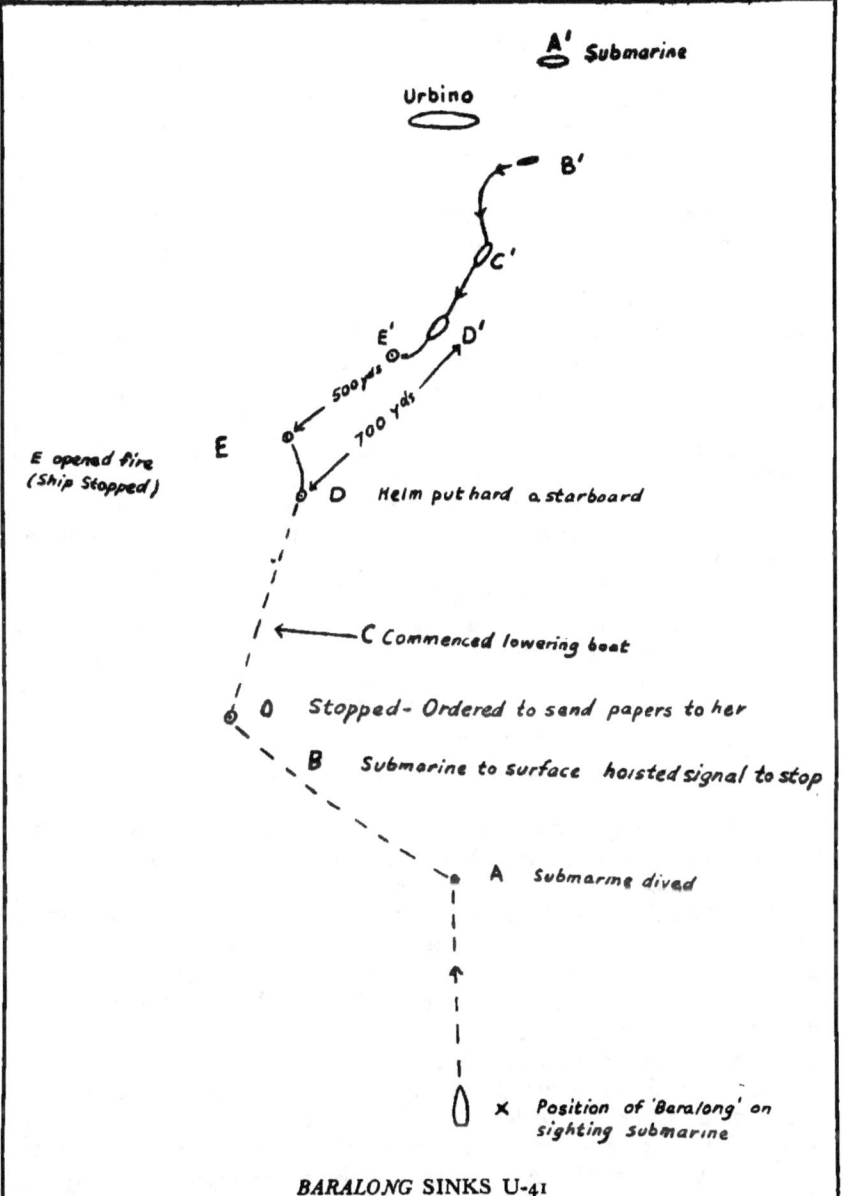

BARALONG SINKS U-41

This was on September 24, 1915. Simultaneous positions of Q-ship and U-41 are shown by lettering. A dash following a letter indicates submarine. Thus, E^1 is where U-41 was sunk.

was an interval half a minute later when bows and top of conning tower showed just above water, with a large volume of smoke and steam escaping. Then she submerged, finally accompanied by a large burst of air and of oil-fuel spreading over the surface. Hansen (who formerly commanded U-16) had at last gone to his doom, U-41 could not cheat destruction again, and four times in forty-five minutes there was smashing of the bulwarks before she sank 75 fathoms down to the seabed in Lat. 49.10 N., Long. 7.23 W.

Wilmot-Smith, after the neatest of engagements, had given U-41 her due, and proceeded to rescue the crew of *Urbino* comprising forty-two officers and men, but in one of these boats was a German seaman and Ober-Leutnant J. Crompton who had hardly yet recovered from their amazement. According to Captain Hick, master of the Wilson liner *Urbino*, the submarine had begun shelling at nine o'clock, and when they took to the boats to row alongside, the nineteeen German sailors standing on U-41's deck jeered and laughed. There had been thirty-seven German officers and men, but the only two survivors were lucky to be alive.

Course was now shaped back to Falmouth ; Lieut.-Commander Wilmot-Smith received a D.S.O., whilst a D.S.C. was awarded the engineer, two of the crew being given the D.S.M.

Of course, with the Teutonic curious inappreciation for the fortune of battle, this incident, when made known in Germany, caused "indignation and horror" exceeded only by the *Baralong* affair. Crompton was on deck in charge of the two guns, and immediately ran for the conning tower when *Wyandra's* guns opened fire. He and Helmsman Gudan escaped death through an open hatchway.

Many amusing stories have been related during the course of this first war against Germany, her submarines, and mines, but the yarn about the fisherman who came into Grimsby towing a German mine with all the horns knocked off happens to be true : he explained that he had smitten these with a boat-hook for safety, as he heard that the projections were the dangerous bits. Another fisherman at night secured his boat to what he thought was a buoy. Dawn showed that it was a German mine.

And the fisherman was still alive.

Since hostilities started we had swept up round our shores 1128 enemy mines up to the end of September, and it is even more wonderful that men and ships of that perilous clearing service should have survived. And using the word "sweeping" in a quite different sense, we still kept making excursions towards Germany and helping ourselves to a few trawlers. Thus at the end of September in one of Commodore Tyrwhitt's sweeps we captured a total of nine and sank two. Such steam trawlers as the *Stuttgart*, *Sophie*, *Burhave*, *Darmstadt*, and others were added to a few days later, when fifteen more trawlers were "fetched", such as *Blumenthal* and *Doktor*

Kingler. By the middle of October we had taken twenty-six of them, and the fish realized £700.

Did Germany ever use the "pigeon post" as we used to employ it from trawlers off the East Anglian coast? It was certainly employed during the autumn of 1915 off the Flemish coast by the smaller submarines of the UB and UC type, for we managed to pick up one bird sent at 11.15 a.m. from 4 miles north of the Middlekerke Buoy (where we have noted were the look-outs against Admiral Bacon's vessels) to the Zeebrugge Seaplane Station, requesting that the lock be ready for entry at 4 p.m. when the submarine was to come in.

The enemy were affected by a certain anxiety about these smaller craft, for on or about October 6 they lost UC-9 which was blown up by her own mines in the southern part of the North Sea. And when we remember that such mines were a boat's weekly cargo, that occasionally the mine would jam in its chute, that we also would countermine ambush areas, it was hardly surprising that Flanders lost some of its boats.

The North Sea was a complicated area in those days. There were German and British minefields, British smacks and steam trawlers, decoys and submarines, German Zeppelins swooping low near the Smith's Knoll, sometimes a British armed trawler carrying a seaplane, but even in October, 1915, one of our "C"-class submarines was co-operating with an armed trawler off the Dogger Bank. Of course the losses of purely peaceable steam and sailing fishing vessels throughout the North Sea had been very heavy, and in spite of the many which we had commandeered for the Navy, and those lost by mines or U-boats, there were still in the North Sea about three hundred and fifty hard at work fishing, and every morning the fish carriers came out from London for the supplies that were destined for Billingsgate.

You never knew where mines could be found after a submarine had worked her way down—say—through the Dover Straits. On October 20 the unarmed, but naval drifter *Star of Buchan* off the Nab was hauling in her nets over the bows when it "grew" heavy and awkward, so the rope was taken to the capstan. Then it became barely possible to lift this weight from the water. Was there a mine thus located 500 yards east of the Nab? Another trap from a submarine that hovered round frequented seamarks?

The answer quickly came. Suddenly as the fishermen toiled, a violent explosion shook the world, the sea was in turmoil, the whole of the ship's fore part was blown away and with it seven men were killed. But when salvage operations were being conducted two days later, another heavy explosion was caused. More men were injured including the diver, and two riggers lost their lives.

Yet still German submarines were not having things entirely their own way. UC-8 was yet another lesson of uncertain losses.

Sent from Kiel to Flanders, this minelayer on the way down past the Dutch coast had the misfortune on November 4 to get ashore off Terschelling among the tides and sandbanks. Although afterwards refloated, the Hollanders interned her and she became merged with the Dutch Navy. So, also, after those trawlers had been brought across the North Sea from Germany, they were fitted out and armed at Lowestoft before being renamed and sent to patrol in the Mediterranean. They became known as the "Seven Deadly Sins" Class, being called *Calumsin, Corinsin, Charlsin,* and so on.

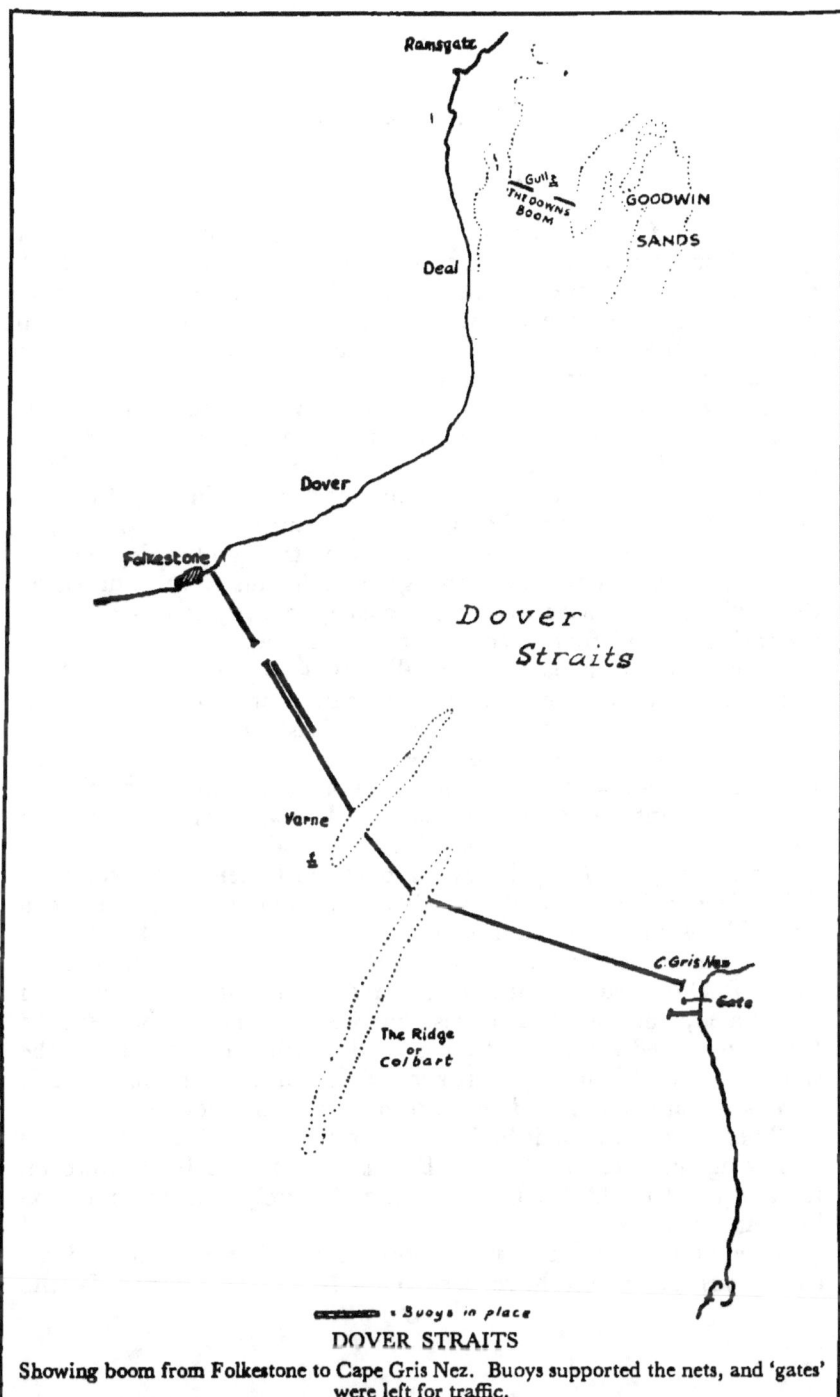

DOVER STRAITS
Showing boom from Folkestone to Cape Gris Nez. Buoys supported the nets, and 'gates' were left for traffic.

CHAPTER 20

IN THE MIDDLE SEA

APART from the fact that that UC-13 (which had been sent from the Adriatic to Constantinople and then to the Black Sea) got ashore and was finished by a Russian destroyer on November 29, no more U-boat sinkings of any sort happened until UC-12 was blown up off Taranto on March 16. We have noted the reason for that in northern Europe.

A new phase was about to open in this war against submarines, for by the end of 1915 an efficient kind of depth charge had been designed and was about to be put aboard our patrols. Their general adoption was necessarily a matter of some time, and the use of bomb-throwers meant that a new important weapon was brought against the U-boat. No other reply availed than by keeping beyond the zone of explosion. But although experiments were initiated on the Firth of Forth with hydrophones early in 1915, it was not until the spring of 1917 that directional types were evolved.

Although British patrols marvelled that for three months there had been a mysterious cessation of submarine activities in the autumn of 1915, yet suddenly during Christmas at 1.35 p.m. the British S.S. *Van Stirum* (3284 tons) was pounced on in the Irish Channel 9 miles west of the Smalls. For a time this ship tried to escape and sent a wireless call, but two U-boats were co-operating against her and she at last foundered.

Still voyaging south, the two U-boats on December 26 sank the S.S. *Ministre Beernart* and the *Cottingham*—the latter having run down UC-2 on the previous second of July. On December 28 was shelled the British oil-tanker *El Zorro* (5989 tons), 10 miles south from the Old Head of Kinsale. Afterwards she was torpedoed and abandoned, but still farther west the S.S. *Huronian* of the Leyland Line was torpedoed about 8 miles south of the Fastnet. It was the sudden arrival from Queenstown of Admiral Bayly in H.M.S. *Adventure* that saved the *Huronian* from further interference.

Then, as quickly as it had started on Christmas Day, this spasm of sinking died down. Why? Because the two U-boats were on their way out to the Mediterranean, and merely took these attacks in their stride.

One of the quaint developments in warfare is that to-day's enemy yesterday may have been our ally and vice versa. In the

Second German War we find the Italy of Mussolini one of the powers against us, but some months after the First War started, Italy decided in a different direction. An uncharitable critic might say that so anxious always is that country to emerge on the winning side that she never makes up her mind till late in events which is to be her partner.

On May 10, 1915, after nine months of hostilities, an Allied Naval Convention was signed whereby British light cruisers with French destroyers and submarines were to join up with Italian light cruisers and destroyers against Germany, but that British battleships were to work with the Italian Battle Fleet. The French Battle Fleet, however, would continue to act independently. When, a few days later, U-21 arrived from Germany and burst her way into the Adriatic, the sharpness of division became even still more accentuated, but it was from May 24 that Italy established a state of war with Austria and Germany.

We are, however, concerned in this, our study, with submarines only. In the late spring and summer of 1915, and subsequent months, we became interested by the attacks from Austrian U-boats up the Adriatic, presently to be strengthened by the coming from northern Europe of the railway-carried small craft from Germany, followed by the seaborne U-21 and other full-sized submarines. In course of time, then, underwater hostilities increased along the Mediterranean north, south, east, and west, but based on Cattaro and Pola.

British, Italian, and French men-of-war quite early and frequently became the targets for Austrian torpedoes, as for instance when H.M.S. *Dublin* was struck on June 9, but limped into Brindisi; when the Italian cruiser *Amalfi* was torpedoed and sunk on July 7; and the Italian cruiser *G. Garibaldi* destroyed in a similar manner. It was because of the submarines passing up and down the Otranto Straits that we sent many drifters out from the North Sea to work their nets.

Frankly the Italian naval units were something of a disappointment to us: they lacked that enterprise which had been expected. Thus on June 12 the Italian submarine *Medusa* became the early victim of UB-15 which by now had been handed over to the Austro-Hungarian Navy.[1] In command of UB-15 was Lieut. von Heimburg, but he and his German crew during July turned over to UB-14 which sank our submarine E-20 in the Dardanelles on November 5. The latter was awaiting the French submarine *Turquoise* in the Sea of Marmara. The Frenchman, meanwhile, had been captured, and UB-14 ingeniously impersonated the craft that should have kept the rendezvous. Von Heimburg was certainly very efficient if ruthless, for already on August 13 whilst on passage from Cattaro to Constantinople he sank the transport *Royal*

---

[1] For a detailed account of Italy's share in the Mediterranean war I would refer to my *Seas of Adventures*.

L

Edward 6 miles west of Kandeliusa in the Aegean. He was wont to hide especially in Orak Bay, 10 miles east of Budrum.

From the autumn of 1915 onwards, U-boats gradually established themselves in the Mediterranean, some of them commencing their hostilities almost as soon as they got inside the Straits of Gibraltar. Amongst other objects, they essayed to thwart the coming of military transports and munition ships to the Aegean, but when the Dardanelles campaign concluded after the first week of January, 1916, the submarine had still British and French and Italian warships, as well as mercantile vessels, for targets. One of the outstanding successes down here was U-35, but even when Kophamel, at the end of 1915, was transferred to Pola in charge of German U-boats, a very remarkable officer replaced him.

This was Lieut.-Commander Arnauld de la Pèriere. His surname of course suggests one of the most historic French families, distinguished in the Navy and other professions. But how came it that one bearing this honoured name should be a German?

The answer is that Lothar Arnauld de la Pèriere's father as an officer in the French Army, took part in the Franco-Prussian War and was made prisoner. After peace he became naturalized, remained in Germany and there married. Of this marriage Lothar was the son who grew up and entered the Kaiser's Navy, specializing in submarines. In the course of this Mediterranean campaign he became not merely famous, but unique as the "ace of aces". For he surpassed everyone else by the tonnage which he destroyed. Thus, for the whole war, his accredited amount is 400,000 tons, then came Forstmann (U-39) with 380,000 tons, and Max Valentiner (U-38) with 300,000 tons. Lothar's technique was quite simple: he relied chiefly on his guns, opening fire from 6000 yards and gradually decreasing to 3000, rarely closing any nearer till he saw the victim abandoned. He had a first-class gunner lent him from the High Sea Fleet. An excellent officer (though hated by his contemporary family connections on the French side), he remained in the Mediterranean and in command of U-35 until the spring of 1918 when he transferred to northern Europe, but in U-139.

After this First German War we pass over a generation and find that in 1941 he rose to the rank of Vice-Admiral, but during that spring when he was once again in the France of his ancestors, he was suddenly killed from the air and at last his brilliant career came to a close.

But we must resume our story in the Mediterranean, and indicate something of the effort which was being made down there by the British Admiralty in the use of special ships that looked the very opposite of their reality. It is true that men-of-war of all sorts were being employed at the Inland Sea, that dockyards of Malta and Gibraltar were being kept busy, that Italian bases in Taranto and Brindisi became crowded because of British warships; nevertheless our principal effort against the enemy's U-boats must be met as the latter came to and from their bases up the Adriatic via the Straits of Otranto. In a general sense, however, the U-boat was liable to be trapped whilst operating along the shipping tracks of the Mediterranean that should be watched. And if armed ships, externally resembling ordinary traders, had gulled whilst near the British Isles, such astute submarine specialists as the captains of U-36, U-27, and U-41, perhaps similar success might also be ours in the Middle Sea.

Now from the autumn of 1915 the British Admiralty resolved to have five of those so-called "Mystery" or Q-ships based on Malta, but cruising separately along the Mediterranean sea-lanes. Of about 4000 tons, externally the most normal sort of "tramp" of the "three-island" design, they concealed at least a couple of 4-inch guns with carefully trained naval personnel disguised as a rough crowd of mariners.

This quintette comprised the steamers *Margit*, *Penhallow*, *Saros*, *Werribee* (alias *Wonganella*), and *Wyandra*, which under the name of *Baralong* had recently added a wonderful chapter to our naval history and driven the Kaiser so frantic with anger that £1000 reward was waiting for her captain's arrest. On August 19 she had sunk U-27 and a month later, U-41 with the neatest effort and in the west of the British Isles. Little did Hersing, Valentiner, and company ever suspect that *Baralong*—of all ships—should be roaming the blue Mediterranean now.

Things really began to happen on January 17, 1916, when the *Margit*, about 9.30 a.m., being 170 miles east of Malta along the Port Said route, intercepted with her wireless the following message: "S O S. . . . Am being shelled. . . . Submarine gaining on me."

From the signals' strength it was evident the drama must be happening not far off. Presently the 4943-ton S.S. *Baron Napier* could be seen 4 miles away, and shells falling all round her.

In accordance with legal ruse, *Margit* now hoisted Dutch ensign as false colours, and her commanding officer (Lieut.-Commander G. L. Hodson, R.N.) took the Q-ship within 2 miles of the visible U-35. The submarine promptly transferred her attentions to *Margit* who, by cleverly edging away, enabled the *Baron Napier* to make a complete escape. Thus the first trick was won by Hodson.

But a veritable deluge of steel was being fired terribly close to *Margit*, both ahead and astern. The disciplined crew never flinched, their commander pretended to abandon ship, hoisted the signal "I am stopped", and sent away his boat with a party representing all hands; yet the guns' crews, plus five riflemen on the foredeck under Sergeant Kelly of Marines, together with Midshipman Hovenden, R.N., and Chief Petty Officer Hines who carried rifles and hid themselves right aft, continued aboard.

Lying prone on the bridge, invisible, though peeping through holes in the canvas screen, Hodson, with suppressed excitement, watched the periscope coming nearer. For the German (having been warned by his Admiralty of the *Baralong* surprises) had temporarily ceased fire, submerged, and began to investigate cautiously.

Eight hundreds yards away! . . . Now only fifty yards! Only 2 feet of periscope showing!

At last, having motored down the port side and then back again, the enemy decided *Margit* was a poor old "tramp" which could be shelled to destruction. The German, therefore, began choosing his distance off the starboard bow, rising to the surface, and then opened the conning tower hatch from which poured three men.

Hodson seized the vital chance, lowered false colours, sent up the White Ensign.

"Down screens!"

And the mystery steamer's guns began barking. Range 700 yards.

The latter was increased to 1100, and the tenth shot looked like a hit: in fact U-35 now hurriedly dived for safety stern first. Gone away! Hodson ordered "Cease fire", waited a while, then steamed to pick up his men in the boat, and the davit falls had barely been hooked on . . .

"There she comes, sir!"

Again that ugly conning tower was breaking surface. Seventy yards away, this time. Most awkward. Too short a range for the guns. However, these were given extreme depression, fire was resumed at a target hardly visible. *Margit* rolled lazily to the swell. Boom! Crash!

Hines' starboard foremost gun seemed to have registered a hit immediately, but most unluckily through being fired at such depression it dismounted itself, fell on this C.P.O. and killed him.

The U-boat delayed no longer, fled below, some days later reached her base up the Adriatic, and on January 29 Germany's wireless broadcast the episode with the usual additional untruths. But this, of course, merely showed the intense annoyance that the enemy had been robbed of his prey by another dirty old "tramp".

A few days later—February 9—the Q-ship *Werribee* (3848 tons) under Lieut.-Commander B. J. D. Guy, R.N., was steaming along that same busy route, when about 9 a.m. she picked out of the air this pathetic message from the 5593-ton S.S. *Springwell*: "Torpedoed and sinking by the head. Position Lat. 34.10 N., Long. 23.10 E."

At once Guy set forth at full speed towards the spot which on the chart was worked out as 20 miles away. More than occasionally a merchant vessel happened to be a little bit wrong in her reckoning, and so it was so to-day. Presently *Werribee* sighted on the starboard bow in Lat. 34.12 N., Long. 22.56 E. a steamer obviously in difficulties down by the head, listing to port, her boats just leaving.

Sure enough this turned out to be *Springwell*. Coming up amid the boats, Guy hailed the master and inquired:

"Where's the enemy?"

The naval vessel was flying the Red Ensign, and guns' crews were at their stations, hidden, but ready.

"Sighted her last close alongside," came the answer, "half an hour after torpedoing us."

Guy was certain the German could not be far away. Without stopping engines, the former went near the *Speedwell's* stern to read her present draught. Later he would come back and try salving, provided she had not sunk more deeply.

"Look out!"

All of a sudden—5000 yards from the starboard bow—there burst through the sea's polished surface a great whale-like hull, 210 feet long and 20 feet wide. It was Max Valentiner's U-38, painted that brownish-green which the Austrian Navy used to employ for camouflage. Strange apparition on this lovely calm day, with blue sky and the air so clear that the coast of Crete, some 60 miles northeastward, was in sight.

German bluejackets ran to get ready their two deck guns, whose first couple of rounds fell 50 and 20 yards "over", and the third struck *Werribee* right aft, riddling both of her lifeboats. Valentiner's plan was by extremely accurate and rapid fire to knock out the second English ship as he had the first.

But already Guy had sounded "Alarm" stations, and it was going to be a deadly duel. One smart captain matching his wits against the other. Both conceding nothing. And the Briton knew it were useless to attempt the abandon-ship tactics here. Only thing to do was to put up a straight fight.

The U-boat remained on his beam, distant 4000 yards, when the *Werribee* broke out White Ensign and ten seconds later began action with the 4-inch quickfirer. Then, with cinema-like celerity, Valentiner received the shock of his life.

"Accursed trap ship! Those damnable Englishmen!"

The first few shots had fallen short of the camouflaged "whale", the sixth silenced her gunners, the eighth struck abaft the conning tower, so that she heeled towards the *Werribee* and at 11.10 a.m. in a cloud of smoke dived quickly to avoid most certain death. For Guy's men, having got the range exactly and with such advantage of height, could scarce have avoided dropping shells in the right spot each time.

Startled and wounded, U-38 only just cheated doom, wisely not daring to surface. Thus did one more of the "star turns" learn that Germania could not rule the waves. Now one skipper by purest chance watched this short, sharp, contest from beginning to end.

The master of the S.S. *Bakana*, which happened to be passing quite near, he simply could not believe his eyes as he saw "an old tramp with a few patches of paint" hurling terror into a tyrant. But nothing could save *Springwell*, which foundered that afternoon.

In those days the unexpected became almost part of life's routine. On April 4, H.M.S. *Wallflower* (one of those flower-class, small cruisers) during less than half an hour tasted enough excitement to last a long commission. She was travelling along the track between Malta and Cape Matapan when, without warning at 11.12 a.m., two periscopes of a submarine momentarily rose on the port beam and then dipped. Out gushed a silver torpedo, and straight it sped. Only by quickly putting helm hard astarboard did *Wallflower* dodge the missile which passed 15 yards astern.

They were smart people in that sloop. Lieut.-Commander Guy Livingston, R.N., her captain, went full speed towards the enemy's estimated position and dropped a depth charge. Curiously, this bomb did not explode and *Wallflower* cruised about the spot in tense wonder. Next, apparently without any reason, the charge burst at 11.35 sending up a great column of water 20 feet high. Evidently the depth-charge originally fell on to the U-boat's deck whilst the latter was stationary, but when she moved to avoid *Wallflower*, off jerked the bomb and it was detonated.

This submarine was either U-34 or U-39, but you can imagine what sort of a nerve shaking up her crew suffered.

Eight days passed, and now it was for *Wyandra* (*Baralong*) that events awaited. Her new captain, Lieut. F. M. Simon, R.N., an hour before midnight, steaming by the south of Sicily and zig-zagging at 11 knots, looked out over the sea that glistened under a bright moon.

Something away beyond the port bow flashed. Then again. Shells began to flop into the surrounding water, some falling so near as 50 yards. The Q-ship wasted no time, guessed the almost invisible object to be a submarine, estimated her as 3000 yards away, and by the time the German had fired six shots *Wyandra* replied with five. Then sudden peace again. Why?

Neither party knew the other's identity, but Simon did take note that his ship's fifth shell (which apparently caused the enemy's discontinuance) burst with particular brightness. Nothing further occurred until seven the next morning near the Messina Straits, when the respective foes sighted each other, both having made good during the dark hours at 10 knots. Shots were exchanged, Simon gave chase, the U-boat dived at 7.40 but came up again five minutes later.

This confirmed Simon's suspicions that she had been too badly damaged for long submergence, and though the separating distance was 6000 yards—3 sea miles—*Wyandra* tried very hard to give the knock-out blow. Nineteen rounds the steamer fired, till the German dived again, altered course below water, and finally by sheerest luck passed through the Otranto Straits to her Austrian base.

Not till years afterwards, by collating all the facts, dates, and times, did I discover that this submarine was the historic U-21 which previously had sunk H.M.S. *Pathfinder* in the North Sea; *Triumph* and *Majestic* at the Dardanelles; and the French *Amiral Charner* in the Mediterranean. Otto Hersing did not know this April night (and probably has not since learnt) that it was Germany's most hated enemy *Baralong*, whose fifth shell exploded on impact with such effulgence. But he will never forget that three pieces of it struck him in the face and drew blood; that he then ordered a smoke-screen, and dived into obscurity. This was Hersing's first (and I believe only) encounter with a trap ship, and he didn't like the experience. "We ran for dear life," he admitted.

Gradually this Mediterranean campaign grew so important that many other U-boats, including minelayers, were sent south from Germany; but our enemies found that when once we had begun to employ the convoy system, the number of our shipping losses diminished and the submarines could attack only with slender hope of emerging alive.

Ruthlessness is a most dangerous game to play on the sea, for when blind justice after long patience demands that the penalty be paid, the culprit suffers bitterly. One of these Mediterranean U-boat captains, whose name I have, was little better than a pirate. Before sinking an unarmed steamer, he nearly always sent a party aboard to remove all portable provisions and articles of value. Thus in fifteen months he collected a hundred chronometers, large quantities of champagne, whisky, and tinned foods, which he distributed among his personal friends in Austria and Germany.

Occasionally he gave some tinned beef and cheaper food to his crew, who showed heated resentment at his meanness and took to pilfering, wherefore the Kapitan-leutnant threatened to have the delinquents court-martialled. Defiance, however, made him think again of his own shortcomings, and the matter dropped. Some time later he was appointed to another command, sudden and terrible danger overtook this submarine, many of his crew went down with her though miraculously he was among the rescued and became a British prisoner. I wonder whether after hostilities his conscience ever gave him respite?

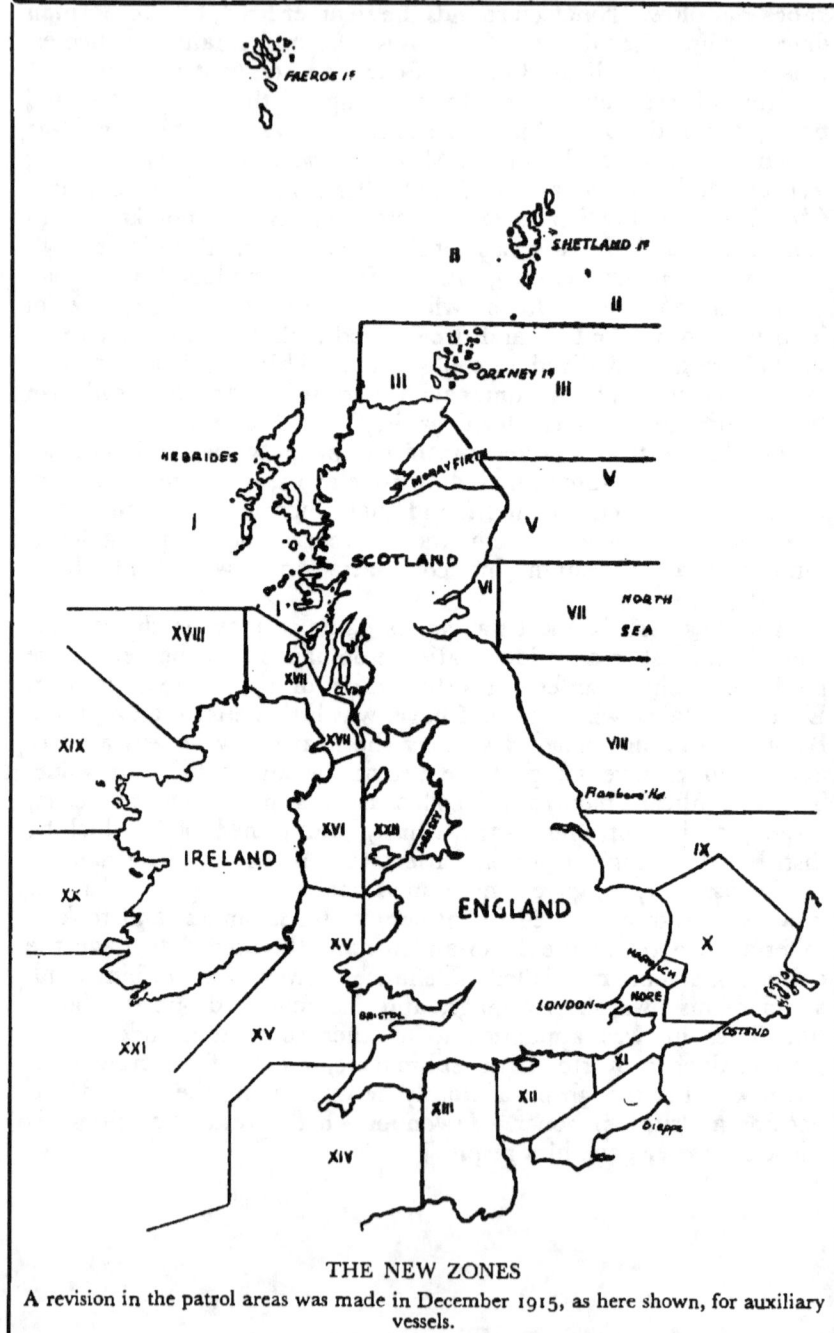

THE NEW ZONES

A revision in the patrol areas was made in December 1915, as here shown, for auxiliary vessels.

CHAPTER 21

AMERICA INTERVENES

WITH nerves keyed up, no one could relax, for the unexpected was never far away.
So the men in the *James Fletcher* realized all of a sudden. She happened to be neither private yacht, nor passenger ship, not even a cargo carrier. The Admiralty had taken her up from the Lancashire and Western Sea Fisheries Joint Committee, armed and commissioned her, appointed Lieut.-Commander E. L. B. Boothby, R.N., in command, and she began patrolling the Dover Straits. Of 263 tons (gross) she was less than ten years old, and her twin propellers gave her that handiness which she might need very badly.

But nothing ever seemed likely to occur. All these weeks were just the same, one season melted into another. Life was so uneventful.

On the night of January 11, 1916, the *James Fletcher* was about $1\frac{1}{2}$ miles southwest of the South Goodwins Lightship, patrolling towards the northeast alert for any of those U-boats which sought to work their way through the Dover Barrage of nets. Midnight had passed, Lieut.-Commander Boothby was off watch below in his bunk, the bridge being in charge of Sub-Lieut. N. O. Burnham, R.N.R. Fresh breeze, choppy sea, night black as an elephant.

It was just about quarter to one when Burnham distinctly heard voices, which surprised him more than a little. They seemed to be off the starboard bow somewhere. Instantly his keen eyesight descried the conning tower of a submarine well above water, and two or three men standing on deck. Ten yards away. No further.

The *James Fletcher* was quietly doing her sentry job at 4 knots: the enemy was trying to rush the Straits at 12 knots. Thus, before anybody could alter course or do anything at all, a mighty wallop of a collision occurred. The first blow caught the German abaft her conning tower, then followed an ugly grating noise for about two seconds duration as hull rasped against hull; next came another crash as the steamship smote violently against the submarine's tail —with such force as practically to stop all way on the patrol vessel and cause the stranger to heel over at an alarming angle.

They say that sailors, like watchful dogs, sleep with one eye open. The sudden impact almost threw Lieut.-Commander

Boothby out of his bunk, and he raced on deck with night-glasses, focused them in time to observe the submarine's form now 150 yards away but off the ship's quarter.

"Full ahead !" he rang down the engine-telegraphs, sent up a red rocket to attract the other patrols, and the twin screws turned *James Fletcher* quickly in the direction where intruder had last been sighted. Range of visibility was small, yet the atmosphere clear. Unfortunately no moon illumined the leaden waters.

In answer to the rocket signal, several drifters and a couple of destroyers arrived to join in the search. They combed the area with thoroughness during that middle watch, they went down the tide, against the tide ; east, north, west, and south. Dawn broke. No submarine. But as the light got stronger the drifter *Cosmos* came across a patch of oil some 20 yards wide and a 100 yards long, south-west of the lightship. No mistaking this oil "slick", for whilst everywhere else the wind against tide lashed water into broken waves, here the surface was smooth as glass.

They never found that submarine, but when *James Fletcher* was brought into Dover's tidal basin and examined, distinct signs of collision were evident on the hull. Five days after the event, a dockyard diver went down to the spot SW. of the lightship, groped about on the bed, came up, and reported the presence there of a submarine. His report being accepted as conclusive, the Admiralty rewarded *James Fletcher's* people with the sum of £1000. It was believed that this U-boat, bound west down Channel, must have been the one which broke through our line of explosive nets and tore away two nets plus mines near the North Goodwins, but for all that probably she did not sink. There is much wreckage near the South Goodwins.

Yes : the unexpected had become almost routine. Only three months after *James Fletcher's* first submarine suprise, the S.S. *Shenandoah* seemed to be making her way up the English Channel quite nicely. Soon be safe in port now, already she had the land aboard, and Folkestone lay only 1½ miles to the eastward. But at that moment she hit a mine which a U-boat had laid.

To the steamer's assistance hurried the armed trawler *Macfarlane* (Lieut. A. H. Barnes, R.N.R.).

"Put your helm hard astarboard," the latter hailed, "and we'll beach her."

The Master complied, but ere the shore could be gained down she sank. Promptly Barnes lowered his own boat to the rescue, picked up two of *Shenandoah's* boats, and was searching the tideway for any other survivors when the *Macfarlane* came across a third boat, but bottom up. Three men were clinging desperately to it, and he rescued them, another trio were close by hanging on to wreckage and these also he saved.

Then somebody said :

"Underneath the capsized boat . . . men inside . . . I can hear them knocking."

Here, then, was a big problem. Boat drifting with the tide, and its occupants imprisoned. What to do? How to get them out?

Anyone who has tried righting a dinghy at sea knows how difficult is the task. But a heavy ship's lifeboat? Barnes realized the problem, hailed another armed trawler—the *Returno*—and ordered her alongside.

Then they put a tackle on to one side of the boat, hove away, persuaded it to come right over on to its keel, and behold two of *Shenandoah's* personnel, more than half-dead, were discovered. Wireless operator and a fireman. They had given up all hope, and soon would have breathed their last. The Admiralty much admired Lieut. Barnes' "coolness and resource", sent him their appreciation in writing.

The attacks against Lowestoft sailing (unarmed) fishing smacks still continued in the New Year. Once Skipper James Crooks of the ketch *Acacia*, which had come out of Lowestoft was at his job about 28 miles southeast of Lowestoft in company of several other smacks. It was 10.30 p.m. on January 17 with a fairly fresh breeze blowing from the southwest, when suddenly Crooks saw a submarine making straight for the *Acacia* and from a mile distant the German opened fire sending machine-gun bullets on board in all directions, damaging sails as well as rigging.

Skipper Crooks watched the approaching enemy, and evidently the latter just now suspected every sailing trawler that came out of Lowestoft. But the Englishman was watching and waiting, for in his previous ship he had been sunk by a submarine in August, 1915, but now resolved not to be taken again. So, waiting his chance, the Lowestoft man with a mighty blow chopped away the trawl rope, put his helm hard up, and went straight for the submarine. The effect of this sudden freedom was that the sailing ship leaped for the submarine as it might have been a tiger pouncing on his enemy. It put fear into the German, missed him by only a few feet, and whilst the latter sought safety in diving, the *Acacia* trimmed sheets and escaped in the darkness of night nearly as fast as the other could be driven by Diesels, though about 1 p.m. next day three of these smacks were sunk by the enemy in the neighbourhood. She had a fish's head painted on the bow in red and white, with two fins coloured black.

It was not merely in such ways as Q-ships and decoy sailing smacks, in tramp steamers and armed trawlers, that the enemy was being put off his guard. Some of our patrol vessels had an efficient manner of concealing a gun by using a condemned boat. The latter was cut and the hinged sides could be dropped apart, the flattened surface within forming the gun platform.

In an earlier chapter we saw that submarine attacks in the

Narrow Seas had cooled off, but meanwhile Britain during the winter of 1915–1916 had been busy arming her merchant ships defensively. This sensible procedure infuriated the Germans who sent a Note to the United States stating that on and after March 1, 1916, such vessels would be treated as warships, so from that date we find Germany resuming her former submarine campaign. It looked, then, as if our enemy would now be able to behave on the sea just as submarine commanders wished, and that respect for American feelings would be ignored. Barely, however, was this decision enforced than before that month ended there occurred a dramatic incident within the English Channel.

For on March 24 the S.S. *Sussex*, whilst crossing the Channel, was at 4.30 p.m. torpedoed in Lat. 50.42 N., Long. 1.11 E., the bows being completely blown off as far as the foremast. Many American passengers were on board at the time, several being killed. This again raised the question of relations between the United States and Germany. The *New York World* asked "whether anything is to be gained by maintaining any longer the ghastly pretence of friendly diplomatic correspondence with a power notoriously lacking in truth and honour."[1]

The late Admiral Scheer,[2] commenting on this incident, remarked:

> "The American Government took occasion, in consequence of this incident, to send a very sharp Note to the German Government protesting against the wrongfulness of the submarine campaign against commerce. It threatened to break off diplomatic relations with Germany. . . . As a result of this Note, presented on April 20th, 1916, our Government decided to give in and sent orders to the Naval Staff to the effect that submarine warfare was henceforward to be carried in on accordance with Prize Law. This order reached the Fleet by wireless telegraphy when it was on its way to bombard Lowestoft (April 25th, 1916). As war waged according to Prize Law by U-boats in the waters around England could not possibly have any success. . . . I recalled all the U-boats by wireless, and announced that the U-boat campaign against British commerce had ceased."

As a fact no further sinkings by the U-boats in home waters occurred after May 8 until July 5 and 8 : two months, that is to say. Meanwhile the Submarine War in the Mediterranean continued.

The isolation of Germany was therefore impossible as a working proposition : she must come into line with recognized civilized standards or rue the bad results. We have seen the whole trouble

---

[1] It is pertinent to observe how similar were the remarks criticising Germany made in the American Press of 1915 and 1916 to those made in the years 1940 and 1941.
[2] *Germany's High Sea Fleet*, page 242.

HOW GUNS WERE HIDDEN

This shows how, by means of a ship's boat, by lockers, or other device, the gun was rendered invisible to the enemy

beginning with the sinking of *Lusitania*, intensified with the treatment of *Arabic*, and still more affected by the *Sussex*. Actually very few sinkings by torpedoes occurred in Home Waters until September. Why did figures now begin to rise again?

The reason was that after the failure of the Battle of Jutland, and the realization that victory on the sea against England would rest on U-boats rather than the High Sea Fleet, it was no good looking in a wrong direction. Germany had blundered from the first by her political policy, by not having the prevision to realize how one set of circumstances would bring about certain results; but in perceiving the most obvious truths she remained blind wilfully—until too late. Either she must carry on the Submarine War in accordance with the rules, i.e. before sinking a ship the U-boat must rise to the surface, stop the vessel, examine her papers, and allow all passengers and crew to leave in safety—or else the war vessel must ruthlessly sink at sight and keep on sinking ships all the while wherever there was an opportunity.

Germany therefore cast international prudence to the winds, and in so deciding she could not have chosen more foolishly. The United States entered the war officially within a year later.

From September, 1916 (when the blunt resolve to "go all out" unconditionally, by means of U-boats, became the leading motive) until April, 1917 (when the peak of submarine warfare was reached and began to drop) the amount of British seaborne mercantile tonnage increased gradually from 42,553 tons to 516,394 tons, with a slight temporary falling in November, 1916, to 36,672 tons.

Can we not see that Nazi Germany in this war that began in 1939 made the same strategical error leading to the same disastrous end?

It is curious, however, to note how generous were some of the mistakes made by the Admiralty. In the employment of those Lowestoft armed smacks a big monetary award was given hardly in full accord with the facts. Thus, although on March 6, 1916, as many as four German submarines were sighted about 40 miles EbyS. of Lowestoft and three of them were engaged, two at least being thought to have been hit (the Skipper of *Fame* being given a D.S.C. and £1000 being divided among the crew), no longer is the loss of any submarine in any part of the world on that date credited.

In any war similar scenes may be the areas of contention. Just as the year 1941 brought to our minds continuous fighting along the North African coast, so with the Navy's co-operation the first stage in the reoccupation of the Egyptian coast line west of Marsa Matruh was in the first week of March, 1916, completed. Sloops, trawlers, and supplies arrived off Barrani, but visits to that coast from U-boats had certainly been daringly made. On March 14 Sollum was occupied, the Navy moving with the advancing columns to support the soldiers.

With the German U-boats in the Mediterranean thus extending

the war to Africa ; with both German and Austro-Hungarian craft developing the Adriatic zone ; the Dardanelles and Aegean were by no means the only busy war areas. In the Adriatic Flotilla was serving UC-12 which on March 17 was laying mines off the entrance to the Italian harbour of Taranto. She had indeed succeeded in laying eight such explosives in position, when she was blown up by a terrible incident in a spot 20 fathoms deep. The probable cause of disaster was that the safety catch was not acting. All the mines were subsequently brought to land, including two found aboard her, and two seen from a kite-balloon. Thus UC-12 instead of laying a trap for battleships emerging from harbour, blew herself up in two halves which lying among the clear waters of Italy were easily visible and presently could be salved.

Thus had Lieut. E. Fröhner and his crew passed beyond the sphere of contention to frightful destiny. But with the return to Northern Europe of this resuscitated U-boat menace came also a new confidence, for in just over five weeks were sunk five more German submarines. One enemy loss practically every seven days. Could we expect anything more wonderful than this?

We must examine the five individually.

CHAPTER 22

GERMAN DEVICE

WHEN the two successes of *Baralong* against submarines south of Ireland ; when also the enthusiasm of naval officers, and the support given by Admiral Bayly ; produced a new phase against the enemy, curious developments were apparent in the disguised Q-ships and "slovenly" dressed crews which now went to sea in armed, but apparently innocent, tramp-steamers and colliers. In September, 1916, there were taken up, fitted out, and commissioned the 3207 ton S.S. *Lodorer*, and 2917-ton S.S. *Zylpha*, but others followed.

The return of spring, coinciding with the new offensive in March, 1916, brought a new purpose : time had also afforded the chance for constructive thinking-out of anti-submarine measures. We will confine ourselves to the *Lodorer* which was commanded by Lieut.-Commander Gordon Campbell, R.N., and was sent from Devonport to work under Sir Lewis Bayly at Queenstown. On the way across she changed her name to *Farnborough*, and throughout that long trying winter had cruised thousands of miles without any luck. It was exactly a repetition of what had happened to Lieut.-Commander Herbert in *Baralong*.

March came in like a lion off the west of Ireland, and on the 21st at least one large submarine was prowling about the coast seeking whom he might devour. The S.S. *Aranmore* fell a victim. Next morning at 6.40 *Farnborough* came steaming along at 8 knots when about 5 miles away she espied U-68 awash. Commanded by Lieut.-Commander Güntzel, she was one of those who had specialized in the Western Approaches area, having previously sunk shipping off the Scillies. It was U-68 also who had escorted over the North Sea the raider *Möwe* when the latter just after Christmas, 1915, started out on her first ocean raiding voyage.

A desperate person, Güntzel fired a torpedo after twenty minutes —but missed the *Farnborough*, which stopped, blew off steam, and "abandoned ship" in the manner so previously well rehearsed. Commander Campbell and his gun crews were waiting concealed at their stations, whilst the German closed to 800 yards on the surface and again fired.

This was the psychological moment, whereupon Campbell dropped all disguise, replied with her three 12-pounders, and hit the enemy several times so that U-68 disappeared. Then steaming at full speed (only 9 knots) *Farnborough* let go a depth charge, and immediately the submarine rose from the sea almost perpendicularly with a large gash in her bows. At close range five more rounds were fired into the conning tower, so that again the boat disappeared. And for the last time (though to make doubly sure) two more depth charges were loosed off, whereupon over the sea spread much oil and many pieces of cabin panelling.

U-68 with all her men numbering thirty-eight, became a total loss; Campbell was given promotion and a D.S.O., whilst £1000 came to the ship. The sinking of this submarine laid the foundation for Commander Campbell's career as our "ace of aces" among Q-ships, but it also raised so much enthusiasm among other naval officers that service in such vessels was eagerly sought.

On the last day of this March the enemy started a new idea of frightfulness. His main intention being that of crippling us as an island nation, he therefore resolved to cut our service of the sea. But how? He was trying very hard by sinking our cargo-carriers, but so far that did not hold out complete promise. So what?

When the S.S. *Goldmouth* was torpedoed 60 miles WNW. of Ushant at 2.30 p.m., the U-boat allowed the survivors to escape in the boats, except the Master. Him they took prisoner and retained on board the submarine, for detention in Germany would prevent his professional help afloat. This was the first known instance of a U-boat making such a capture, but later from other ships the Chief Engineer was also taken. Sometimes on the contrary it was the German crew who became captive, and that very shortly after setting out from home.

Take UB-26 for instance. Under Lieut. W. Smiths she left the Ems at 3.30 p.m. on March 19, 1916, and went slowly down the coast past Holland, keeping about 3 miles off the land and using the cloak of a long night. At 10.30 a.m. of March 21 she reached Zeebrugge, entered the lock, and after three hours arrived in Bruges There, having loaded stores, she left again and proceeded at the end of the month down Channel beyond Dover Straits to Havre. Now the visits of submarines to that port were becoming so frequent that some British drifters were sent from England with their nets.

The Germans loved to lie in wait near the Whistling Buoy in Havre roads to trap steamers bringing to France munitions of war. On the morning of April 5, 1916, UB-26 was somewhere in that neighbourhood, so half a dozen of these net drifters—*Endurance, Welcome Star, Stately, Comrades, Pleiades,* and *Pleasance*—commanded by Lieut. J. M'Loughlin, R.N.R., went to shoot their nets near the buoy. Nor had they long to wait for the *Comrades* felt the curious shock of something bumping the ship's bottom. Next it was the *Endurance*, which realized without a doubt that a submarine had got into her nets.

As if to dispel the slightest uncertainty, the submarine poked her periscope violently upward so that it struck the *Endurance's* rudder with such force as to knock the steering out of action. The British toilers of the sea were now acting as one man angling for a fish who plays the game with some skill, sometimes yielding, sometimes holding his own. By paying out the nets, *Endurance* allowed the submarine to become thoroughly wrapped up in the tangle of netting, and then the fishing crew let the bundle go.

In response to *Endurance's* signal the other drifters surrounded this complicated mass, and a French torpedo boat obliged by coming to drop bombs. This was more than Lieut. Smiths could tolerate, so the German was compelled to rise along the surface and surrender with all hands. Both Lieut. M'Loughlin and Skipper T. C. Wylie of the *Endurance* were given the D.S.C., whilst the usual £1000 was divided among the drifters.

Now in the North Sea we managed to teach the enemy that their U-boats were playing a risky game, even when none of our warships happened to be in sight. It was on April 1 that Captain F. Beeching was bringing the S.S. *Cromer* from the Hook of Holland bound for Tilbury. One of those Great Eastern Railway steamers which pluckily carried on despite all the threats of Germany's submarines. A fine night, spring-like, clear, though dark. Time, just after 11 p.m. and the Maas Lightship (off the Dutch coast) half a dozen miles still to the westward.

Suddenly the form of a U-boat revealed itself beyond the starboard bow. A favourite locality this. Whether lurking about for mercantile victims, or on passage between Germany and their Flanders base, submarines often used this lightship for fixing their position. But Beeching was too wide awake to have his ship torpedoed like others, and his mind reacted instantly. The railway steamer was travelling at 13½ knots. More rapidly than the low-lying craft could move along the surface, except in a calm.

"Hard aport!" he ordered the quartermaster.

"Hard aport, sir," the man obeyed.

"Now then, steady . . . steady as she goes."

"Steady as she goes, sir."

A few tense seconds. Then a dull, heavy bump.

From out of the darkness a chariot-shaped conning tower seemed to leap at the steamer, a great commotion had arisen, a German officer was bellowing out commands, the *Cromer's* steel stem had clashed against steel, then the U-boat had slid along the steamer's starboard bow. Just that—nothing more. For the blow had been a glancing one; to ram with exactness and without adequate warning is, as we have so often noted, always a difficult manoeuvre.

So the steamer raced on without stopping, glad to have saved herself from destruction, but leaving one hostile craft with a

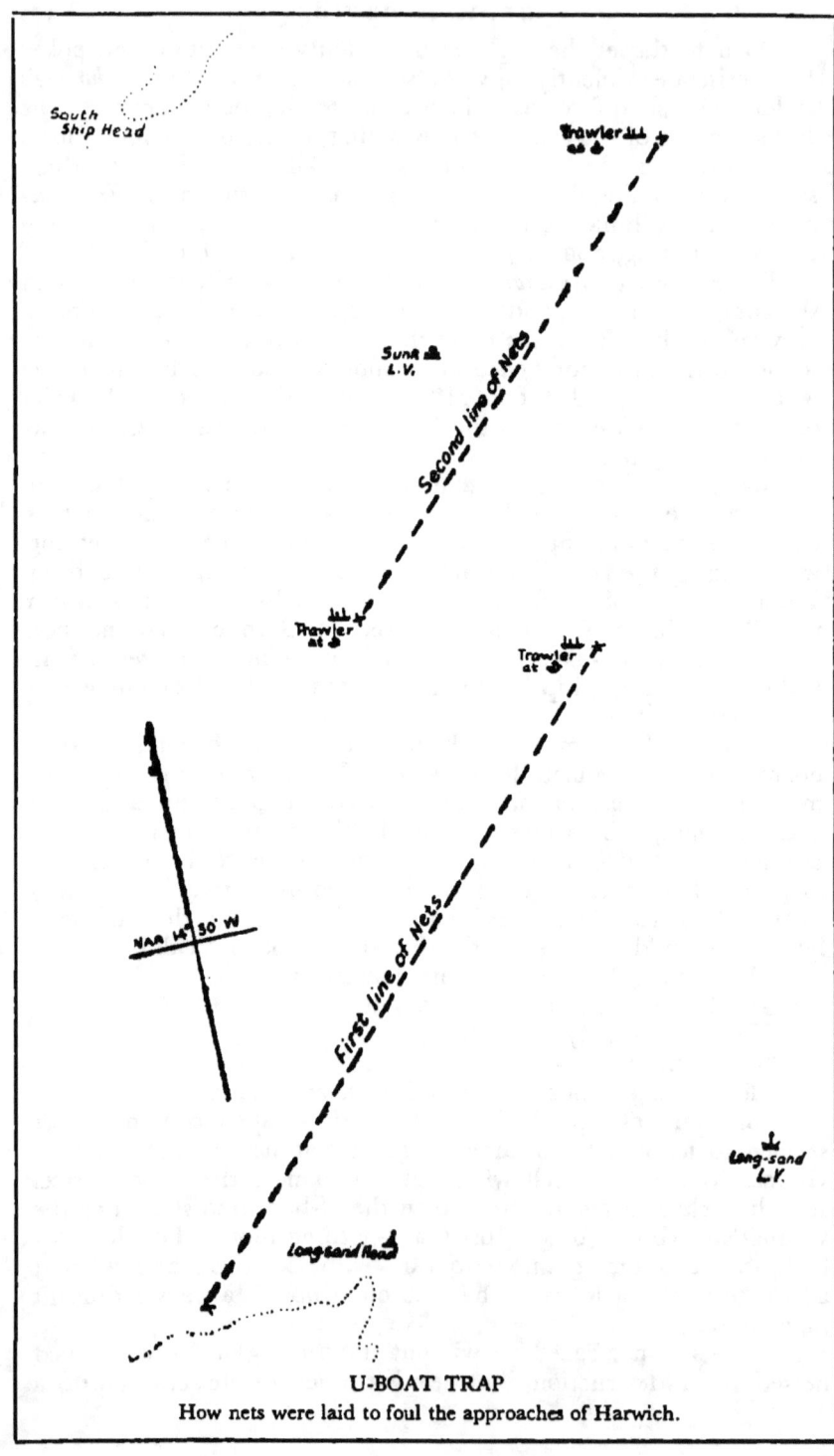

U-BOAT TRAP
How nets were laid to foul the approaches of Harwich.

reminder that every unarmed merchantman has in her forefoot a powerful defensive weapon. You can imagine something of the Teutonic excitement when the submarine developed a violent temporary list, and all hands imagined their final moment had arrived. Those men in future would never quite recover from the blow.

When, presently, in an English port and dry dock, an examination was also made of this steamer, plenty of visible proof on the starboard side 18 inches below waterline, as well as along the starboard bilge-keel 9 feet below, sufficed to convince the most sceptical.

That was why Captain Beeching was given a D.S.C., and the sum of £750, whilst £250 was awarded to the crew. Yet no U-boat was sunk.

This April brought no permanent good to Germany, though with diabolical scheming she tried to take fullest advantage of political treachery. It was the month when disaffection in Ireland was approaching its zenith and a Sinn Fein revolution had been planned for Easter Monday, April 24. This is what actually happened.

On April 9 Germany despatched from Kiel a steamer with a cargo of rifles, bombs, cartridges, trench tools, surgical dressings, and other warlike stores ready to assist the rising in Ireland. This cargo was camouflaged on the top by tin baths, enamelled steelware, window-frames, and the like, in case a British blockade ship should examine her. Also the steamer (whose real name was *Castro*) had been given the name *Aud* with faked logs, certificates, manifests pretending that she was Norwegian, whose colours were painted on her hull. Actually the *Castro* (1228 tons) was one of the Wilson liners trading from Hull and had fallen into German hands at the beginning of the war.

Hidden manholes, dummy bulkheads, concealed entrances, were all added and Lieut. Karl Spindler of the German Naval Reserve appointed in command. She came over the North Sea, passed through the blockade off the north of Scotland, down the west of Ireland, but Spindler was not aware that the British Navy knew all about him and had been shadowing the *Aud*. Thus on April 20 she passed near the River Shannon's mouth and next afternoon (Good Friday) was seized by H.M.S. *Bluebell* and *Zinnia*. The former then escorted *Aud* as captive towards Queenstown, but at 9.25 a.m., just outside that harbour on Saturday, Spindler stopped engines, lowered boats with his crew, and blew up the gun-runner so that she sank. Thus Germany's material help did not reach the rebels.

But it had been part of the German-Irish plan that Sir Roger Casement, the notorious renegade who had settled in Germany, should reach the west coast the same time as *Aud*. He therefore left Kiel about April 12 in the submarine U-19, and should have made contact with *Aud* on the night of April 20 one mile NW of

Inishtooskert, an uninhabited island at the NW. end of Tralee Bay. A proper muddle ensued. U-19 was sighted in the darkness, bows on, and mistaken for a British destroyer! The night passed and during the early hours of Good Friday this Casement, despairing of *Aud's* arrival, landed in a small collapsible boat from U-19.

This black-bearded stranger was seen by a girl named Mary Gorman, who informed the Royal Irish Constabulary. From that moment Casement sealed his own fate. He proceeded to the local railway station, but an officer sent by Admiral Bayly (Commander-in-Chief at Queenstown) arrived there, too. Casement at first denied identity, tried to rid himself of a secret code for communicating with Germany, but a boy picked up the paper and gave it to the police. So Casement soon found himself sent as prisoner to England and on trial in Bow Street. The following August he was hanged at Pentonville Prison. Thus did a curious, mad, visionary who had once been a British Consul end his career.

As everyone knows to-day, the rebellion could not begin in western Ireland, but it did break out in Dublin on Easter Monday. What the public scarcely realizes is the further co-operation which Germany planned in the usual effort to upset our nerves and throw British measures into confusion. It was a wicked, foolish, complicated plot, lacking any strategic sense, yet well expressive of the German bullying mentality.

The *Aud* expedition and the voyage of U-19 had merely made us a present of some interesting prisoners, though the Kaiser's admirals were still kept unawares. The enemy now imagined that synchronization of events over the North Sea would intimidate us. On the night of Easter Monday Germany therefore sent a Zeppelin to drop bombs on East Anglia. At 4 a.m. on Easter Tuesday a German naval force comprising four battle-cruisers, six light cruisers, and a flotilla of destroyers, arrived off Lowestoft and Yarmouth, did a brief spectacular bombardment, damaging house property to the extent of £36,000, killing also four people. The sudden appearance, however, of British light cruisers and destroyers from Harwich caused the enemy to rush away in a hurry.

Not only had the Germans failed to do their cause any good, but they paid such an excessive price as to lose by this expedition. For, on the way out, their crack battle-cruiser *Seydlitz* (25,000 tons) struck a mine, which killed eleven of her crew, made a big hole into which 1400 tons of water poured, and with difficulty she returned home to spend a long period in dockyard hands. That night, too, a Zeppelin raid was effected over Essex and Kent, which likewise had no sort of result on the war.

The "best laid schemes of men" turned out curiously unfruitful.

If, however, the Flemish submarines no longer were mystery craft, they were still persistent pests to our shipping. And the Smith's Knoll Pillar Buoy area still the danger zone.

Behold, then, the smack *Cheero* on April 23, 1916, coming out of harbour and at 5.45 p.m. being some 10 miles northeast of the usual Smith's Knoll Buoy. She was commanded by Lieut. W. F. Scott, R.N.R., who had under him two Petty Officers, and one Leading Seaman as fighting crew; whilst fishing Skipper, Second Hand, and three deck hands were responsible for the handling of *Cheero* with her nets.

Actually the latter were now of special design, being fitted with mines, and it had been found that with 600 yards of these nets towing astern, the smack could still sail ahead at 3 knots. From for'ard of the smack a bridle, made out of a trawler's warp, was stopped down the towing wire, so that it would look exactly as if a genuine smack were working her trawl. All that the men desired was that some submarine should get foul of these nets.

At the above-mentioned hour, wind being light and the weather foggy, nets were shot and connected with an electric battery. The only neighbouring vessel was the steam trawler *King Stephen*. Now the *Cheero* had been fitted with a hydrophone and thus for more than an hour she could hear the slow steady throb of reciprocating engines. Suddenly at 7 p.m. a totally different noise overlaid this sound: a quick, buzzing, unmistakeable indication of a submarine. And increasing momentarily, whilst that of *King Stephen* grew fainter. And now it was 7.40 p.m.

Ting! Tong! Pang!

The wire leading to the nets immediately became tight as a piano, stretched to its limit and bearing a terrible strain. Then it eased a little and became again rigid. Without further warning an awful explosion burst in the mine-nets, the sea rose 20 feet in the air, and just as the water was calming off went another upheaval sending up heavy oil.

Ten minutes. Crew were waiting at their stations ready for the next development, but nothing happened, wherefore Lieut. Scott ordered the nets to be hauled. At first the meshes came aboard easily, then so heavy was the strain as to require six instead of two men. And, next, the weight took a sharp angle down from the ship's side as if tumbling out before getting free. Small pieces of steel were recovered, others flopped back into the sea, and the smell of oil became more foul. Yes! and now it was evident that one of the of the net-mines had exploded.

Further examination proved that unquestionably the submarine had taken nets down to the sea-bed (150 feet deep), for bits of seaweed were still clinging. So, finally, Lieut. Scott burnt a flare to attract *King Stephen* who marked the place with one of his fishing buoys. Three days later, as it was too deep for a diver to work, minesweepers were sent to the spot who located the German. She turned out to be UC-3 (Lieut. G. Kreysern), which had been a busy minelayer off the East and southeast coasts. Since there were no survivors, Germany never learned her fate till long after the war. And this was the first occasion when the newly adopted hydrophone had been used in destroying the enemy.

Curious and inexplicable is time's sequence. UC-3 had been sunk on the evening of Easter Day. Early in the morning, of Easter Tuesday, German battle-cruisers, light cruisers, and destroyers, arrived off Lowestoft and Yarmouth to bombard the buildings. But the German destroyer G-41 also sank the *King Stephen*, taking the crew as prisoners. There were some vessels less lucky than others: for, during the last two months this trawler had been working hereabouts as one of our decoys.

Yet between the loss of UC-3 on April 23 and the Lowestoft bombardment of April 25 two most interesting sea-affairs occurred off the Belgian coast, both involving boats from the Flanders Flotilla. And here once more the "Fortune of War" played its hand.

Whilst still the German squadrons were on their way towards East Anglia, UC-10 was trying to come forth. About midnight she motored out of Zeebrugge, but at 12.40 a.m. got caught in the newly laid barrage of nets and mines deposited off the Belgian coast by Admiral Bacon's units sent from Dover for this precise purpose.

Unsuspecting the trap, she became properly entangled, tried to dive beneath, got caught again, off went a mine, followed by another, then several more. The experience by night was terrifying, nerve-snapping. During two hectic hours UC-10 sought to free her hull of encumbrances. Then, just when things seemed impossible, she rose to the surface, rid herself of mines, discovered that the circuits were cut and—scared out of her enterprise—hurried back thankfully into Zeebrugge.

Yet was her destiny only delayed. On August 21, 1917, she was torpedoed—not so very far away—off the Schouwen Lightship by the British submarine E-54.

Now the other incident off the Belgian coast took place on the afternoon of April 24, 1916. Lieut. A. Mety in UB-13 was trying to negotiate the Belgian barrage when he bungled badly.

H.M. Drifter *Gleaner of the Sea*, guarding the mines and nets, lay at her anchor with 15 fathoms of chain out and a further 25 fathoms of wire shackled on to the chain. Total, 40 fathoms. Suddenly the watch on deck heard something grinding on the wire, rushed for'ard to investigate, and discovered UB-13 caught against the wire.

"Skipper," they called below. "You're wanted."

Up came Skipper R. G. Hurren who seized a lance-bomb, hurled it straight at the submarine's fore-deck with perfect result. Such a violent explosion followed that the water flew right over the drifter's foredeck.

It was an amazingly complete attack, for UB-13, having been

holed, sank bodily down the wire which, no longer able to bear the 142 tons weight, parted. He then ordered his engines "Full Speed Ahead", fired a signal rocket, saw the large boil of water still rising, gave it one more bomb, and buoyed it.

Answering his summons arrived the drifter *E.E.S.* who let go a third bomb, where oil and bubbles steadily rose up. Leaving *E.E.S.* standing by, *Gleaner of the Sea* hastened off for a destroyer, found H.M.S. *Afridi* who now steamed exactly over the wreck, made doubly sure and fired her explosive sweep.

That was why UB-13, with all hands, never saw Zeebrugge again. That was also why Skipper Hurren was given the Distinguished Service Cross plus £389, whilst his crew got the balance out of £1000 and one man won the D.S.M.

From instances already given in preceding chapters the UC-class, whether in the Adriatic, or North Sea, or Black Sea, were not more fortunate than the UB's; and the following narrative, covering a period of ten months, shows something of the persistency, but also the risks, with which many of the voyages from Zeebrugge were accompanied.

UC-5 (Lieut. Mohrbutter) was one of those five (UC-1, 3, 5, 6, and 7) submarines which were daily occupied, since the summer of 1915, in laying mines off East Anglia and the southeast coast. The areas he fouled included off the Sunk Lightship; about 2 miles NE. of the Kentish Knock Lightship; in the Stanford Channel (Lowestoft); off the South Goodwins; and Elbow Buoy. She was usually painted a slate colour and had no distinguishing number. Reaching Zeebrugge from Germany on July 27, 1915, she started out on August 20 from Bruges at 6.40 a.m., went down the coast to the Straits, crossing the Dover Barrage close by No. 3 Buoy on the surface "at utmost speed". That night she sat on the seabed, but next morning at 6.30 laid a dozen mines off Boulogne. This was regarded by the Flanders Submarine Flotilla as the first real success achieved on the far side of the line Dover—Calais, for at the end of June the boats had been forbidden to cross Dover Straits, and August 20 was the first time when a German minelayer successfully got through.

The work done by UC-5 quickly revealed itself when the S.S. *William Dawson* was blown up. It was found that these mines measured 5½ feet high, 3 feet in diameter, and carried 200 lb. weight of charge. On August 27 at 3.13 a.m. she dropped twelve mines west of the Longsand Lightship, on September 7 she laid six mines off the entrance to Boulogne Harbour at 6.48 a.m., then crossed the English Channel, and at 10.10 p.m., laid the other six off Folkestone. Nine days later she came down channel, once more laying mines off Dymchurch and off Folkestone, the object being to entrap ships passing through the gate.

A month later, at midnight, her twelve mines were dropped off

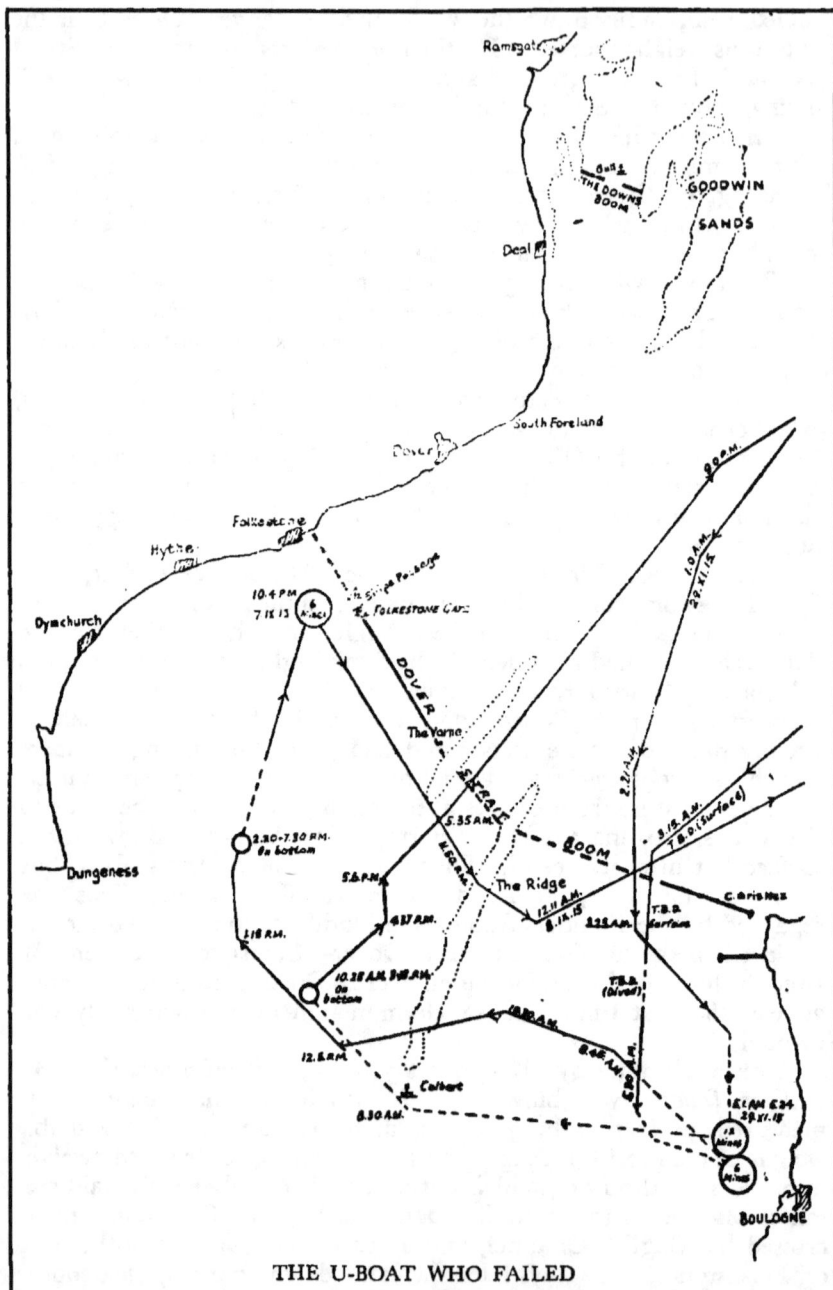

THE U-BOAT WHO FAILED

This shows the track of UC-5 when she laid mines in the Dover Straits during September and November 1915. The broken lines show the nets or boom defence already in position.

the Kentish coast just east of the Elbow Buoy, being set for 7 ft. 9 in. below Low Water Springs. In that October also she laid her cargo off the Nab Lightship and SW. of the Needles. Curiously her mines laid off the Sunk Lightship in November did no harm, but eleven days afterwards she laid another dozen off Dover at four o'clock in the morning.

During the New Year this submarine still continued in her subtle work, on January 17 laid two rows of mines off the Shipwash Lightship, and a fortnight later off the Sunk Lightship: it was when the Dutch S.S. *Juliana* struck one of these "eggs" that the Harwich sweepers located them. The following month found UC-5 selecting the Kentish Knock Lightship for the region of her labours, and a couple of steamers thus soon were victims. Her next visit was in mid-March to the Sunk Lightship, followed a fortnight later by visiting the Corton Lightship area. Here she released not twelve, but eleven, mines: for the safety lanyard jammed in the chute, and the dangerous object could not be persuaded farther.

All these months, then, UC-5 had been paying her visits around our lightships with a regularity which enabled the date of each visit to be foretold almost exactly. If the weather was not quite suitable, then there would be a slight delay. Her final coming occurred when she left Zeebrugge at 8 a.m. of April 26, 1916, and proceeded via the Thornton Ridge and North Hinder. She then shaped a course for the Galloper Buoy. It was one of those typical North Sea spring days, with a light easterly wind accompanied by mist which rendered navigation less easy.

Off the Norfolk coast this evening she had to avoid several steamers, but spent some time in edging along the Galloper Sand, ascertaining the position of a newly placed lightship. Before dawn of April 27 Mohrbutter was again under way, having evidently sat on the bottom hereabouts for the dark hours. His familiarity with this coast—its landmarks, the set of the tides, the buoyage and lightships—had bred a certain contempt. True, the sight of a steamer at 5.15 a.m., made him dive out of sight, yet it was only for five minutes before he rose to the surface.

On that day either the fog or carelessness made Mohrbutter lose his customary ability—or his usual luck—for, immediately, his craft struck the sands violently. Yet he did manage by emptying his tanks of the sea-water to float off, and before six o'clock he retrimmed the boat and dived below water where, in $8\tfrac{3}{4}$ fathoms he once more lay on the North Sea floor till after breakfast. At first he now cruised at periscope depth, but at 10 o'clock (G.M.T.) got hard aground, doubtless because Mohrbutter had not made allowance for the tidal set. This time his mistake was extremely serious, for the ebb would soon leave him high and dry. Many an exciting adventure had this craft experienced, occasionally there had been breakdowns with the Diesel engines, water in the cylinders and so on, narrow escapes from being run down by chasing and converging steamers. Occasionally at sea she had even sighted British mines adrift, and sunk them with rifles.

Certainly to-day she had submerged at $26\frac{1}{4}$ feet, but instead of endeavouring to get her afloat once more by going full speed (500 revolutions), i.e. 4 knots, her captain tried "Utmost Speed" (575 revolutions), but that could not shift her from the bed she was making. No human power could alter the fact that aground on the Shipwash in Lat. 52.03 N., Long. 1.146 E. with a falling tide, and off a hostile coast, the minelayer, having her tell-tale cargo, was in an impossible situation.

She bleated for help, but her wireless was heard by H.M.S. *Firedrake*, and to this destroyer she must indeed surrender intact with all her crew. Thus, at last, the voyages of UC-5 across the North Sea came to a sudden end.

CHAPTER 23

TO THE BOTTOM

CONCERNING the fate of U-10 there will always continue to be some uncertainty. It has been claimed that she was lost up the Baltic, but the cause of disaster cannot be given : the date alleged is sometime during May, 1916.

Other authority will tell you that U-10 was definitely destroyed in Lat. 51.26 N., Long. 2.50 E. between May 7 and July 15 of that year, for the Dover Drifters laid a fleet of nets in the above position on May 7, but whilst the nets were being hauled aboard on July 15 (so as to replace by new ones) the eighth net was missing. Presumably it had been carried away by U-10 attempting to negotiate the Straits, because both mines of the net had fired and— still more notable—the gear revealed the corpse of a German Petty Officer telegraphist on whose body (clad in a double-breasted coat with white metal buttons) were found a pass and identity disc. The former allowed him to move about Bruges : the other indicated that his ship was U-10.

Whilst, therefore, it is not improbable that this submarine foundered on a Baltic mine, we should like to have explained to our satisfaction : (1) the appearance of the cleanly removed drifter net, and (2) how the German telegraphist managed to leave his remains in that net.

But as regards the fate of the Austrian submarine U-6 there is no ambiguity. This boat had been built at Fiume in 1909, and her immersed displacement was of 236 tons. Her cruises during the war had been generally confined to the Adriatic, but only occasionally extended to Corfu and the Gulf of Taranto. On March 18, 1916, she torpedoed the French destroyer *Renaudin* off Durazzo. When, on May 12, this U-6 set out again from Cattaro, she sighted about 9 p.m. a British drifter working her nets in the Otranto Straits and dived, but felt herself caught by the nets. Her captain (Lieut. von Falkenhausen) realized that though one propeller continued to work all right, the other had fouled the nets.

Very well, then ! Blow tanks, and rise to the surface !

He did this, only to discover that he was surrounded by drifters burning powerful lights and that the British fishermen were firing on him. Falkenhausen, therefore, saw the game was up, ordered his men to put on lifebelts, open the Kingston flooding-valve, and jump into the Adriatic. Although the commanding officer, two junior officers, and seventeen men were all picked up by the drifters and brought into Brindisi, the submarine sank; but £1000 was divided among three little drifters named the *Dulce Doris, Calistoga,* and *Evening Star II.*

Off Belgium we had completed by May 26 a Blockade Obstruction of nets which, had been laid within 15 miles of that coast, by thirty British drifters. At the most they could never do more than 8 knots even with a clean bottom, but it was characteristic of these fishermen's courage that the latter continued to go about their work even when totally unsupported. On the other hand we know from the captured UC-5 and other sources that these nets with their mines and buoys were a serious nuisance to German submarines coming in and out of Zeebrugge. There were indeed times when navigation became entirely suspended.

The bigger U-boats direct from Germany were now to be kept busier than ever in the North Sea, for Scheer was completing his plans which led to that historic clash that we know as the Battle of Jutland. Well ahead of time he sent these submarines to take up positions off what the enemy considered our "main bases"—Humber, Firth of Forth, Moray Firth, and Scapa Flow—and by luring warships out into the U-boats' ambush "give battle under conditions favourable" to the Germans.

As this volume is concerned with the German underwater craft, we may content ourselves with two examples in the reverse order of their occurrence. It was part of Scheer's plan to lay a cargo of mines from U-74 off the SE. corner of the Firth of Forth—obviously to trap Admiral Beatty's battle-cruiser fleet. During May 27 the four armed trawlers, *Searanger* (Lieut. H. J. Bray, R.N.R.), *Oku, Rodino,* and *Kimberley,* were on patrol more than 100 miles seaward of Peterhead at 12.30 p.m., when suddenly a sail and some smoke were sighted coming eastward. Presently this distant disguise revealed U-74, against whom the first three trawlers opened fire. It was a smooth day, the trawlers had been cruising about in no sort of formation, but just resembled fishing vessels at work, and evidently the German had so regarded them.

But they bluffed the U-boat, what is more they soon found the distance, and when *Searanger* sent a shell crashing across the water into the enemy's hull, the latter lowered sail and returned the fire alternatively of all four trawlers. The latter gradually closed in upon their opponent, who lost part of the periscope, got the worst of the engagement, and finally ceased fire entirely, preferring rather to submerge. But the trawlers were too quick, for the U-boat came still nearer with their guns so that such concentrated fire was now deadly. Suddenly, like some drunken wounded creature, the submarine rose from the surface with a heavy list and erratic course. *Kimberley* tried to ram, but was too close, and fired three consecutive shots. Range, point blank! The enemy must have been riddled with shells.

In less than an hour from the start this engagement was over and ended. To the bottom departed U-74 for the last time, taking with her all hands and leaving behind only a well-defined patch. So that particular cargo of German mines did not affect the Battle of Jutland which, after four days, drew nigh.

Now U-74 belonged to a new class intentionally built for mine-laying: two months before the above incident she laid a field off the Forth eastern approach, and a fortnight preceding the climax laid another area there southeast off the Bass Rock. But U-75 (one more of these novel types which carried their cargoes from Germany to Scottish waters) was operating this month off the Orkneys. You perceive how a particular locality was given over to a selected officer.

To Lieut.-Commander Beitzen of U-75 the order came that he was to deposit these horned explosives off the Brough of Birsay, at the western side of the Orkneys. He laid them on May 29, only two days before the battle, yet although no fewer than thirteen German submarines operated off Scapa, Kinnaird Head, the Firth of Forth, the Humber, and in the North Sea, it was not on U-75's mines that Beitzen afforded help to Scheer, though the help given was sensational enough.

Lord Kitchener, on June 5, came north, bound for Archangel. After the journey by train from London he crossed to Scotland, lunched with Admiral Jellicoe in the *Iron Duke*, went aboard the cruiser *Hampshire*, round the west side of the island because it was blowing a gale from the northeast; but unfortunately the wind was already backing. It was June 5 and by the time *Hampshire* was off the Brough of Birsay a heavy sea, besides a dangerous ambush, awaited the ship. She plunged into the invisible dangers, blew up, foundered, and Field-Marshal Earl Kitchener perished, too.

Beitzen had laid his mines more dangerously than ever he anticipated.

At its best, and at its worst, U-boat life always was a gamble. We mentioned just now Arnauld de la Perière. In less than three weeks of June he sank in the Mediterranean from aboard U-35 no fewer than twenty steamers and twenty-one sailing vessels. So, also, after a submarine had recently laid her mines near the Corton Lightship, one of them evidently was caught by the tide adrift from her moorings and blew up this mark vessel.

There is about the fate of U-77 an unsettled mystery, which neither Britain nor Germany can make clear. During July there was a determined and successful series of attacks against our North Sea fishing vessels. On the night of the 5th these were very spread, when assaults occurred about 20 miles NE. of the Tyne. By allotting such areas to newly armed drifters and armed trawlers, these raids partially were stopped with the assistance of two destroyers; but attacks off the Tyne, Coquet Island, and elsewhere in the North Sea this summer, were even yet not too successful.

But about U-77?

She disappeared during July 5–7, but though Germany believes that one of our trawlers sank her off the East Coast, the matter cannot precisely be explained. Nevertheless, I believe that it happened on July 7 when in Lat. 58.20 N., 0.48 E. the Peterhead trawlers sighted one submarine at 7.15 a.m., and another at 7.40 a.m. The first was chased by two armed trawlers, and the second by three. Heavy fire was exchanged at different hours of the day, until about 8 p.m., the seventeenth round from *Albatross* in the second contingent, seemed to strike the submarine's forward gun, causing an amount of black smoke to rise.

Did one of the trawler's shells, then, strike a box of German ammunition? Or was there one of her mines later that day which was destined to explode? It might so have happened, but the submarine quickly made off to the eastward, and there will be some who could suggest, like U-74, that U-77 blew up on her own mines.

Yes: the North Sea seemed to contain nearly as many surprises as fish. Consider the motor-boat *Salmon*. She was just a very fast little craft of 20 knots, measuring 40 feet long and 8 feet beam, with a large cockpit and no cabin. Very suitable, perhaps, for a nice day up the river. But as a warship? Well, even if she had changed her name to *Shark*, she hardly looked hostile.

She was only a year old, had been presented with five other motor-boats to the Admiralty by Mr. Cochrane, a wealthy American yachtsman, and sent to Lowestoft under the command of Sub-Lieut. E. T. West, R.N.V.R. Fitted with one of those newly invented hydrophones, she was patrolling off this port just before midnight of July 6–7, and we who have perused the above chapters, know how regularly was the area off Lowestoft visited by the UC-minelayers.

Now, to-night, *Salmon* kept hearing on this instrument a buzzing which sounded extremely interesting. At 1.30 a.m. it commenced again, but seemed to be much nearer. Then the noise shifted to right underneath, so *Salmon* went full-speed ahead and dropped a depth charge. This exploded, but was followed by a still more violent detonation, and a column of water 50 feet high rose in the air accompanied by pieces of white-painted wood, gratings, bubbles, and a smell of gas.

But there was no further sound on the hydrophone.

German Diesels had stopped suddenly as German mines went off. That was the sudden end of UC-7: it happened to be the first occasion when the smallest ship settled the enemy by employing the most simple method. But it is significant that ten days later six smacks were sunk in the Lowestoft vicinity all by another submarine.

Quite another sort of surprise happened on July 14 to H.M. Submarine H-5 (Lieut. Varley) who for some time had been stalking about the coast of Northern Germany. On the surface he sighted a German off the Ems estuary. In spite of the short sea, he made to attack her, fired two torpedoes, hitting her forward of the conning tower most successfully. The craft then disappeared for the last time and so ended the career of U-51. It was another aspect of the Submarine Campaign when on June 23 the mercantile German submarine *Deutschland* started out from Kiel on June 23, arrived at Baltimore with a mixed cargo on July 9, and left the American port on August 2. Special arrangements were made by Admiral Bayly for intercepting her by six different Q-ships, but she managed to evade attention, reaching the port of Bremen on August 24. Her sister-ship, *Bremen*, also essayed the voyage to America, but to this day Germany cannot say what happened to her on the way out. There is, however, reason for supposing that she was in collision with one of the armed merchant cruisers belonging to 10th Cruiser Squadron. The same mist and fog which were such aids to the *Deutschland's* return may have been the cause of the other submarine's destruction.

It seems remarkably extraordinary that despite a submarine's modernity and all sorts of gadgets she still became subject to fishermen's nets worked from drifters : that the crews who normally caught herring now enmeshed submarines. Was it not this spirit, that gallant audacity, which British sailormen from the Narrow Seas brought to the Adriatic ? How well were the submarines of Austria and Germany being frustrated !

About 6.30 a.m. on July 30, the drifter *Quarry Knowe* was working her nets when the Mate called Skipper W. Bruce on deck.

"Something wrong," pointed the former. "Heavy strain on these nets. And they seem to be going down."

In fact, the rope was straight up and down, so it was hove in as much as possible and then shackled on to wire which gave more play. Bruce signalled to the drifter *Garrigill* for help.

"My nets are sinking," was quite enough to bring *Garrigill* alongside with two more of these craft. The strain and the air-bubbles rising to the surface could not be disputed. Was a submarine caught ?

But the time was to act rather than wonder, so *Garrigill* dropped one depth charge and then another. The strain still remained. One of two things. Either a submarine in the net, or else a whale. (For occasionally such creatures as the latter were noticed in the Adriatic.) *Quarry Knowe* now began towing the net into shallow water, but after half an hour it looked as if this wire would break owing to the weight, whereupon *Garrigill* passed a wire round the nets, but eventually nets and submarine sank. The position was approximately Lat. 40.12.30 N., Long. 18.46.30 E., and whilst many felt sure that a submarine had been sent to her doom, the Admiralty were far from convinced. Then, at last, truth came into its own, and the fishermen were undoubtedly right.

For this turned out to be the new UB-44 which had been constructed in Germany, and put together again at Pola. In command was Lieut. Wager: he had failed to appreciate just exactly what drifters' nets and depth charges meant. So he lost his life, so did the crew, and the submarine had to be crossed off the list as now merely a steel coffin.

Life aboard such craft continued to be a huge gamble of uncertainty.

Yes: in more ways than what you might think. Contrary to the general impression of the public, the High Sea Fleet did come out in force some weeks after Jutland. Indeed, there seemed on August 19 every probability that the clash between the north-steaming German squadrons and the south-steaming British Grand Fleet must terminate in another Jutland. But a great battle was rendered impracticable because of an unsatisfactory message from the airship "L.13", whose signal threw Scheer's plan completely out of focus; and what would have been a most thrilling occasion must be admitted.

But the submarines at this period were kept very busy. Just as in the days immediately preceding Jutland, so now an unusually large number of U-boats in the North Sea hinted at something unusual. Actually H.M.S. *Nottingham* was on August 19 twice torpedoed by U-63, and then U-52 torpedoed her so that the cruiser sank next morning. But U-53 and U-35 were active, U-65 fired two missiles at the battle-cruiser *Inflexible*, U-66 sank the *Falmouth*, but was badly depth charged. In fact, by employing submarines disposed in a movable line was a more efficacious method than merely stationing them outside British ports of issue.

But one of the best instances of lucky, and unlucky, submarines was associated with the port of Zeebrugge and UC-10. Out from the former was proceeding the latter on April 24, 1916, when she got caught in one of the net mines of our Belgian Barrage. Then she observed the net floats, tried to dive under them, but for a while got caught up. This caused several explosions in the vicinity, and in turn our watching drifters imagined that this noise meant a German submarine was destroyed. Eventually, however, UC-10 came to the surface, found some net-mines foul of the hull with the circuits cut. These she cleared, and by good fortune got safely into port.

A few months passed, this same submarine on August 21 was in Lat. 51.45 N., Long. 3.20 E. (near the Schouwen Bank Lightship), and it would have been expected that a minelayer would find it convenient in that neighbourhood to ambush a British warship. But H.M. Submarine E-54 was there, also, who overtook and got on the bow of this UC-10. At a distance of 400 yards both torpedoes were fired, and one was a hit. Down descended UC-10, unlucky at last. There were no survivors.

We have frequently given examples to show that in the 1939 war with Germany the latter was in many a respect merely repeating the lessons of U-boat warfare already employed on a smaller scale twenty years earlier. On August 26, 1916, the British drifters were at their nets in the Adriatic when three aeroplanes were seen coming from the north.

After nearer approach they were identified as Austrian. Two of them swooped low over the drifter *Rosies*, and the second bomb hit so explosively on forehatch that the ship sank and there was barely time for the crew to escape in their boat.

At home we were still intrigued with that trawler-plus-submarine method beguiling the enemy. Several times had circumstances compelled us to give up the idea, though it was a notion so excellent that we kept returning to the plan. The final abandonment of this device was after August 28, 1916, when H.M. Submarine C-29 (Lieut. Schofield) was being towed by the disguised trawler *Ariadne*. The latter whilst working off the Humber came in contact with one of the mines either at the NW. end of the Outer Silver Pit area or of the Humber minefield. The submarine struck the object, and blew up with all hands.

Doubtless for the purpose of intimidating the United States, the submarine U-53 was on September 17 sent from Heligoland to attack shipping off the American coast. She proceeded under Lieut.-Commander Rose via north of the Shetlands, thence across via the Newfoundland Banks to Long Island Sound and entered on October 7 Newport, Rhode Island, where she remained only two and a half hours. Then she made next for the Nantucket Lightship which is the meeting place of many trade routes. Thus on October 8 she sank five steamers, and the same night began her return Atlantic voyage. Coming back via the Hebrides and the Shetlands, she reached Heligoland on October 28. Certainly this was a fine achievement and Rose proved himself an extremely able commander, but although American naval officers told me that the feat impressed them, it had very little political value, for within a few months the United States began sending their destroyers to co-operate with us in the war.

It was characteristic of German submarine enterprise at this time that U-46 on September 19 left Emden for the Arctic and proceeded to the entrance of the White Sea. She sank not less than eight vessels and got back on October 24. That was the limit of her fuel endurance. Off Lowestoft, with rare persistency, submarines still used to come over, and our armed smacks still located them on the hydrophone. But the Germans were very incensed by the employment of those decoys and on three occasions sent in warnings

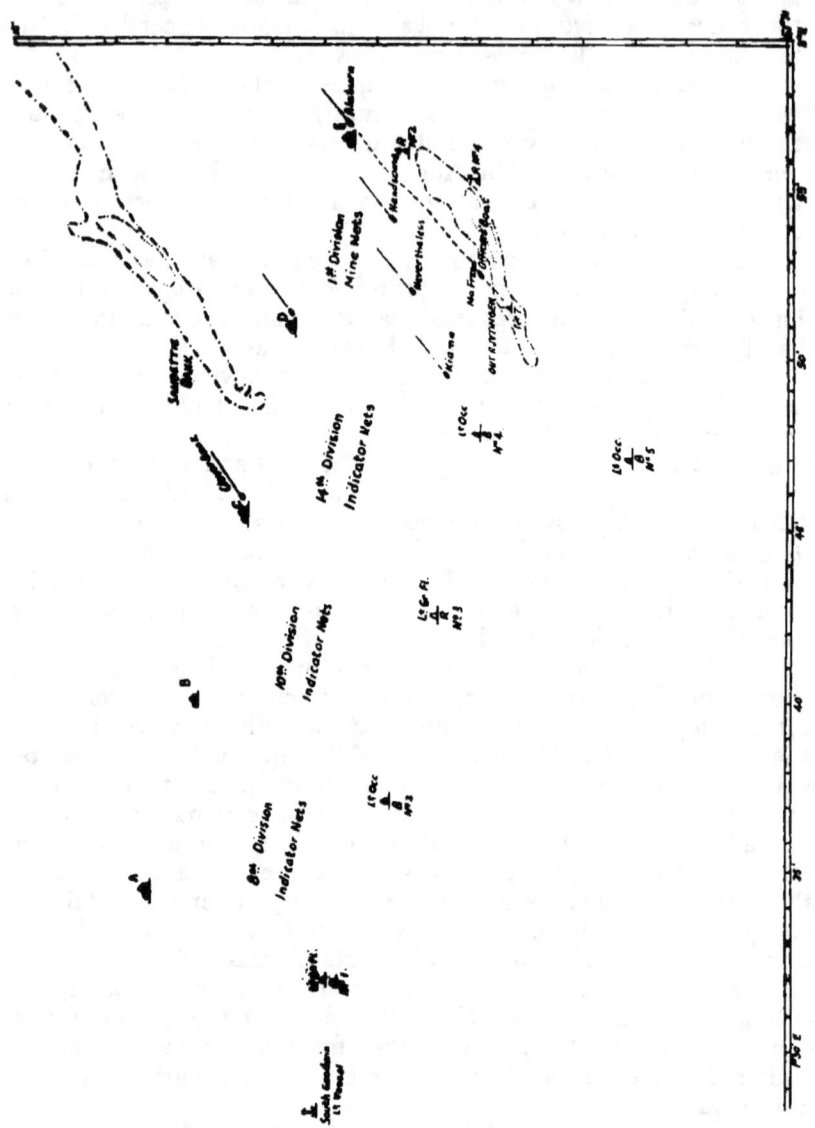

GUARDING DOVER STRAITS
The above shows how divisions of drifters riding to their indicator nets with a N.E.-going tide thwarted the passage of U-boats.

that as the submarines could not tackle the smacks they "will send over something that can". No doubt this fearsome threat was not unconnected with the Lowestoft raids, but certainly it did not frighten North Sea fishermen.

In the southern waters events not always turned out with such simplicity and directness. There is a little ambiguity about the Austrian Submarine XVI, which in October was operating in the Gulf of Taranto. According to one account she was lost on October 16, because in torpedoing the Italian destroyer *Nembo*, the destroyer's depth charges were detonated and thereby the submarine was damaged and sunk. A report from Vienna, however, says this submarine sinking was on October 17 through being rammed by an Italian.

CHAPTER 24

THE STORY OF SCHWIEGER

NOW in October, 1916, a new barrage was being placed across Dover Straits just as during the summer a barrage had been laid off the Belgian coast. In both cases the object was to thwart submarines, but since it was not considered possible to patrol the Belgian obstruction during winter months much was expected of the Dover area which ran from the SE. of the Goodwins to the SW. end of the Outer Ruytingen, thence eastward towards Dunkirk. This barrage consisted of wire nets clipped to a jackstay supported every 500 yards by large mooring buoys, but watched night and day by drifter divisions. There were about 70 miles of moored nets laid out, but by the spring—what with the virulent weather and strong tides—not 25 per cent of this barrage was really effective.

During the last week of October, or the first week of November, the smaller German submarines sent south still tempted fate with the perils of the Black Sea minefields. It is thus that UB-45 was destroyed by accident, and UB-7 also ; though as to the latter no details are known other than the locality. So also little is known about U-56 except that she had been sent north to prevent stores reaching their destination. One of the Russian patrols destroyed her off Lapland. Very different, however, is the detailed story which it is possible for us to piece together concerning a German U-boat much farther south.

Even in the realm of fiction it would be difficult to find a better submarine yarn than that which centres round U-20 and U-30, yet every word is literal historical truth.

Their early war careers began together, then respective duties separated them, yet the flimsiest touch of fate drew them once more and, by their accidental but combined efforts, they produced an amazing result.

Doubtless many readers will recollect that first naval air raid which was made over Cuxhaven on the morning of Christmas, 1914, when British seaplanes took the sky after reaching Heligoland Bight in the three carriers *Riviera*, *Engadine*, and *Empress*. These three ex-cross-Channel steamers were supported by Harwich light cruisers, against which the Germans sent out U-20, U-22, and U-30. Only the first managed to loose off a torpedo, but our destroyers were too quick for the others.

THE STORY OF SCHWIEGER

The winter passed, spring brought to German submarines an adolescent consciousness of their unrealized strength, and young commanding officers sought to surpass each other's feats. Thus when on April 30, 1915, U-20 departed from Borkum Roads for the south of Ireland, she had barely reached her allotted locality than she torpedoed *Lusitania*, created a world sensation, and was back home at Wilhelmshaven by May 13. Walter Schwieger, within a brief fortnight, had become a marked man.

Every time these boats got to Germany they were given a detailed overhaul, crews were rested, and off they started—usually to the same area as before, so that they developed into regional specialists. Thus did Schwieger's craft find herself busily sinking ships *en route* through Irish waters, but on July 9, 1915, when 30 miles south of Queenstown—not so very far from the scene of *Lusitania's* tragedy—U-20 seemed to have another chance of sinking a Cunarder. This time it was the 15,499 tons *Orduna*, the silver missile was fired from its tube, but most fortunately missed the target.

So, likewise, in September, 1915, Schwieger on a subsequent cruise 80 miles SW. of the Fastnet destroyed the 10,920-ton armed merchant cruiser *Hesperian* (Allan Line) and, after sinking other vessels in the Bay of Biscay, got home, refitted, before setting out on an exploratory trip in November, 1915. This was to be off north Scotland, east of Cape Wrath for, on New Year's Day the surface raider *Möwe* was to lay 252 mines, which, incidentally, caused the loss of the battleship *King Edward VII*.

One year after torpedoing the famous Cunarder, by the same manner did U-20 on May 8, 1916, sink the White Star S.S. *Cymric* (13,370 tons) in the Atlantic, 140 miles WNW. of the Fastnet, whilst the liner was on her way to America. Oh, yes! Schwieger's conscience was tougher than leather. The anniversary of a sea massacre meant nothing to his insensitiveness.

That August he paid another visit to his secondary area, the Bay of Biscay, but never down there won successes as off the coast of Ireland. Then on October 13—mark the unlucky date—being again ready for sea, U-20 left Germany for her usual SW. Irish hunting area, and before the end of that month had begun her voyage home via the north of Scotland, Orkneys, thence across to hug the Norwegian coast, down the west side of Denmark, and so towards the Heligoland Bight.

However, she did eventually resume her service, and a year later —November 1, 1916—was at work off the southwest coast of Norway below Bergen. On that day she torpedoed and sank the British S.S. *Brierley Hill*, 18 miles WNW. of Helliso Lighthouse. Quite a small steamer, of 1168 tons, bound for Hull with a very necessary cargo of Norwegian pit-props for our collieries.

Next day U-30 was coming north and some distance from the land, being now some 25 miles west of Bergen. The curses which her previous crew had bequeathed—for she once sank off Borkum—were well active, as the new personnel realized all too mournfully. For, having sunk another small British steamer (*Spero*, 1132 tons), this time 95 miles WSW. of the Helliso Light, she developed a serious engine breakdown. Both Diesels had "packed up". Nothing would persuade these machines to move.

The situation off a rock-bound coast, to which the next south-west gale would quickly hurl her, was not pleasant to contemplate. Again going to play the role of coffin-ship for most of her men, as she holed herself on the sharp pinnacles? Or just present herself as a nice target for British light cruisers on their way home from another of their Skagerrak expeditions?

Altogether a most anxious and ridiculous predicament for any U-boat commander. Only one thing he could do. Call for help. But Heligoland lay 450 miles away. Would U-30's radio carry thus far? Long-distance wireless for submarines was still in its experimental stage. On the other hand her sister-craft, Schwieger's U-20, had already established a record that year when she made connection with Germany from a distance of 770 miles.

So to-night at seven o'clock U-30 began bleating on her wireless for aid, and her message was picked up by another submarine, which—with remarkable coincidence—chanced to be in this Norwegian neighbourhood and only 40 miles away. Homeward-bound from SW. Ireland. Yes: it was actually her old friend U-20 of Cuxhaven association.

Schwieger altered course, the time ticked by full of suspense for both boats, anything might happen during a few hours in that uncertain locality. By 8.30 p.m. he was quite certain of her latitude and longitude, he had flashed his reply, but searching for a submarine in the darkness is no simple job. He could only hope neither inquisitive neutral steamer, nor British cargo-carrier might meanwhile intervene.

Now Schwieger was not the only party to have intercepted U-30's radio. Among those who heard was the British Navy, but by another strange coincidence Admiral Sir John Jellicoe on the night of November 2 temporarily had relinquished command of the Grand Fleet. Why? Because he had departed by train to London. "I left the *Iron Duke* at Cromarty," he publicly announced later, "and proceeded to the Admiralty at the request of the First Lord, Mr. Balfour." It was in order to discuss the submarine problem.

So Vice-Admiral Sir Cecil Burney from November 2-4 was in charge but he had gone to sea with the 2nd Battle Squadron, 4th Light Cruiser Squadron, and 11th Destroyer Squadron for exercises eastward of the Shetlands. By the time he could wireless orders, and these could be obeyed, it was 4 a.m. of November 3. Picture at that cold, dark hour, H.M.S. *Botha* with a quartette of destroyers steaming out from Scapa Flow to sweep along the Norwegian coast, whilst H.M.S. *Faulknor* with six other destroyers from Cromarty the same day went forth on a similar quest.

Unfortunately they were all too late, for by 2 a.m. of the 3rd already U-20 had located U-30, passed a line, and got the lame duck in tow. Had the latter now changed her character at last? Was good fortune in future to be hers? Lucky she had been to receive help. And now away southwards at best possible speed she was being hauled, lest surprise attack should come with daylight. However the hours passed uneventfully, no suspicious smoke smudged the horizon at dawn, steady progress at 6 knots was being made towards the Skagerrak approach. When at length that should have been crossed, and the low-lying western side of Denmark picked up, Germany's waters would not seem so far away.

This afternoon at three o'clock U-30 signalled good news to her consort. The mechanics after much effort had persuaded both Deisels to function. Everything was now all right in the engine-room, so tow-rope could be cast off, and the two boats continued in company but freely on the surface at 12 knots. A great improvement, though 4 knots slower than their designed rate.

Lucky again! For, without their mutual knowledge, the *Botha* destroyer division having passed ahead of the German couple at 6.40 p.m. turned back towards Scapa with negative news.

Seven hours of peace and progress, then at 10 p.m. U-30 resumed her ugly tricks, the Diesels died once more, this U-20 again passed the tow-rope, and a dull but anxious monotony settled down. Not yet out of the risky region—by a long way! Another dawn of suspense, but one of them bereft of power to attack any British naval force.

Still more unluckily, November 4 brought no gleam of sunshine but one of those genuine autumn fogs which the North Sea knows so well. At least the act of towing kept both boats together, yet as noon passed and night shut down without the damp impenetrable blanket lifting, Schwieger became anxious concerning his navigation. By evening he hoped to have crossed the Skagerrak and got hold of the Danish coast at its northwest shoulder. Thence, having fixed his position, he could edge away from the land and set a course for Heligoland.

Were the ghosts of those dead men, whom U-30 once drowned off Borkum, having their revenge to-night? Drawing both boats into danger? At the best and brightest of sunlit days this Jutland shore is a treacherous place, where everything is fine drift-sand with tufts of coarse grass and flat heath-like plains extending from the sea. An occasional windmill, a church spire, a red circular tower, or a lighthouse, varies the endless line of dunes; but, when southwesters blow, a nasty short sea is kicked up in the shallows which quickly follow the 4-fathom (24 feet) line.

At 7.20 p.m., whilst lookouts were still unable to sight a streak of land, U-20 felt a bump, soft and gentle. Then she came to a full stop, and no power of engines could make her shift. U-30 likewise slid into the sand, with similar result, so that when the fog lifted they found themselves lying within Danish territory, abreast of Harböere which is about 5 miles north of Bovbjerg, and rather more than that distance south of Limfjord entrance.

Another harassing situation, where it needed only a British submarine bound between Heligoland and Harwich to torpedo them both in the morning. This time it looked less like luck than doom, but a quick calculation revealed that the tide was rising and had another two hours to flood. U-30 began lightening herself, dumped thirty tons of oil-fuel over the side, floated from the tenacious sand by high water, though now buoyant like a balloon and as unmanageable.

But U-20, having seated herself in a sand-pocket, would not budge and the southwest swell with boisterous wind held her firmly on a lee shore. Well, what could be done now?

The same as before. Wireless for help!

That call was answered promptly, and by 10 p.m. German destroyers were on their way north. Half an hour later Admiral Hipper was sent with a mighty force that included battle-cruisers and battleships. Why such strength displayed merely on behalf of two U-boats?

The reason is that naval history shows many an instance where big battles develop out of small occasions. British light cruisers frequently made incursions towards Heligoland Bight, often supported further up the North Sea by battle fleets. Who knew whether light cruisers might not already be shelling U-20 and U-30?

It was 6.30 a.m. when Schwieger on November 5 sighted the destroyers arriving, and approximately half-flood. At once the destroyer-leader anchored to seaward of U-20, got a good hawser aboard, and then steamed ahead. But the submarine, having scooped for herself too solid a bed declined to shift. As the tide rose, further efforts were made, but the only result consisted of snapped hawsers. And the rough seas did not help operations. A final effort, made that forenoon with the ten o'clock high water, failed signally. Her ends were afloat but amidships U-20 was firmly aground; wherefore, she had to be abandoned, she was blown up with a great wide wound for'ard, her crew were put aboard the fleet, and at 11 a.m. Admiral Hipper's forces began making homeward. Such was the last picture of the submarine which had sunk *Lusitania*.

And now, though U-30 was brought safely into port, her baneful influence which indirectly had caused the loss of U-20, besides fetching Hipper's units out of harbour, was to exert itself again—but in the most dramatic manner possible.

The exact times are worth noting. At 11.41 a.m. Admiral

Hipper signalled his squadron that at noon they were to alter course and reduced speed to 12 knots. An unforgettable Sunday, sea getting worse all the time, the fog changing to mist and rain. Visibility no better than 2 miles. Who among sailormen to-day would not "swallow the anchor" and buy a farm?

At 11.50 a.m., 30 miles SW. of Horn's Reef, buffeted about by the waves, a grey British submarine was keeping her damp patrol. H.M.S. *J1*, Commander Noel Laurence, giant in stature, one of Britain's greatest submarine pioneers, already had won a great reputation and the D.S.O. for his exploits in the Baltic, where he also torpedoed the famous German battle-cruiser *Moltke*. To-day in *J1* he glanced through his periscope to behold not a battle-cruiser, but four of Hipper's 25,000-ton dreadnoughts approaching. They were *König*, *Markgraf*, *Grosser Kurfurst*, and *Kronprinz Wilhelm*, each of them 21-knotters with over 1000 men and ten 12-inch guns.

Commander Laurence told me that he reckoned the range as 4000 yards and the enemy's speed at 16 knots when he fired his first torpedo, the exact hour being 12.8 p.m. Three and a half minutes later he heard a loud explosion. . . . Then two minutes interval. His second torpedo had also found its target. And despite *J1's* lively desire to break surface in the heavy swell!

Two German depth charges soon burst unpleasantly near; for two hours destroyers' propellers could be heard thrashing the sea just above, and their sweep-wire actually scraped over the submarine's hull, with an uncomfortable rasping sound.

This time the Germans were far too late. Laurence's first torpedo had struck the *Grosser Kurfurst*, and the second torpedo hit *Kronprinz Wilhelm*, making a hole below waterline big enough to admit a motor-car. The *Grosser Kurfurst* shipped 300 tons of sea, and her rudder was damaged. By strenuous efforts both battleships were finally brought into harbour. Why didn't they sink? Because German battleships were built with a most elaborate series of water-tight compartments, and tightly-packed layers of cork inserted.

All the same, U-30 had within so few hours proved herself the most expensive nuisance. One submarine abandoned for all time, and two dreadnoughts to be laid up in dry-dock for months. For his unprecedented achievement, Commander Laurence won a bar to his D.S.O. To-day Admiral Sir Noel Laurence, K.C.B., occupies one of the highest responsibilities in the service.

As for Walter Schwieger, he was given charge of U-88, but on September 7, 1917, and not far from where the above two battleships were holed, the slayer of *Lusitania* plunged right into a Horn's Reef minefield and not a soul was saved.

Thus did fate write the final act of justice to a wicked crime.

CHAPTER 25

DODGING DEATH

IMMENSITY always affects our puny minds.
When on November 21, 1916, the 48,158-ton White Star Liner *Britannic* was sunk in the Mediterranean, people could not fail to be impressed. But when it was further learnt that she was coming through the Zea Channel and there foundered on mines laid just an hour previously by U-73 (Lieut.-Commander Siehs) one thought less of the great tonnage wasted than the loss of twenty-one lives. Siehs was a comparatively newcomer, having left Cuxhaven for the Mediterranean on April 1 with thirty-four mines. It seems an unnecessary risk thus before setting out to have filled the chutes with so many explosives rather than waiting for shipment till the boat itself had ended her voyage; but she appears to have invited attention. On April 11, whilst going round past Ireland she sank the sailing vessel *Inverlyon*,[1] and six days later laid some of her mine-cargo off Lisbon.

But she had her reward. U-73 never came out of the Mediterranean. At the end of October, 1918, just before the Armistice and when she saw how things were shaping, she blew herself up at Pola as she had been accustomed to explode shipping.

The closing days of 1916 are a period of hope, of confidence that the German submarine if it meant to succeed would have many things to contend with: ill fortune, minefields, disguised trawlers, Q-ships, motor launches, steam yachts, armed patrols, depth charges, nets having explosives, and alike the fast destroyer or the slower fishing vessel with steel stem that would go through a submarine's hull as a knife through butter. Yet of course there were some events which were greater than the actual results.

The S.S. *Penshurst*, otherwise known as Q-7, was commanded by a very modest and extremely able, courteous, retired naval officer supported by a highly efficient personnel. Commander F. H. Grenfell, R.N., steamed up and down the English Channel but especially in that area between Guernsey and the Dorset Coast. No seafarer could have imagined that this steamer was of hostile intent, for externally she appeared a typical trader.

It was on November 29 at 8.20 a.m. she engaged a submarine in Lat. 49.45 N., Long. 4.40 W. The sun was just rising at 7.45,

[1] Not to be confused, of course, with the Lowestoft smack *Inverlyon*.

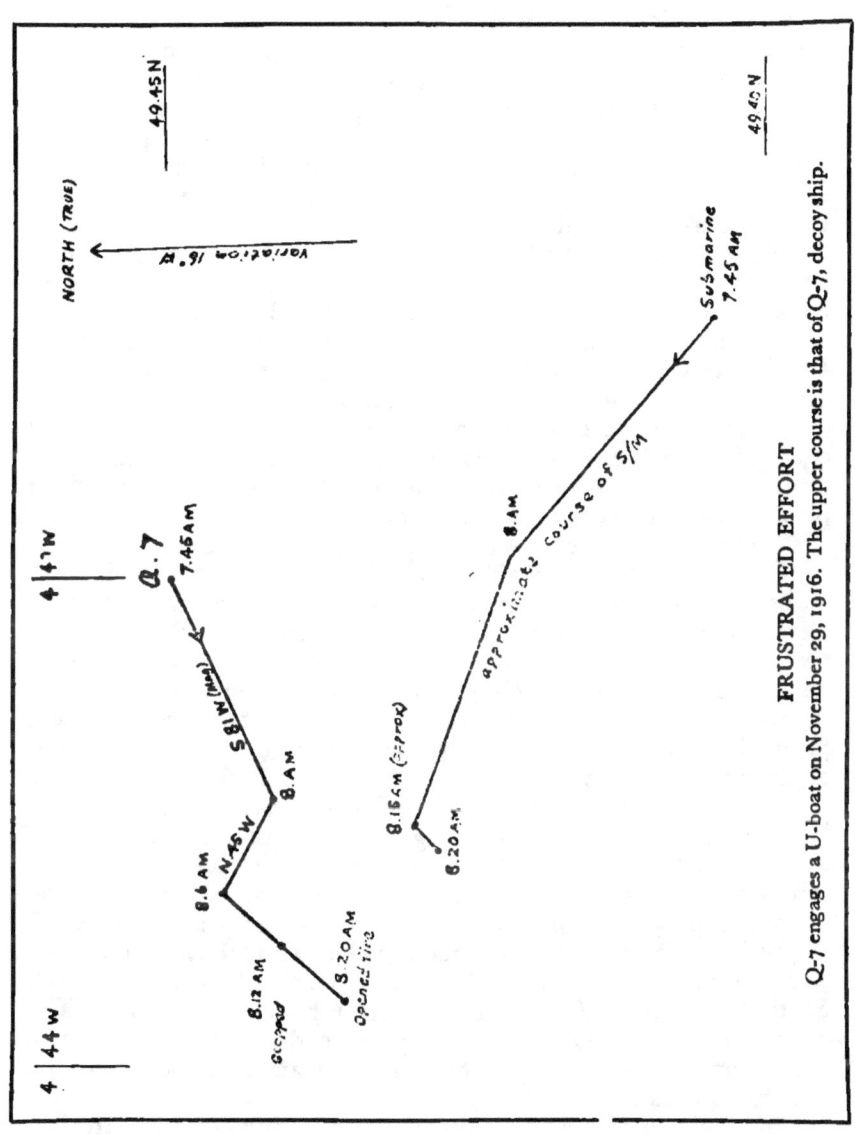

FRUSTRATED EFFORT

Q-7 engages a U-boat on November 29, 1916. The upper course is that of Q-7, decoy ship.

the wind southwest and gentle, when against the glare of the horizon something was descried. Its nature or distance was however difficult to ascertain until at 7.52 a.m. the object declared itself a U-boat by firing a shot, which fell 60 yards short. After two more shells the *Penshurst* at 8.12 stopped engines and pretended to "panic" in the usual manner with boats lowered clumsily; but at 8.20 a.m. as it was impossible to induce the stranger to come closer than 3000 yards, Captain Grenfell opened fire against this black spot in the glare. There was barely time for a few rounds to be fired at the enemy, than the German dived out of sight. Further action was thus rendered impossible.

Meanwhile the *Penshurst* went in the direction of Alderney, changed the ship's camouflage so that she was painted a different colour and her mizzenmast taken down. Even if the strange submarine had wirelessed the description of her opponent to another U-boat, this would not be in accord with the *Penshurst's* present appearance. So next day at noon came another chance.

Being in Lat. 50.11 N., Long. 2.31 W., and steering on a westerly course down Channel the *Penshurst* plucked out of the atmosphere a message sent by wireless from the cross-Channel S.S. *Ibex*, which plied between Guernsey and Weymouth.

"Submarine sighted diving 20 miles NW. of Casquets."

Course was therefore altered by the Q-ship towards this spot, and sure enough at 1.50 p.m. a submarine's conning tower could be seen 5 miles to the southward chasing a steamer to the west, but then the enemy turned eastward and submerged. Why? It may have been the British seaplane which soaring overhead dropped a bomb, but this did not hit the German. Furthermore, it was particularly awkward that the 'plane should now break down and alight on the surface.

Commander Grenfell was preparing to hoist the wreckage on board when at 3.14 p.m. shells began dropping around the Q-ship, so the derrick was swung in and the seaplane with broken wing and minus floats cast off. Proceeding at 3.24 p.m. to the southwest slowly, keeping the submarine on the port quarter, Captain Grenfell stopped engines at 4.12 p.m. when the German had overhauled him and watched the steamer's two boatloads "abandoning ship". So the confounded Englishmen in terror had left the ship? The attention of every German was therefore directed towards these oared boats: from the ship's Master the steamer's papers could be obtained preparatory to boarding.

Suddenly something rent the air. At a range of 250 yards all the *Penshurst's* guns banged, but so surprised were the Germans that no attempt was made to return the fire. The submarine's engine-room was penetrated, and at this close range every one of eighty-three shells hit the target so that at 4.36 p.m. the submarine foundered as the Q-ship's boat rescued the survivors, who included her captain, Lieut. Erich Noodt, Lieut. Karl Bartel, and fourteen others, but seven had been killed. She had come out of Zeebrugge eight days ago. Commander Grenfell was awarded the D.S.O. and distinctions were given to other members of the crew.

It was UB-19 which the Q-ship sank, but about this date UC-13 was sunk somewhere in the Mediterranean and UC-15 was sunk in

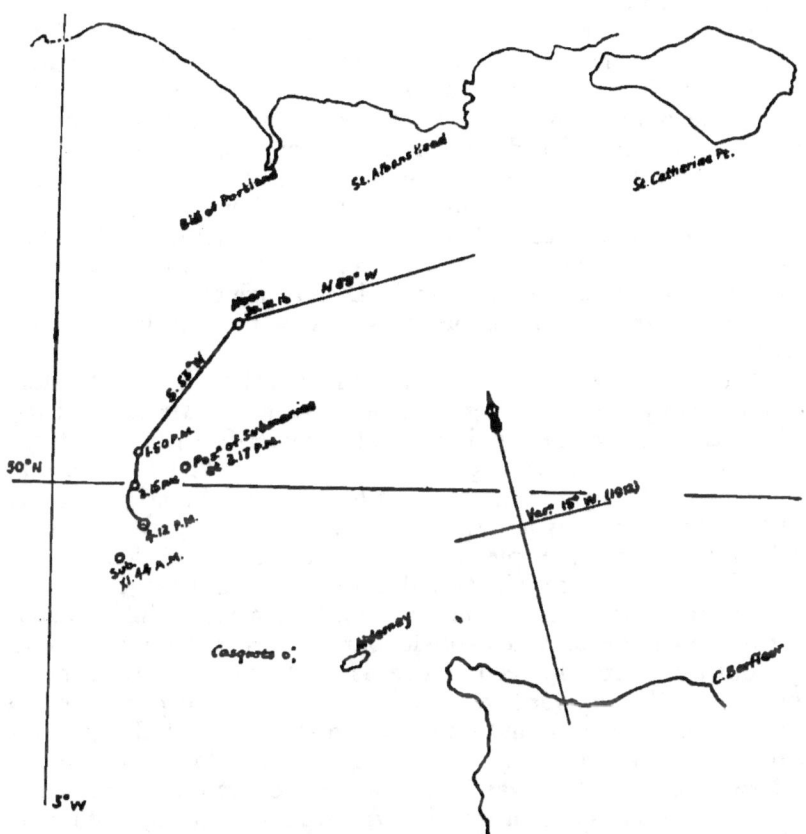

SINKING OF UB-19
by Q-ship on November 30, 1916, in the English Channel.

the Black Sea by mines off Sulina. No further details are known yet it is ascertainable that in the three months beginning from September 1 the Q-ships from Queenstown had no fewer than thirteen actions with U-boats.

Germany was not relaxing her pressure on the Mediterranean by these submarines, and on December 3 sent out from Kiel UC-35 which joined the Adriatic Flotilla until she was sunk by the French

Ailly in May, 1918, off Sardinia. This submarine had specialized as a minelayer in the Gulf of Genoa.

Truly this menace, whether in the North or the Mediterranean, was far from ended; but recent happenings had proved that a tight grip was being kept. In December this year concluded with four more sinkings, of which two were in the North and two up the Mediterranean.

The first happened at 9.40 p.m. on December 4 in Lat. 51.8 N., Long. 1.40 E. (the Straits of Dover), when H.M.S. *Llewellyn* sighted UC-19 awash and distant 300 yards. It was just the sort of place where one of these minelayers might be encountered, but night time is less convenient for destroyer than submarine. The *Llewellyn* tried to ram the German but missed: next, however, was dropped a depth charge beautifully directed. When light returned, a large area of oil was revealed and four days later this fuel was still welling up from below. To make extra sure, a sample was taken and it proved to be mineral oil suitable for Diesel engines.

That, indeed, is the simple story of how the minelayer UC-19 was sunk.

Perhaps the reader may recollect in an earlier chapter the story of the destroyer *Ariel* sinking U-12 off Scotland on March 10, 1915. She had since been repaired and on December 6, 1916, was off the south of Ireland in Lat. 49.41 N., Long. 6.30 W. when some 1¼ miles away she sighted the conning tower of a submarine. It was UB-29, by no means a surprising visitor to these parts, but such submarines were never pleased when destroyers came along.

UB-29 at once dived, *Ariel* dropped a depth charge and this should have meant the immediate finish of a foe. Unfortunately the depth charge failed to explode, but with great alacrity the vessel got out a high-speed sweep and repassed the submarine's supposed position. With 35 yards of wire out, the starboard paravane was fired at 30 feet depth, and up came a mass of black bubbles to the surface, followed by large quantities of light-coloured oil shortly afterwards. And that was how UB-29 bade farewell to the world. Units of that class and of the UC-type are found north, south, east, and west being sunk this year, as for instance when UB-46 was mined on December 7 off the Bosphorus.

There was one which had a second life. The reader will call to mind that UC-12, whilst laying mines on March 17 off Taranto blew up in two portions: but afterwards she was salved by the Italians and repaired. So on December 9 she was relaunched and added to the Italian Navy as Submarine No. *X. 1*.

But there is still some doubt regarding the Austrian submarine No. XX. According to one document the incident may be summed up as follows:

On December 17, 1916, about 2.30 p.m. our drifters in the Adriatic were using their anti-submarine nets where the water was 500 fathoms deep. It was blowing a strong southerly wind when suddenly the drifter *Fisher Girl*, with eight 180-foot nets out, fouled something hard and heavy. A submarine? Well, she signalled the *DHS* and *Guerdon* to come and help. The *Fisher Girl's* skipper (Arthur H. Sago) found it impossible to haul in the nets. The *Guerdon* dropped a depth charge, as also did the *DHS*.

By 6.19 p.m. it was blowing a moderate gale, and *Fisher Girl* was convinced that a submarine was still in the nets. A lance bomb was thrown, she blew on her whistle, fired rockets, and Very's lights. Then *DHS* came up and dropped a depth charge where she imagined was the artful U-XX. Although it was now dark, raining, and blowing harder than ever, the *Fisher Girl* noticed that the explosion caused the sea for the next half-hour to be "smooth as if it were a calm". Next morning at 6.15 a.m. small quantities of oil were found.

Still the rope, as before, could not be hauled in : it was more like a bar of iron, and finally the nets parted owing to the immense weight, and oily patches were visible until 11.30 a.m. In due course a Court of Inquiry was held who decided that the Austrian submarine No. XX had been sunk.

On the face of it this seemed decisive and was generally believed. Yet U-XX was not sunk then : at least, that is the contention. For later on the Italians claimed that their submarine F-12 sank her on July 4, 1918, whilst in Vienna during 1930 it was claimed that an Italian torpedoed her on May 1, 1918. Which of these stories then is true? On the whole I think the first (December 17–18) still holds the position for credence. And that was the last enemy submarine to be destroyed this year.

Such, then, is the long and varied story of the U-boat which began so mildly and with such diffidence when hostilities with Germany first started. If we have chosen for our study that period until the end of the year 1916, it is because only by examining this enormous canvas carefully, and in detail, can we hope to interpret accurately the motives and methods of the First German War in comparison with the Second. Although more than two decades intervened between the two stages of hostilities and it was a fresh generation which grew up in the meanwhile, there has been one war : a continuation of the first part but with an emphasis on the lessons previously gained and now re-presented.

The final and decisive half of hostilities—1917 and 1918—after having been written will be offered to the reader shortly under the title *Beating the U-Boats*. As in the above chapters, an endeavour is made not only to indicate the atmosphere, but also the motives, the difficulties, and the results of German striving by means of her underwater craft.

INDEX

Aboukir, H.M.S., 26
Acacia, H.M.S., 101
Acacia, ketch, 171
Achilles, H.M.S., 24
Acworth, Lieut.-Comdr., 143, 144
Adolf, schooner, 102
Adventure, H.M.S., 86, 160
Afridi, H.M.S., 183
Agamemnon, trawler, 121
Aguila, 65
Aillebrand, Lieut.-Comdr., 63
Ailly, French ship, 206
Ajax, H.M.S., 18, 35
Alarm, H.M.S., 32
Albatross, minelayer, 19, 20, 21, 22, 190
Alberta, 22
Alex Hastie, trawler, 57, 119
Allied Naval Convention, 161
Allman, Sub.-Lieut. A. C., 124, 125, 126
Amalfi, Italian cruiser, 161
Amazing Adventure, 39
Amethyst, smack, 144
Amiral Charner, 167
Amiral Ganteaume, French steamer, 33, 47
Amphion, H.M.S., 15, 20
Andalusian, S.S., 63
Andromache, H.M.S., 31, 53
Antwerp, H.M.S., 63, 136
Apollo, H.M.S., 31
Arabic, S.S., 21, 146, 148, 149, 173
Aranmore, S.S., 175
Arctic, trawler, 100
Arethusa, H.M.S., 51, 89
Argyll, H.M.S., 108, 112
Ariel, H.M.S., 33, 62, 206
Askold, Russian cruiser, 78
Asturias, hospital ship, 52
Attentive, H.M.S., 27, 40
Aud, 179, 180
Audacious, H.M.S., 34, 35
Aurora, H.M.S., 51
Austrian U-boats, 161
 ultimatum to Servia, 12
Auxiliary Patrol, 23
Auxiliary Patrol Areas, 47, 48, 49

Bacon, Rear-Admiral R. H. S., 74
Bacon, Admiral, 150, 151, 152
Badger, H.M.S., destroyer, 33, 34, 50, 89

Bakana, S.S., 166
Balfour, Arthur, 86
Ballater, S.S., 85, 99
Bamford, C. A., 132, 133
Bang, Capt., 131
Baralong, Q-ship, 136, 146, 147, 148, 149, 150, 151, 153, 155, 175
Barnes, Lieut. A. H., 170, 171
Baron Napier, S.S., 163
Bartel, Lieut. K., 205
Bauer, Comdr. H., 13, 17
Bayano, H.M.S., 58, 63, 146
Bayly, Vice-Admiral L., 35, 45, 46, 86, 150, 153, 160, 175, 180, 191
Beating the U-boats, 7, 207
Beatty, Admiral 45, 51, 188
Beeching, Capt. F., 177, 179
Behncke, Admiral, 18
Beitzen, Lieut.-Comdr., 189
Bellglade, barque, 105, 106
Bempton, trawler, 119
Ben Cruachan, 52
Berlin, German liner, 34
Berlin, German minelayer, 42
Bethmann Hollweg, 149
Bickford, Lieut.-Comdr. E. O. B., 114
Biermann, Comdr., 14, 15
Birmingham, H.M.S., 18, 27, 51, 108
Bismarck, German battleship, 102
Blonde, A. E., 90
Blücher, 40, 43, 51
Bluebell, H.M.S., 179
Blumenthal, trawler, 156
Bond, C. C., 103
Boothby, Lieut.-Comdr. E. L. B., 169, 170
Botha, H.M.S., 198, 199
Branksome Chine, 59
Bray, Lieut. H. J., 188
Bremen, German mercantile submarine, 191
Brierley Hill, S.S., 197
Brighton Queen, 30
Britannic, S.S., 202
British Expeditionary Force, 1914, 18, 19, 20, 28
British Grand Fleet, 19, 20, 34, 36, 40, 41, 42, 43, 87, 89, 104, 192
British Submarines
 C-23, 143, 144
 C-24, 110, 111, 112, 134, 135
 C-27, 110, 127, 135

208

British Submarines (*Continued*) :—
  C-29, 193
  C-33, 128
  C-39, 74
  D-3, 38
  D-4, 109
  D-5, 25, 38, 39
  D-8, 136
  E-3, 32, 42, 146
  E-4, 117, 152
  E-9, 25
  E-13, 149
  E-14, 153
  E-16, 73
  E-20, 161
  E-22, 149
  E-54, 182, 192
  H-5, 191
  J-1, 201
  S-1, 114, 115, 116
Brock, trawler, 84
Brodie, Lieut. D., 39
Bruce, W., 191
Brutus, trawler, 42
Burhave, trawler, 156
Burney, Vice-Admiral Sir C., 198
Burnham, Sub.-Lieut. N. O., 169
Butler, W. H., 101
Buttons, C., 123

Calgarian, H.M.S., 21
Caliban, S.S., 130
Calistoga, drifter, 188
Calumsin, trawler, 158
Cambank, S.S., 54, 119
Cambria, H.M.S., 35
Cambridge, 30
Cameo, trawler, 122, 123
Campbell, Lieut.-Comdr. G., 175, 176
Canada, troops from, 35
Candidate, S.S., 80
Cannel, Lieut., 84
Cantlie, Lieut. C., 127, 128
Carmania, S.S., 78
Casement, Sir Roger, 179, 180
Castro, S.S., 179
Caucasian, S.S., 119
Cayo Romano, S.S., 80
Centurion, H.M.S., 35
Centurion, S.S., 81
Charlsin, trawler, 158
Cheero, smack, 180

Churchill, Winston S., 41, 85, 86
City, S.S., 43
City of Belfast, 22
Clarke, F. B., 128, 129
Coates, Comdr. O. U., 109
Coke, Admiral, 82, 86
Comrades, drifter, 176
Corinsin, trawler, 158
Cosmos, drifter, 170
Cossack, H.M.S., 59
Costello, S.S., 139
Cottingham, S.S., 120, 151, 160
Cowie, J., 103
Craigard, S.S., 119
Crawford, Lieut., 131
Cressy, H.M.S., 26, 27, 29, 32, 46, 64, 78
Cromer, S.S., 177
Cromorna, drifter, 105
Crompton, Lieut.-Comdr. J., 156
Cromsit, trawler, 116
Crooks, J., 171
Crown of India, barque, 104
Curlew, trawler, 100
Cuxhaven, barrage of blockships at, 13
Cymrie, S.S., 197

Dardanelles campaign, 14, 152
Dardanelles Dilemma, 75
Dare, Admiral, 90, 106
Darmstadt, trawler, 156
Davies, H., 66
Davis, U.S. destroyer, 98
Defensive arming of liners, 74
Demerara, S.S., 85
Deptford, S.S., 58
Depth charge, 160
Derfflinger, 43, 51
Deutschland, German mercantile submarine, 191
Devonia, 30
Devonshire, H.M.S., 109
Dinorah, S.S., 55
Dobson, Lieut.-Comdr. C. C., 127, 128
Dogger Bank, Battle of, 51
Doktor Kingler, trawler, 156-7
Dorothy Gray, trawler, 41, 42
Dover, Air observation over Straits, 104
  nets across Straits of, 55
  Straits Boom, 159

INDEX

Downshire, S.S., 119
Dreadnought, H.M.S., 18, 64
Drifters as Navy auxiliaries, 23
  Bases for net, 50
Droescher, Lieut.-Comdr., 52, 81
Dryad, H.M.S., 137
Dublin, H.M.S., 161
Duke of Wellington, trawler, 87
Dulce Doris, drifter, 188
Dulwich, S.S., 55
Dumfriesshire, 106
Dundee, H.M.S., 21, 24
Dunedin, S.S., 67
Dunslay, S.S., 145
Durward, S.S., 50

Earl of Lathom, 80
Eastward Ho! trawler, 122, 123
Edgar class of cruisers, 32
Edwards, Lieut.-Comdr. H. D., 110, 112, 143
Eileen Emma, 67
Ellison, Captain, 20
Elterwater, collier, 43
El Zorro, tanker, 160
Empress, seaplane carrier, 196
Endurance, drifter, 176, 177
Endymion, H.M.S., 32
Engadine, seaplane carrier, 196
Equinox, trawler, 142
Eske, trawler, 96
Esterburg, German trawler, 117, 152
Euclid, trawler, 87
Evans, Comdr. (Admiral), 60
Evening Star, drifter, 188

F-12, Italian submarine, 207
Fair Maid, minesweeper, 38
Falaba, S.S., 67
Falkenhausen, Lieut. von, 187
Falmouth, H.M.S., 192
Farnborough, S.S., 175, 176
Faulknor, H.M.S., 199
Fearless, H.M.S., 27
Feldkirchner, Lieut.-Comdr., 32
Ferguson, Lieut. H. J., 101, 102, 103
Fichandel, trawler, 152
Fiery Cross, 120
Fimreite, S.S., 128, 129
Firedrake, H.M.S., 116, 186
Fisher Girl, drifter, 207
Fisher, Lord, 46, 85, 136

Flanders U-boat Flotilla, 64, 93
Formidable, H.M.S., 21, 46, 72, 86, 144, 145
Forstmann, Lieut.-Comdr., 87, 118, 119, 120, 121, 140, 141, 162
Forstner, Lieut.-Comdr. F. von, 65, 66, 67, 68
Forth Bridge, 23
Forth Destroyer Patrol, 24
Fröhner, Lieut. E., 174
Fulgent, collier, 80, 93
Fuller, Petty Officer, 103
Fürbringer, Lieut.-Comdr. G., 108, 111, 112, 113
Fürbringer, Lieut.-Comdr. W., 108
Fury, H.M.S., destroyer, 36

Gadsby, S.S., 119
Galilean, H.M. drifter, 94
Gallipoli, 76
G. and E., smack, 142, 143, 144
Gansser, Lieut.-Comdr., 72, 140, 141
Garland. G., 89
Garrigill, drifter, 191
Garry, H.M.S., 41
Gayer, Capt., 17, 49, 53, 57, 72, 73, 87, 102, 123, 134, 144
Gazehound, trawler, 100
General de Sonis, barque, 68, 69
George and May, 85
German character, 11
  High Seas Fleet, 12, 13, 20, 25, 28, 87, 93, 114, 192
  military arrogance, 20
  naval policy, 17, 31
  Navy, operational methods, 12, 13
  Secret Service, 19
  Submarines
    U-5, 13, 17, 19, 23, 40
    U-6, 17, 19, 73, 153, 187
    U-7, 13, 17, 19, 49
    U-8, 13, 17, 19, 54, 58-60, 62
    U-9, 13, 17, 19, 26, 32, 87
    U-10, 17, 19, 187
    U-11, 17, 19, 33, 40
    U-12, 17, 19, 33, 40, 62, 63, 206
    U-13, 17, 18, 19
    U-14, 13, 17, 19, 101, 102, 103
    U-15, 17, 18, 19, 27
    U-16, 13, 17, 19, 54, 55, 63, 74, 87, 102, 103, 134, 135, 156
    U-17, 13, 17, 19, 32, 141
    U-18, 13, 17, 19, 27, 28, 40, 41

INDEX

German Submarines (*Continued*):—
  U-19, 18, 19, 21, 25, 33, 50, 87, 89, 95, 179, 180
  U-20, 19, 25, 28, 52, 58, 81, 118, 119, 196, 197, 198, 199, 200
  U-21, 18, 19, 23, 25, 27, 28, 41, 50, 52, 54, 75, 76, 77, 78, 145, 161, 167
  U-22, 18, 19, 25, 49, 140, 196
  U-23, 93, 127, 128, 135, 143
  U-24, 18, 21, 25, 33, 47, 72, 145
  U-25, 17, 87, 89, 95
  U-26, 139
  U-27, 21, 33, 34, 42, 58, 63, 146, 147, 148, 149, 163
  U-28, 25, 65, 66, 67, 68, 141
  U-29, 63, 64, 136
  U-30, 54, 57, 58, 119, 196, 197, 198, 199, 200, 201
  U-31, 49
  U-32, 49, 50, 72, 94
  U-33, 50, 72, 140
  U-34, 64, 65, 68, 85, 86, 97, 98, 140, 166
  U-35, 64, 65, 85, 86, 105, 108, 140, 162, 163, 164, 189, 192
  U-36, 87, 92, 128, 129, 130, 135, 163
  U-37, 65, 68
  U-38, 109, 112, 141, 150, 162, 165
  U-39, 87, 118, 119, 120, 121, 140, 162, 166
  U-40, 108, 111, 112, 113, 135
  U-41, 122, 123, 124, 125, 126, 134, 136, 153, 154, 155, 156, 163
  U-46, 135, 193
  U-51, 191
  U-52, 192
  U-53, 192, 193
  U-56, 196
  U-63, 192
  U-65, 192
  U-66, 139, 192
  U-67, 139
  U-68, 139, 175, 176
  U-69, 139
  U-73, 202
  U-74, 188, 190
  U-77, 189, 190
  U-88, 201
  U-103, 65, 98

German Submarines (*Continued*):—
  U-139, 162
  UB and UC types, 71, 72, 100, 136
  UB-1, 73, 139
  UB-3, 41, 73
  UB-4, 72, 136, 137, 142, 143, 144
  UB-6, 81, 93, 95, 96, 152
  UB-7, 73, 196
  UB-8, 73
  UB-10, 94, 95
  UB-13, 95, 182, 183
  UB-14, 73, 161
  UB-15, 73, 161
  UB-16, 95
  UB-19, 205
  UB-26, 176
  UB-29, 206
  UB-44, 192
  UB-45, 196
  UB-46, 206
  UB-72, 109
  UB-74, 36
  UB-110, 108
  UC-1, 94, 95, 139, 152, 183
  UC-2, 94, 95, 119, 120, 151, 160
  UC-3, 94, 139, 181, 182, 183
  UC-5, 139, 183, 184, 185, 186, 188
  UC-6, 139, 183
  UC-7, 139, 183, 190
  UC-8, 157
  UC-9, 157
  UC-10, 182, 192, 193
  UC-11, 38, 71, 93
  UC-12, 73, 160, 174, 206
  UC-13, 73, 160, 205
  UC-14, 73
  UC-15, 73, 205
  UC-19, 206
  UC-35, 205

Germany's High Sea Fleet, 43, 51, 172
G. Garibaldi, Italian cruiser, 161
Ghurka, H.M.S., 60, 61
Gibson, Capt., 68, 69, 70
Glance, barque, 131
Gleaner of the Sea, drifter, 182, 183
Glen Avon, 30
Glencarse, 73
Glenholm, 84
Glitra, S.S., 32
Gloria, trawler, 144

INDEX

Goldmouth, S.S., 176
Good Luck, trawler, 108
Gorleston, German raid on, 37, 38, 44
Gorman, Mary, 180
Gossamer, H.M.S., 43
Graeff, Lieut.-Comdr., 128
Graudenz, 40
Green, Capt. J. R., 65, 66, 67
Green, Lieut., 96
Greif, see Rena.
Grenfell, Comdr. F. H., 202, 204, 205
Gross, Lieut. C., 136, 137
Grosser Kurfurst, German battleship, 201
Guerdon, H.M.S., 207
Gulflight, S.S., 84
Gull, trawler, 101, 103
Güntzel, Lieut.-Comdr., 175
Guy, Lieut.-Comdr. B. J. D., 164

Hacker, Lieut., 81, 93, 96, 97
Hague Convention, 1907, 14
Halcyon, H.M.S., 20, 37, 38, 40, 142
Hamburg, German cruiser, 19, 87
Hamburg-Amerika Line, 12, 14
Hamlet, trawler, 42
Hammerle, Lieut., 101
Hamond, Lieut. C. E., 142, 143
Hampshire, H.M.S., 189
Hansen, Lieut.-Comdr. Claus, 103, 122, 123, 124, 125, 126, 134, 136, 153, 154, 156
Harpalyce, S.S., 72
Hartlepool, German raid on, 43, 44
Hawke, H.M.S., 32
Hawk, trawler, 101, 102, 103
Heimburg, Lieut. von, 161
Hela, German cruiser, 25
Heligoland Bight, Battle of, 25, 28
Hennig, Lieut.-Comdr. von, 17, 27, 40, 41
Herbert, Lieut.-Comdr. G., 25, 38, 39, 63, 136, 146, 148, 175
Hermes, H.M.S., seaplane carrier, 33, 42, 63
Hersing, Lieut.-Comdr. Otto, 23, 24, 25, 28, 31, 41, 50, 52, 64, 75, 76, 77, 78, 79, 140, 141, 163, 167
Hesperian, H.M.S., 197
Hick, Capt., 156
Hildebrand, H.M.S., 130

Hillebrand, Lieut.-Comdr., 134, 135
Hines, C.P.O., 163
Hipper, Admiral, 40, 43, 51, 200, 201
Hirose, trawler, 85, 98, 99
Hodson, Lieut.-Comdr. G. L., 163, 164
Hofe, Rear-Admiral K. von, 107
Hogue, H.M.S., 26
Hohenloh-Schillingsfurst, Prince Zu, 127
Hohenzollern, German royal yacht, 12
Homer, steam tug, 68, 69, 70
Horton, Lieut.-Comdr. Max, 25
Hovenden, Midshipman, 163
Hughes, A., 107
Humby, A. E., 107, 108
Hunt, Lieut.-Comdr. W. W., 77
Huronian, S.S., 160
Hurren, R. G., 182, 183
Hydrophone, 181, 182, 190, 193

Ibex, S.S., 204
Ikpria, 52
Ina Williams, trawler, 85, 119
India, H.M.S., 140
"Indicator" nets, 50
Indomitable, H.M.S., 51
Inflexible, H.M.S., 192
Ingenohl, Admiral von, 12, 13, 19, 42
Inglemoor, S.S., 119
Intrepid, H.M.S., 31, 53
Inverlyon, sailing ship, 202
Inverlyon, smack, 137, 139, 142, 144
Invincible, H.M.S., 24
Iphigenia, H.M.S., 31
Iron Duke, H.M.S., 18, 189, 198
Isabella Alexandra, yacht, 16
Ivy Green, drifter, 105

Jackson, Admiral Sir H., 86
Jacqueline, trawler, 90
James Fletcher, 169, 170
Japonica, trawler, 100, 101
Jason, H.M.S., 43
Jeannette, steam yacht, 91
Jehan, E. M., 137, 139
Jellicoe, Admiral, 18, 30, 35, 42, 45, 46, 123, 189, 198
Johnson, Capt. C. D., 59
Juliana, S.S., 185
Jurassic, S.S., 100
Jutland, Battle of, 51, 173, 188, 189

INDEX

Kaphreda, trawler, 29
Kellett, Lieut.-Comdr., 114, 115
Kelly, Sergt. R. M., 163
Kennedy, Lieut., 115, 116
Kilcoan, 52
Kilmarnock, trawler, 29
Kimberley, trawler, 188
King Charles, trawler, 87
King Edward VII, H.M.S., 197
King George V, H.M.S., 35
King's Channel, 15
King Stephen, trawler, 181, 182
Kitchener, Lord, 189
Knorr, Capt. von, 141
Kolbe, Lieut.-Comdr., 95
Kolberg, 40, 43, 44
König, German battleship, 201
Konigen Luise, minelayer, 14, 15, 16
Kophamel, Lieut.-Comdr., 65, 85, 105, 107, 140, 162
Kratsch, Lieut.-Comdr., 62
Kreysern, Lieut. G., 181
Kronprinz Wilhelm, German battleship, 201

L.13, airship, 192
Lady Ismay, 30
Laertes, S.S., 54
Lappland, S.S., 102
Latona, H.M.S., 53
Laurence, Comdr. N., 201
Layton, Lieut.-Comdr., 149
L. C. Tower, 119
Leader, smack, 142
Leake, Capt. Martin, 24
Lee, G. M., 151
Leeuwarden, S.S., 65
Leopard, H.M.S., destroyer, 37
Lepsius, Lieut.-Comdr., 73, 153
Lightvessels
   Corton, 185, 189
   Cross Sand, 37
   Galloper, 26
   Haaks, 15
   Haisborough, 152
   Horn's Reef, 114
   Inner Dowsing, 25
   Kentish Knock, 185
   Kish, 91
   Longsand, 26, 121, 183
   Maas, 15, 16, 18, 26, 50, 54
   Nab, 183
   Nantucket, 193

Lightvessels (*Continued*):—
   North Hinder, 26, 95
   Outer Dowsing, 22, 25
   Outer Gabbard, 18, 26
   Ruytingen, 26
   Sandettie, 26
   Schouwen, 182, 192
   Shipwash, 26, 99, 121, 185
   Smith's Knoll, 25
   South Goodwins, 32, 71, 93, 99
   Sunk, 99, 185
   Terschelling, 15
   West Hinder, 26
Limewold, trawler, 101, 102, 103
Linda Blanche, 52
Linsdell, 22
Lion, H.M.S., 27, 45, 51
Lively, H.M.S., destroyer, 37, 38
Liverpool, H.M.S., 36
Livingston, Lieut.-Comdr. G., 166
Llewellyn, H.M.S., 206
Loch Shiel, trawler, 108
Lodorer, S.S., 175
Lord Nelson, 46
Lord Roberts, 80
Lorna, yacht, 36
Louise, S.S., 130
Lowca, bombardment of by U-boat, 145
Lowestoft, bombardment of, 44, 180
Lowestoft, H.M.S., 27, 51
Lusitania, S.S., 58, 64, 81-2, 84, 95, 118, 140, 145, 146, 148, 149, 172, 197, 200, 201

Macfarlane, trawler, 170
Ma Freen, drifter, 59, 61
Maid of Honour, yacht, 125
Majestic, H.M.S., 78, 167
Malachite, S.S., 41
Malley, Capt., 63
Manchester Commerce, S.S., 34
Manning, Capt. C. H., 148
Maori, H.M.S., 60
Margit, Q-ship, 163, 164
Maricopa, S.S., 89
Marion Lightbody, barque, 118
Markgraf, German battleship, 201
Marlborough, H.M.S., 45, 46
Marsala, 76
Mary, minesweeper, 38
Marynthea, steam yacht, 91
Marys, drifter, 105

Mathieson, Gunlayer, 103
McBride, Capt. W., 148, 149
Medea, S.S., 65
Mediterranean, U-boat campaign, 75–9, 140, 160–7
Medusa, Italian submarine, 161
Medusa, steam yacht, 91
Megantic, S.S., 85
Merion, S.S., 78
Meteor, minelayer, 141
Mety, Lieut. A., 182
Mey, Lieut., 119
Minefields
  Dogger Bank, 87–9
  Elbe, 13
  Ems, 13
  Gorleston, 43
  Humber, 21, 43, 193
  Jade, 13, 38
  Lister Tief, 13
  Lowestoft, 99
  Moray Firth, 141
  Scarborough, 43, 44
  Silver Pit, 74, 92
  Southwold, 20, 43
  Swarte Bank, 75, 152
  Tory Island, 34, 35, 42, 43
  Tyne, 22, 28, 42, 43
Mines, British attitude to, 14
  anchored contact, 14
Minesweeping trawlers, 20
Ministre Beernat, S.S., 160
Minterne, S.S., 80
Mitchell, Capt. C., 120
M'Loughlin, Lieut. J., 176, 177
Mobile, collier, 80
Mohawk, H.M.S., destroyer, 32, 60, 99
Mohrbutter, Lieut., 183, 185
Moltke, German battle-cruiser, 40, 43, 51, 201
Monarch, H.M.S., 18, 35
Morton, Lieut. L., 127
Morwenna, S.S., 85, 90
Motagua, H.M.S., 128
Motor launches, 72
Möwe, German surface raider, 175, 197
Moy, H.M.S., 104
Müller, Capt. Frick von, 12

Narcissus, steam yacht, 91
Nautilus, minelayer, 20, 21
Nebraskan, S.S., 84

Nembo, Italian destroyer, 195
Neptune, H.M.S., 64
New York World, 172
New Zealand, H.M.S., 21, 27, 51
Nicholson, Rear-Admiral S., 78
Nicosian, S.S., 146, 147, 148
Niger, H.M.S., 33, 40, 62
Nimrod, H.M.S., 152
Noodt, Lieut. Erich, 205
Norbreck, trawler, 84, 85
North German Lloyd Line, 12
Nottingham, H.M.S., 51, 109, 192
Nymphe, H.M.S., 92

Oakby, 59
Oceanic II, trawler, 101, 103
Oku, trawler, 188
Olympic, S.S., 35, 36, 65, 74, 98
Ontario, trawler, 89
Orcades, 22
Orcoma, H.M.S., 132
Orduna, S.S., 197
Oriole, 52
Orion, H.M.S., 18
Orlando, S.S., 131
Orsova, S.S., 74
Osprey II, trawler, 108
Ost, German trawler, 115, 116
Osterley, S.S., 74
Outhouse, J. F., 29

Pallada, Russian cruiser, 139
Partridge, H.M.S., 64
Pathfinder, H.M.S., 24, 27, 28, 29, 50, 75, 167
Pearl, trawler, 124, 125, 126
Peckelsheim, Lieut.-Comdr. S. F. von, 72
Peik, S.S., 121
Pelz, engineer officer, 61
Penhallow, Q-ship, 163
Penshurst, Q-ship, 202, 204
Perière, Comdr. L. von A. de la, 41, 162, 189
Persimmon, trawler, 100
Pet, smack, 150, 151
Peterson, Lieut. F. H., 134
Phillips, Lieut.-Comdr. G. C., 114
Phillips, Skipper, 139
Piercy, Lieut.-Comdr. B. H., 64
Pleasance, drifter, 176
Pleiades, drifter, 176
Pohl, Admiral, 18, 25, 28, 52, 93, 149

INDEX

Portia, H.M. yacht, 109
Portia, S.S., 139
Prestridge, Sub-Lieut., 105
Primo, S.S., 41
Prince Charles, collier, 130, 135, 136
Princess Juliana, trawler, 131
Princess Louise, trawler, 127, 128
Princess Olga, S.S., 43
Princess Royal, H.M.S., 51
Propert, Capt., 54

Quarry Knowe, drifter, 191
Queen, S.S., 33
Queen Alexandra, drifter, 105
Q-ships, 130, 136, 141, 146, 148, 151, 163, 176, 191, 202

Ratapiko, trawler, 143, 144
Ratibor, Prince E. von, 127
Recruit, H.M.S., 81, 93, 96
Rena, 24
Renaudin, French destroyer, 187
Returno, trawler, 171
Reverto, trawler, 87
Revigo, 22
Ribbons, A., 111
Richardson, Lieut.-Comdr. R. W., 61
Richmond, S.S., 119
Rio Parana, 59
Riviera, seaplane carrier, 196
Robeck, Admiral de, 78
Rodino, trawler, 188
Rose, Lieut.-Comdr., 193
Roses, drifter, 193
Rostock, German light cruiser, 19, 21, 25, 39
Roxburgh, H.M.S., 108, 109, 112
Royal Edward, transport, 161, 162
Royal Oak, H.M.S., 128
R.R.S., drifter, 52
Rücker, Lieut.-Comdr., 65, 85, 97, 98, 104, 107, 140
Russo-Japanese War, 1903-4, 14

Saidieh, S.S., 95, 96
Sainte Jehanne, 68
Salmon, H.M. submarine, 114
Salmon, motor boat, 190
Salvator, H.M. yacht, 109
Sapphire, steam yacht, 91
Sardomene, barque, 119
Saros, Q-ship, 163
Sayers, A., 122, 123

Scarborough, German raid on, 43, 44
Schafer, Herr, 115, 116
Scheer, Admiral, 43, 51, 54, 104, 172, 188, 192
Schmidt, Lieut. W., 93, 126
Schneider, Lieut.-Comdr., 21, 47, 72, 144, 146
Schofield, Lieut., 193
Schulthess, Lieut.-Comdr., 93, 127, 128
Schwieger, Lieut.-Comdr., 81, 82, 84, 118, 119, 197, 198, 200, 201
Schwinitz, Lieut.-Comdr. Graf von, 18
Scott, Lieut. W. F., 181
Seaplanes, 89
Searanger, trawler, 122, 188
Seas of Adventure, 161
" Seven Deadly Sins " trawlers, 158
Severn, H.M.S., 27
Seydlitz, battle-cruiser, 40, 43, 44, 51, 180
Shark, motor boat, 190
Shenandoah, S.S., 170, 171
Siehs, Lieut.-Comdr., 202
Simon, Lieut. F. M., 166
Skipjack, H.M.S., 43
Smiths, Lieut. W., 176, 177
Sophie, trawler, 156
Southampton, H.M.S., 51
South Point, 65
Speedwell, H.M.S., 123
Speedy, 22
Spero, S.S., 198
Spindler, Lieut. K., 179
Springbank, barque, 129, 130
Springwell, S.S., 164, 165, 166
St. Andrew, hospital ship, 59
Stanley Weyman, trawler, 125
Star of Buchan, drifter, 157
Stately, drifter, 176
Statesman, S.S., 153
Steele, Sub.-Lieut. G. C., 136
Stoch, U-boat commander, 59, 60, 61
Stralsund, German light cruiser, 21, 40
Strassburg, German light cruiser, 19, 21, 25, 40
Strathalladale, trawler, 96
Stuttgart, minelayer, 19, 156
Submarine Blockade, 40, 54, 58
  potentialities not appreciated in 1914, 13
  strength of, in Sept., 1915, 152

Sunlight, barque, 104
Superb, barque, 104
Sussex, S.S., 172, 173
Svorno, Russian S.S., 80, 93
Swan, trawler, 125
Swift, H.M.S., destroyer, 32
Switha Battery, 32
Sycamore, Capt. Edward, 16
Syren, H.M.S., 60

Talbot, Comdr. C. P., 153
Taranaki, trawler, 110, 112, 113, 128, 134, 135, 136
Tarver, Lieut. A. M., 127
Taylor, Lieut. F. H., 110, 111, 112, 134
Teiresias, S.S., 77
Tenth Cruiser Squadron, 32
The Big Blockade, 32, 58
The German Submarines, 57, 87
The Grand Fleet, 46
The Sea Raiders, 14, 24
Theseus, H.M.S., 32
Thetis, H.M.S., 53
Thordis, collier, 153
Thornhill, collier, 35
Tiger, H.M.S., 51, 78
Tirpitz, Admiral, 72, 82, 140, 149
Titania, trawler, 87
Tokio, trawler, 41
Tokomaru, 52
Trafford, S.S., 107, 108
Trawlers, as Navy auxiliaries, 23
  tribute to by German admiral, 107
Triumph, H.M.S., 78, 167
Trondhjemfiord, S.S., 130, 131
Tsushima, battle of, 51
Turnwell, S.S., 107, 108
Turquoise, French submarine, 161
Turkey, 14, 77
Tyrwhitt, Commodore, 39, 51, 89, 141

U-boat Aces, 162
Undaunted, H.M.S., 51
Urbino, S.S., 154, 156
Ure, H.M.S., 60
Ursula, H.M. submarine, 114
Utke, Lieut. Kurt, 38

Vaaren, S.S., 43
Valand, schooner, 132, 133
Valentiner, Lieut.-Comdr. M., 109, 141, 150, 162, 163, 165
Valiant, yacht, 44, 91

Vanduara, yacht, 52
Vanessa, yacht, 125
Van Stirum, S.S., 160
Varley, Lieut., 191
Victoria, trawler, 85, 97, 98, 99
Vigilant, trawler, 101, 103
Viking, H.M.S., 60
Ville de Lille, S.S., 55
Völckner, German merchant marine officer, 62, 74
Von der Tann, 40, 43
Vosges, 65, 66, 67

Wager, Lieut., 192
Wallflower, H.M.S., 166
Ward, F., 98
Wayfarer, S.S., 74
Weddigen, Lieut.-Comdr., 18, 26, 27, 28, 31, 32, 64, 87, 136
Wegener, Lieut.-Comdr., 33, 34, 42, 146, 148, 150
Welbury, S.S., 119
Welcome Star, drifter, 176
Werribee, Q-ship, 163, 164, 165
West, Sub.-Lieut. E. T., 190
Western Coast, 59
Westward Ho!, 30
Weymouth II, trawler, 106
Wilcke, Lieut.-Comdr., 65
Wilhelm II, German Kaiser, 12, 149
William Dawson, S.S., 183
Williams, Sub.-Lieut A. E., 52
Wilmot-Smith, Lieut.-Comdr. A., 149, 154
Wintonia, armed yacht, 67
Wistaria, trawler, 106
Worcester, training ship, 136
Wrightson, Comdr. W. C., 81
Wünsche, Lieut.-Comdr., 95
Wyandra, Q-ship, 154, 163, 166
Wylie, T. G., 177

Yarmouth, German raid on, 39, 40, 180
Yenesi, minelayer, 139
Yorck, German cruiser, 38, 40
Youngson, A., 41

Zeebrugge harbour, 45
Zeppelin, 93, 104, 114, 128, 142, 152, 180
Zinnia, H.M.S., 179
Zylpha, S.S., 175

www.ingramcontent.com/pod-product-compliance
Lightning Source LLC
Chambersburg PA
CBHW071818230426
43670CB00013B/2495